CONCISE DICTIONARY OF PHYSICS

A Perfect Reference for Aspirants of IAS, IIT-JEE, AIEEE, CBSE-PMT, and Students of All Age Groups

Editorial Board

V&S PUBLISHERS

Published by:

V&S PUBLISHERS

F-2/16, Ansari road, Daryaganj, New Delhi-110002
☎ 23240026, 23240027 • *Fax:* 011-23240028
Email: info@vspublishers.com • *Website:* www.vspublishers.com

Regional Office : Hyderabad
5-1-707/1, Brij Bhawan (Beside Central Bank of India Lane)
Bank Street, Koti, Hyderabad - 500 095
☎ 040-24737290
E-mail: vspublishershyd@gmail.com

Branch Office : Mumbai
Jaywant Industrial Estate, 1st Floor–108, Tardeo Road
Opposite Sobo Central Mall, Mumbai – 400 034
☎ 022-23510736
E-mail: vspublishersmum@gmail.com

BUY OUR BOOKS FROM: AMAZON FLIPKART

ISBN 978-93-505715-7-6

Edition 2020

Printed at : Param Offsetters, Okhla, New Delhi–110020

Y,Z

Yield

The yield is the number of secondary particles of the same type that are produced for a given number of primary particle, i.e., the yield for a certain target is 106 pions/1012 protons.

Young's modulus (scalar; n/m^2)

The ratio of tensile stress to tensile strain.

Young's modulus of elasticity

The ratio of normal stress to the longitudinal strain produced in a body.

Z boson

Also known as a Z Particle. A carrier particle of weak interactions. It is involved in weak processes that do not change flavor.

Zeeman effect

The splitting of atomic energy levels of a spectral line by a magnetic field into two or more sublevels under normal conditions.

Zeroth law of thermodynamics

If body A is in thermal equilibrium with body B, and B is also in thermal equilibrium with C, then A is necessarily in thermal equilibrium with C.

Zov

Zinc-Oxide Varistor. Used for detecting Voltage To Ground spurts in Main Ring and Tevatron power supplies.

X

Xbar

Crossbar. A kind of multiplexor for which one of a number of channels are hardware-selected. Crossbars are used extensively in the CATV system, and have applications in the Switchyard as well.

Xerox 530

An obsolete computer, no longer supported by Xerox, which was formerly used to control the accelerator. The most recent, and final accelerator to be converted from the XEROX system to ACNET was the Booster. The MAC-16 computers used by MR.barf are the remnants of the old system.

XMIT button

A button at the keypad of each ACNET console which allows the user to leave an operating program and return to the index page without having to move the cursor. It is used when control of the cursor has been lost. Also known as the application abort button.

X-ray

The part of the electromagnetic spectrum whose radiation has somewhat greater frequencies and smaller wavelengths than those of ultraviolet radiation. Because x-rays are absorbed by the Earth's atmosphere, x-ray astronomy is performed in space.

Publisher's Note

Innumerable books are available in the market on science and its allied branches, like, physics, chemistry, and biology et al, both as textbook and reference manual. Written for different age-groups and class, quite a number of these books come replete with jargon-filled terms; and just fail to connect with readers' inclination and curiosity level. On top of that, new words keep finding their way into the books every other day. Every new addition contributes to difficulty in comprehending the matter.

An average reader is interested only in knowing what a specific word means without getting lost with heavy sounding inputs.

Following an open-ended discussion with a cross-section of students and other stakeholders we realised that many books on science (physics, chemistry and biology) take readers' understanding of scientific terms for granted and make short passing references while alluding to the term in the text. Presentations of this nature in no way assist readers in understanding the subject properly.

You need to suffer no longer.

V&S Publishers has come out with four dictionaries of terms; in science, physics, chemistry and biology. These have been compiled to help readers grasp the meaning of popular scientific terms. For easy reference terms have been arranged alphabetically. Terms that have come into the reckoning even in the early 2012 have been incorporated and suitably explained in such a way that an average secondary and senior secondary student can grasp them easily. High resolution images, illustrations and examples, where appropriate, have been added for reader's convenience. For all readers, who have not made a special study of any science subject, explanations of terms will be found to be easily comprehensible.

An attempt has been made to include important scientific charts, tables, constants, conversion tables as appendices to make this dictionary more useful. A glossary of Nobel Prize winners and their contributions is an added attraction.

We would be happy to have your views and comments about the book.

Introduction

What is Physics?

Physics is the systematic study of the way matters interact. It is really concerned with how things move and what causes things to move. Things can be as large as a star or small as an atom.

Why is study of physics important?

Studying the way things move and interact is fundamentally useful in everyday life. Have you given a thought how our brain functions? It uses an automatic understanding of physics, for example, being able to walk or balancing ourselves requires our brains to make lots of calculations about friction and forces.

Physics is crucial to virtually all of our modern technology, conveniences and infrastructure from computers to cameras and everyday appliances.

It is useful in everyday situations. Having an awareness of physics can help explain:

- Significance of apple falling from a tree
- Difficulty in walking on sand
- How our eyes function
- Big bang and the origin of Earth
- Why we get tired
- How water boils or freezes
- How simple machines work

How is Physics Classified?

Typically physics is classified into traditional areas of study. These include:

Atomic/nuclear - The scientific study of the structure of an atom, its energy states, and its interactions with other particles and with electric and magnetic fields. Atomic physics has proved to be a spectacularly successful application of quantum mechanics, which is one of the cornerstones of modern physics.

Mechanics - The scientific study of motion of bodies under the action of forces, including the special case in which a body remains at rest. In the problem of motion are the forces that bodies exert on one another. This leads to the study of such topics as gravitation, electricity, and magnetism, according to the nature of the forces involved. Given the forces, one can seek the manner in which bodies move under the action of forces.

Electromagnetism - The study of charge and of the forces and fields associated with charge. Electricity and magnetism are two aspects of electromagnetism. Electric forces are produced by electric charges either at rest or in motion. Magnetic forces, on the other hand, are produced only by moving charges and act solely on charges in motion. Electricity and magnetism were long thought to be separate forces. It was not until the 19th century that they were finally treated as interrelated phenomena. At a practical level, however, electric and magnetic forces behave quite differently and are described by different equations.

Thermodynamics - The study of relationship between heat, work, temperature, and energy. In broad terms, thermodynamics deals with the transfer of energy from one place to another and from one form to another. The key concept is that heat is a form of energy corresponding to a definite amount of mechanical work.

Quantum physics - The study of scientific principles that explains the behaviour of matter and its interactions with energy on the scale of atoms and atomic particles (small scale). In classical physics, matter and energy at the macroscopic level (large scale) of the scale familiar to human experience is studied.

Optics - The study of science concerning the production and propagation of light, the changes that it undergoes and produces, and other phenomena closely associated with it. There are two major branches of optics - physical and geometrical. Physical optics deals primarily with the nature and properties of light itself. Geometrical optics has to do with the principles that govern the image-forming properties of lenses, mirrors, and other devices that make use of light.

Acoustics - The study of science concerning production, control, transmission, reception, and effects of sound.

How does Physics Work?

One way that physicists currently study things is by measuring the basic forces that exist in the universe. These forces are:

The Strong Force (forces inside the nucleus of atoms) - The forces that operate inside the nucleus are a mixture of those familiar from everyday life and those that operate only inside the atom. Two protons, for example, will repel each other because of their identical electrical force but will be attracted to each other by gravitation. Nevertheless, because the nucleus stays together in spite of the repulsive electrical force between protons, there must exist a counterforce-which physicists have named the strong force-operating at short range within the nucleus.

The Weak Force (relates to how atoms decay) - The weak force operates inside the nucleus. The weak force is responsible for some of the radioactive decays of nuclei. The four fundamental forces-strong, electromagnetic, weak, and gravitational-are responsible for every process in the universe. One of the important strains in modern theoretical physics is the belief that, although they seem very different, they are different aspects of a single underlying force.

The Electromagnetic Force (forces created by moving electrons including light)
The Gravitational Force (how things fall)

Most everyday physics is a result of the electromagnetic force and gravitational force.

How is Physics Studied?

The basic principle of studying physics is to measure things. For example, how fast is it moving and in which direction or angle?

For example, a series of events have certain duration in time. Time is the dimension of the duration. The duration might be expressed as 30 minutes or as half-an-hour. Minutes and hours are among the units in which time may be expressed. One can compare quantities of the same dimensions, even if they are expressed in different units (an hour is longer than a minute). Quantities of different dimensions cannot be compared with one another.

The fundamental dimensions used in physics are time, mass, and length. The study of electromagnetism adds an additional fundamental dimension, electric charge. Other quantities have dimensions compounded of these. Temperature is measured in Kelvin,

Measurement is done using internationally accepted SI units. The seven basic units, from which other units are derived, are defined as follows:

- Length - metre, defined as the distance travelled by light in vacuum in 1/299,792,458 second.
- Mass - kilogram, which equals to 1,000 grams as defined by the international prototype kilogram of platinum-iridium in the keeping of the International Bureau of Weights and Measures in Sèvres, France.
- Time - second, the duration of 9,192,631,770 periods of radiation associated with a specified transition of the cesium-133 atom.
- Electric current - ampere, which is the current that, if maintained in two wires placed one metre apart in vacuum, would produce a force of 2 × 10?7 Newton per metre of length.
- Luminous intensity - candela, defined as the intensity in a given direction of a source emitting radiation of frequency 540 × 1012 hertz and that has a radiant intensity in that direction of 1/683 watt per steradian.
- Substance - mole, defined as containing as many elementary entities of a substance as there are atoms in 0.012 kg of carbon-12.
- Thermodynamic temperature - kelvin.

Physics is also used in other scientific fields like biology and chemistry. For example: The physics of biology becomes Biophysics, Physics of astronomy becomes Astrophysics and Physics of the earth becomes Geophysics.

Important physicists of all time and their contributions

1. Archimedes (Greek) - Archimedes discovered the concept of buoyancy; developed formulae for the areas and volumes of spheres, cylinders, parabolas, and several other solids. He worked extensively with levers. He also invented the Archimedes screw to raise water. In warfare he developed several siege engines that served to hamper the Roman invasion of his home city of Syracuse.
2. Galileo Galilei (Italian) - Galileo discovered the law of uniformly accelerated motion. He improved on the refracting telescope. He also discovered the four largest satellites of Jupiter. He described projectile motion and the concept of weight. He was, however, best known for his championing of the Copernican theory of heliocentricity against church opposition.
3. Michael Faraday (English) - Faraday showed how a changing magnetic field can be used to generate an electric current. He also described the principles of electrolysis. He is an early

pioneer in the field of low temperature study.

4. Johannes Kepler (German) - Kepler outlined three fundamental laws of planetary motion. He described elliptical motion of planets around the sun. His works served as the precursor to that of Newton's.
5. Isaac Newton (English) - Newton quantified laws of motion and gravity. He also explained the concept of light dispersion and co-invented the Calculus. He invented the reflecting telescope.
6. Albert Einstein (German/Swiss/American) - Einstein developed theories of Special and General Relativity. He also worked on the photoelectric effect and deescribed mass-energy equivalence.
7. Max Planck (German) - He is the father of Quantum mechanics. He showed how the energy of a photon is proportional to its frequency.
8. Georg Ohm (German) - Ohm determined law in electricity that states that current is equal to the ratio of voltage to resistance.
9. James Maxwell (Scottish) - Maxwell developed equations for electromagnetism and the kinetic theory of gases. He predicted that there were other types of radiation beyond that of visible light and showed that light was a type of electromagnetic radiation.
10. Marie Curie (Polish) - Two time Nobel Prize winner, Marie Curie with Henri Becquerel and Pierre discovered radioactivity. She also isolated Plutonium and Radium.
11. Niels Bohr (Danish) - Bohr used Quantum mechanical model to show how electron energy levels are related to Spectral lines.
12. Erwin Schrödinger (Austrian) - Erwin Schrödinger is famous for the equation that bears his name. Describes the wave action and behaviour of matter.
13. Werner Heisenberg (German) - He developed a method to express Quantum mechanics in terms of matrices. Heisenberg is best known for his Uncertainty Principle.
14. Ernest Rutherford (Kiwi/British) - Rutherford is considered as the father of Nuclear Physics. He showed how the atomic nucleus has a positive charge. Rutherford was the first to change one element into another by an artificial nuclear reaction.
15. Nicolas Copernicus (Polish Monk) - Copernicus wrote the 400 page treatise 'On the Revolutions of the Celestial Spheres' that argued that the Earth revolved around the sun. The book challenged the way the world was viewed leading to much ecclesiastical opposition.
16. Christiaan Huygens (Dutch) - Huygens developed Wave Theory of Light and discovered polarization.
17. James Joule (British) - Joule showed that heat is a form of energy and also demonstrated that gas expansion with no work leads to a fall in temperature. His work led to the Theory of Conservation of Energy.
18. Henry Cavendish (British) - He showed that water is made up of the union of two gases and also determined the Universal Gravitation constant.
19. William Thomson Kelvin (Scottish) - A major figure in Thermodynamics. Thomson Kelvin helped develop the Law of Conservation of Energy. He studied Wave motion and vortex motion in hydrodynamics and produced a dynamical theory of heat.

20. Thomas Young (British) - Young furthered the doctrine of wave interference. He is famous for his 'slit' experiments.
21. Enrico Fermi (Italian/American) - Fermi split the nucleus by bombarding it with neutrons and built the first Nuclear reactor in the United States.
22. Richard Feynman (American) - Known for his work on quantum electrodynamics, as well as for his visual representation of the behaviour patterns of interacting particles (Feynman diagrams).
23. Alessandro Volta (Italian) - Volta built the first electrical battery. He is the first scientist to do substantial work with Electric currents.
24. Heinrich Hetrz (German) - Discovered radio waves and determined their velocity.
25. Benjamin Franklin (American) - Franklin worked with electricity and defined positive and negative charges.
26. John Bardeen (American) - Bardeen developed the point contact transistor (won Nobel Prize with Walter Brattain and William Shockley in 1956). He won a second Nobel Prize (1972) for his work on Superconductivity (shared with Leon Cooper and John Schrieffer).
27. Nikolai Tesla (Yugoslavian/American) - Tesla is the champion of alternating current flow (which is the means by which electric power is carried in our modern network). He also improved on the dynamo, transformer and electric bulb and invented the Tesla coil.
28. Paul Dirac (British) - Dirac developed the theory of the spinning electron and proposed the existence of anti-matter.
29. Robert Millikan (American) - Millikan determined the charge on an electron and did vital work with Cosmic Rays.
30. Edwin Hubble (American) - Hubble discovered that the universe is expanding. He established a ratio between the rate of expansion and the distance between galaxies.
31. Pieter Zeeman (Dutch) - Zeeman discovered the Zeeman effect, whereby a ray of light placed in a magnetic field is split spectroscopically into several components. This has helped physicists investigate atoms, study electromagnetic radiation and for astronomers to measure the magnetic field of stars.
32. Andre-Marie Ampere (French) - Ampere worked in field of Electrodynamics. He also showed how an electric current produces a magnetic field.
33. Joseph John Thomson (British) - Thomson showed that Cathode rays were rapidly moving particles. He also worked out that the mass of these individual particles (electrons) was less than 2000 times that of the atom itself.
34. Henri Becquerel (French) - Discovered the natural radioactivity of uranium.
35. Louis de Broglie (French) - Discovered the wave nature of electrons and particles.
36. Charles Coulomb (French) - Determined that positive and negative charges attract one another and showed that the magnitude of the force diminishes with distance.
37. Georges Lemaître (Belgian) - Proposed the Big Bang Theory of the origin of the Universe.
38. Christian Doppler (Austrian) - Doppler discovered that a wave's frequency changes when its

source and the observer are moving relative to one another (the Doppler Effect).

38. Lise Meitner (Austrian) - Meitner discovered with Otto Hahn the radioactive element - protactinium. Known for her work in Nuclear Physics she developed, with her nephew Otto Frisch, the concept of Nuclear Fission.
39. Hans Oersted (Danish) - Discovered magnetic effect of an electric current.
40. Robert Boyle (Irish) - Boyle showed that the pressure and volume of a mixed mass of gas are inversely proportional. He was highly active as a Chemist as well.
41. Hendrik Lorentz (Dutch) - Lorentz clarified the Electromagnetic Theory of light, developed concept of local time. His work would influence Albert Einstein.
42. Joseph von Fraunhofer (German) - First to realise that dark lines in spectra of light can be used to determine the makeup of celestial bodies.
43. Ludwig Boltzmann (Austrian) - Father of Statistical Mechanics. He worked on the kinetic theory of gases.
44. Robert Hooke (British) - Hooke formulated the law of elasticity and invented the balance spring, the microscope and the Gregorian telescope.
45. Evangelista Torrecelli (Italian) - Inventor of the Barometer, Evangelista Torrecelli is considered as the Father of Hydrodynamics.
46. Wilhelm Weber (German) - Weber invented the electrodynamometer. He is the first to apply the mirror and scale method of reading deflections.
47. Ernst Mach (Austrian) - Mach showed how airflow is disturbed at the speed of sound.
48. John Wheeler (American) - Wheeler was a theoretical physicist. He coined the terms black hole and worm hole.
49. Wilhelm Roentgen (German) - Discovered x-rays.
50. Stephen Hawking (British) - Hawking is noteworthy for his work in cosmology especially with respect to singularities. He predicts that a Black hole will convert its mass to radiation, and then disappear.

Of course there were many others that have contributed to physics in many different ways.

The Future of Physics

There have been revolutionary developments taking place in medicine, computers, artificial intelligence, nanotechnology, energy production, and astronautics. The way scientists are applying theory to applications, in all likelihood, by 2100 we will control computers via tiny brain sensors and, like magicians, move objects around with the power of our minds. Artificial intelligence will be dispersed throughout the environment, and Internet-enabled contact lenses will allow us to access the world's information base or conjure up any image we desire in the blink of an eye.

Meanwhile, cars will drive themselves using GPS, and if room-temperature superconductors are discovered, vehicles will effortlessly fly on a cushion of air, coasting on powerful magnetic fields and ushering in the age of magnetism.

Using molecular medicine, scientists will be able to grow almost every organ of the body and cure genetic diseases. Millions of tiny DNA sensors and nano-particles patrolling our blood cells will silently scan our bodies for the first sign of illness, while rapid advances in genetic research will enable us to slow down or maybe even reverse the aging process, allowing human life spans to increase dramatically.

In space, radically new ships - needle-sized vessels using laser propulsion - could replace the expensive chemical rockets of today and perhaps visit nearby stars. Advances in nanotechnology may lead to the fabled space elevator, which would propel humans hundreds of miles above the earth's atmosphere at the push of a button.

But these astonishing revelations are only the tip of the iceberg. There would be emotional robots, antimatter rockets, X-ray vision, and the ability to create new life-forms. Physics of the Future is a thrilling, wondrous ride through the next 100 years of breathtaking scientific revolution.

What are the laws of physics yet to be discovered? This is perhaps the age old question for physics. One big future goal in physics is to somehow unify the basic forces of nature.

One of the main future goals in physics is to unify laws of gravity with quantum mechanics.

While studying physics, we come across hundreds of words. Some of them are comprehensible to us while others are not. To facilitate study of physics properly, the first important element is to grasp what a particular word means. Once done, it becomes easy to read the text and understand its meaning.

The dictionary you are about to read will do just that.

A

A/D, ADC
Analogue to Digital converter (hardware) or the Analogue readback of a device (software). The hardware is a device which converts an analog voltage presented at its input to a binary digital representation of that voltage for use by the control system. Most A/D's in the control system have a measurement resolution of less than 5 mv and accept input voltages in the range -10.23 to 10.24 volts. In some applications (Linac and MRPS regulation) special units are used which have a resolution of less than 1.25 mv.

AAL
Activation Analysis Laboratory of the ES&H Section

Abort
Terminating the acceleration process prematurely, either by inhibiting the injection mechanism or by removing circulating beam to some sort of dump. This is generally done to prevent injury to some personnel or damage to accelerator components.

Abort concentrator module
A CAMAC 200 module in the Main Ring, Tevatron, and Pbar abort system capable of accepting up to 8 inputs from devices in a given service building. If the permit signal originating from a device disappears, an abort is generated.

Abort link generator module
A C201 card located at the C0 Service Building which generates the 5 MHz permit signal broadcast around the abort loop.

Abort logic/pulse shifter interface
Produces status of Main Ring and Tevatron abort loops. Inputs to Linac Keyswitch Module.

Abort loop
The system of electronics which decides to remove the beam from an accelerator in order to protect personnel and/or equipment.

Abort reset command (TEV)
A command sent from the MCR in the form of a TCLK event which clears the latched abort status and restores a beam permit.

Abort system
The Main Ring and Tevatron abort system at Fermilab is designed to dump the beam promptly on a beam dump. During Fixed Target operation both dumps are located near the long straight section C. During Colliding Beams operation the Tevatron abort system is located in the A0 section of the ring to make room for the Tevatron seperators. The abort magnets are triggered by any one of several abnormal accelerator conditions or radiation alarms. It is routinely fired at the end of an acceleration cycle to purge the accelerator of unextracted beam.

Abscissa
The value corresponding to the horizontal distance of a point on a graph from the Y axis and the X coordinate.

Absolute deviation

The difference between a single measured value and the average of several measurements made in the same way.

Absolute error

The actual difference between a measured value and its accepted value.

Absolute humidity

The ratio of water vapour in a sample of air to the volume of the sample.

Absolute pressure

Units to measure gas pressure. Normally referred to as psia (pounds per square inch absolute) with zero being a perfect vacuum.

Absolute zero

The temperature of - 273.16°C or - 459.67°F or 0 K at which molecular motion ceases.

Absorptance

The ratio of the total absorbed radiation to the total incident radiation.

Absorption spectrum

A continuous spectrum interrupted by dark lines or bands that are characteristic of the medium through which the radiation has passed.

Accelerating column

Located in the Pre-Acc pit. Set of seven titanium electrodes (eight gaps) arranged in Pierce geometry to accelerate ions to 750 keV. Situated between -750 kV dome and pit wall.

Acceleration

Time rate of change of velocity.

Acceleration due to gravity

The acceleration imparted to bodies by the attractive force of the earth or any other heavenly body.

Accelerator

Any machine used to impart large kinetic energies to charged particles such as electrons, protons, and atomic nuclei. These accelerated particles are then used to probe nuclear or subnuclear phenomena. There are also many accelerators in industrial and medical applications.

Accelerator studies

Mode of operation of the accelerator where accelerator performance and/or beam dynamics is studied and tested.

Acceptance

The measure of the limiting aperture of a transport line, accelerator, or individual device; it defines how "large" a beam will fit without scraping. More technicaly acceptance is the phase-space volume within which the beam must lie in order to be transmitted through an optical system without losses. From an experimenters point of view acceptance is the phase-space volume intercepted by an experimenter's detector system. The complement of emittance.

Acceptor

An element with three valence electrons per atom which when added to a semiconductor crystal provides electron "holes" in the lattice structure of the crystal.

Accidental rate

The rate of false coincidences in an electronic counter experiment produced by products of the reactions of more than one beam particle within the time resolution of the apparatus.

Accuracy

Closeness of a measurement to the accepted value for a specific physical quantity; expressed in terms of error.

Achromatic

The quality of a transport line or optical system where particle momentum has no effect on its trajectory through the system. An achromatic device or system is that in which the output beam displacement or divergence (or both) is independent of the input beam's momentum. If a system of lenses is achromatic, all particles of the same momentum will have equal path lengths through the system.

Aclkwatcher
A process on the VAX which decodes TCLK events and generates timing information for internal consumption (for such things as the frequency of data acquisition.)

ACNET
Accelerator Control NETwork. A system of computers that monitors and controls the accelerator complex. Interfaced to users through consoles in the MCR and elsewhere.

Acoustics
The science of the production, transmission and effects of sound.

Acoustic shielding
A sound barrier that prevents the transmission of acoustic energy.

AD
Accelerator Division

AD/OPS
Accelerator Division Operations Department

Adhesion
The force of attraction between unlike molecules.

Adiabatic
Any change in which there is no gain or loss of heat.

Adiabatic cooling
The classical description is a process in which the temperature of a system is reduced without any heat being exchanged between the system and its surroundings. At Fermilab this term is used to describe the process in the Antiproton Source Accumulator storage ring where beam emittances are reduced without affecting beam energy. This process is used in accumulating antiprotons.

Adiabatic invariant
An **invariant** of a motion is a quantity which does not change as time advances. For instance, the energy of a system is often an invariant (for a swinging pendulum, or a planet and the Sun), and knowing that it stays constant is a great help in calculating the motion.

Adiabatic process
A thermal process in which no heat is added to or removed from a system.

Adsorbent
The material of an adsorber. Silica gel, Alumina, Charcoal. Characterized by high surface/volume ratio.

Adsorber
Attracts and holds (by Van der Waal forces) molecular layers of dense gases (i.e. very near condensation temperatures) on porous high surface/volume ratio materials.

Aeolus
A process on the VAX which collects alarm information from the front-ends, combines that information with appropriate parametres in the database, and sends the package to the console cpus.

Afocal lens
A lens of zero convergent power, whose focal points are infinitely distant.

Aggregate ON/OFF
A command used to control the digital status of a block of devices.

AGS
Alternating Gradient Synchrotron accelerator at Brookhaven National Laboratory on Long Island, New York. It is a 30 GeV combined function proton synchrotron which started operation in 1959.

Air ionization chamber
Devices used by NTF to monitor neutron flux during patient treatment.

Alara
As Low As Reasonably Achievable. A safety acronym used to describe the radiation safety

philosophy of minimizing occupational radiation exposure.

Alarm

A message, usually generated by the AEOLUS VAX process, indicating that the digital or analogue status of a device is not within the tolerances set for it.

Alarm display monitor

A colour television display in the upper right-hand corner of each ACNET console which lists devices currently in a state of alarm.

Alarm screen

Same as the Alarm Display Monitor.

Albedo

The fraction of the total light incident on a reflecting surface, especially a celestial body, which is reflected back in all directions.

Alpha function

(ax, ay) A measure of the change of the beta function db/dz; a>0 N converging, a

Alpha particle

A helium-4 nucleus, especially when emitted from the nucleus of a radioactive atom.

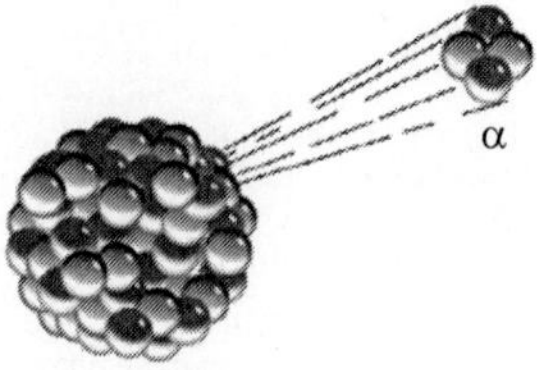

Alternating current

An electric current that has one direction during one part of a generating cycle and the opposite direction during the remainder of the cycle.

Ammeter

An electric metre designed to measure current.

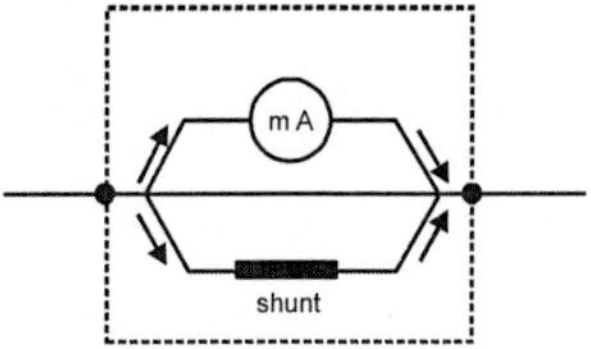

Amorphous

Solids which have neither definite form nor structure.

Ampere

The unit of electric current; one coulomb per second.

Amplifier

Any device that amplifies an electronic signal.

Amplitude

The maximum displacement of a vibrating particle from its equilibrium position.

Amplitude control module

Linac low-level RF system component that controls the amplitude of the RF gradient by varying the size of the modulator input pulse.

Analogue

Typically a device or circuit that expresses a signal in direct proportion to a physical measurement.

Angle of contact

The angle between tangents to the liquid surface and the solid surface inside the liquid, both the tangents drawn at the point of contact.

Angle of incidence

The angle between the incident ray and the normal drawn to the point of incidence.

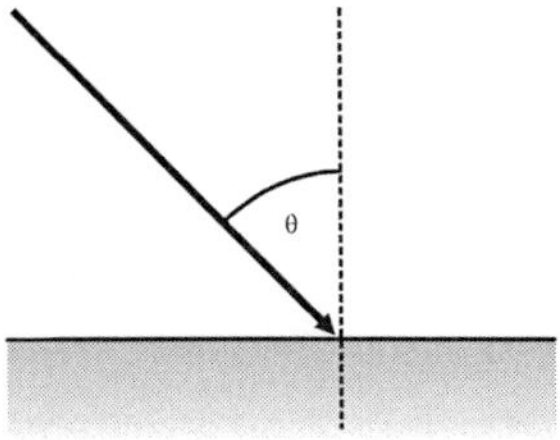

Angle of reflection
The angle between the reflected ray and the normal drawn to the point of incidence.

Angle of refraction
The angle between the refracted ray and the normal drawn to the point of refraction.

Angle of repose
The angle of inclination of a plane with the horizontal such that a body placed on the plane is at the verge of sliding.

Angstrom
A unit of linear measure equal to 10^{-10} m.

Angular acceleration
The time rate of change of angular velocity.

Angular impulse
The product of a torque and the time interval during which it acts.

Angular momentum
The product of the rotational inertia of a body and its angular velocity.

Angular velocity
The time rate of change of angular displacement.

Annihilation
A process in which a particle and antiparticle combine and release their rest energies in other particles.

Annunciator board
Status panel in Linac primary and secondary microprocessors showing status and interrupt levels.

Anode
(1) The positive electrode of an electric cell.
(2) The positive electrode or plate of an electronic tube.
(3) The electron-poor electrode.

Ansi
American National Standards Institute

Antimatter
A substance composed of antiparticles.

Antineutrino
The antiparticle of neutrino, it has zero mass and spin ½.

Antiparticle
A counterpart of a subatomic particle having opposite properties (except for equal mass).

Antiproton
The antimatter counterpart of the proton. The proton forms the nucleus of the hydrogen atom for example. Antiprotons are routinely produced at Fermilab's Antiproton source by slamming high energy protons from the Main Ring into a target. The resulting nuclear collision includes antiprotons as by-products and the source accumulates them over time. After a large "stack" has been built up, the antiprotons are shot out into the Tevatron where they are brought up to the largest energies. They are also found in cosmic rays but the intensity is much smaller.

Antiproton accumulator
After some time in the debuncher, antiprotons are continuously diverted to the accumulator where they undergo further cooling until a large stack of antiprotons is built. At this point, they are funneled out to the Main Ring and accelerated up to where the Tevatron will use them to collide with protons.

Antiproton debuncher

Protons from the Main Ring are presently diverted into a target where among other products, antiprotons are produced. Only 8 GeV antiprotons are accepted and steered into the Debuncher ring where radio frequency manipulations and various cooling systems shrink the size of the size of the beam in phase space in anticipation of its being stored for long periods of time.

Antiquench

The false appearance of a positive resistive voltage (negative resistance). This is the result of the Quench Protection Monitors's calculation during an actual quench in another cell or due to an instrumentation failure.

AP or APCR

Antiproton Control Room, located in AP10. Now more commonly referred to simply as AP10.

AP0

Accelerator building situated above the pbar target vault enclosure. The power supplies, electronics and maintenance equipment for the pbar target station and lithium lens are located here.

AP4

The beamline designed to provide a low intensity beam of 8 GeV protons from the Booster to the Debuncher.

Aperture scan

Process of changing the beam position via 3-bumps in a localized area in order to determine the size of the aperture. The beam is moved until is scrapes the side of the beam pipe or encounters an obstruction.

APM

Applications Programme Manager. A function on the console computer which coordinates application task scheduling by making sure the PA or SA executes at the proper periodic rate, recognizes the keyboard interrupt, etc. It also performs console data collection tasks, determines the visible cursor position, shaft encoder position, touch panel x, y position, and the status of the interrupt button.

Apparent mean thermal conductivity

The effective thermal conductivity of an assemblage of material (Pearlite, super insulation) between specified temperatures.

Apparent power

The product of the effective values of alternating voltage and current.

Application programmes

Software designed for direct use by a console user. The programmes reside on the ACNET consoles.

Arc degree

A unit of angular measure in which there are 360 arc degrees in a full circle.

Arc second

Abbreviated *arcsec*. A unit of angular measure in which there are 60 arc seconds in 1 arc minute and therefore 3600 arc seconds in 1 arc degree. One arc second is equal to about 725 km on the Sun.

Arc tangent

The inverse function to the tangent. Symbol: arctan or $\tan^{-1}$. Interpretation: "An angle whose tangent is

Archimedes principle

A body immersed in a fluid experiences an apparent loss in weight which is equal to the weight of the fluid displaced by the body.

Archive

Permanent storage of information regarding a given accelerator system. Magnetic tape is the primary medium. An archive should be distinguished from a "Save", where information is written onto a disk and is likely to be written over at some future date.

Argus

A process on the VAX which logs off interactive users if the account has been idle for a certain length of time.

Armature
A coil of wire formed around an iron or steel core that rotates in the magnetic field of a generator or motor.

Artifact
A feature which appears in an NMR spectrum of a molecule which should not be present based on the chemical structure and pulse sequence used.

Astronomical unit (AU)
The mean Sun-Earth distance, a unit of distance widely used in expressing distances in the solar system. 1 AU = 149597870 km = 92955807 miles.

Astrophysics
The science of studying the physical processes occurring in and around astronomical objects such as stars and galaxies.

Atmosphere
A convenient measure of pressure. 1 std atm = 14.696 psi.

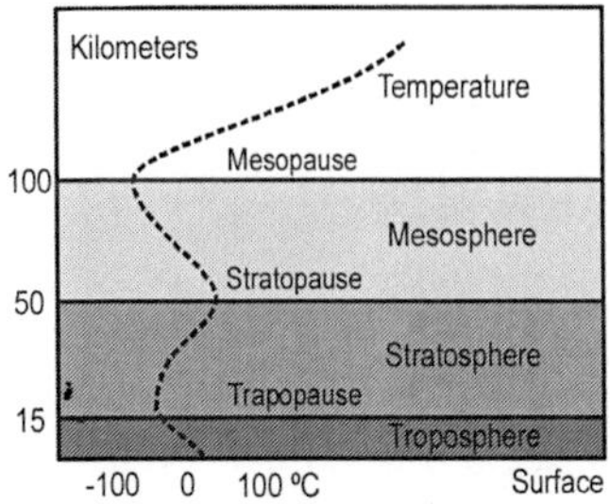

Atom
The smallest particle of an element that can exist either alone or in combination with other atoms of the same or other elements.

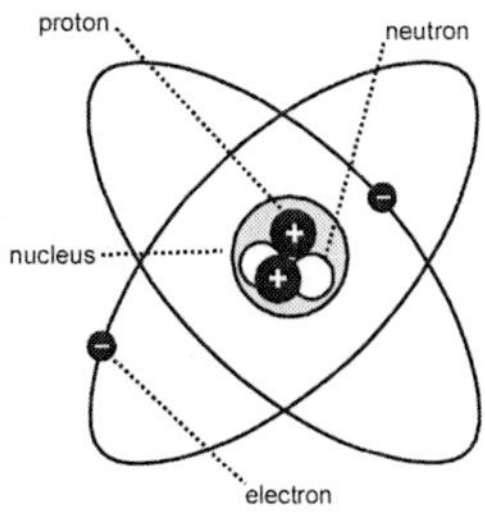

Atomic mass unit
One-twelfth of the mass of carbon-12, or 1.6605655 x 10^{-27} kg.

Atomic number
The number of protons in the nucleus of an atom.

Atomic weight
The weighted average of the atomic masses of an element's isotopes based on their relative abundance.

Attitude (of a satellite)
The direction in which the satellite is oriented in space.

Audio signal
The alternating voltage proportional to the sound pressure produced in an electric circuit.

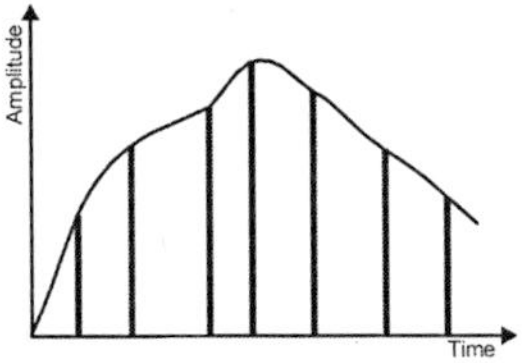

Aurora

A colourful, rapidly varying glow in the sky caused by the collision of charged particles in the magnetosphere with atoms in the Earth's upper atmosphere. Auroras are most often observed at high latitudes and are enhanced during geomagnetic storms.

Aurora (short for polar aurora)

A glow in the sky, seen often in a ring-shaped region around the magnetic poles ("auroral zone") and occasionally further equatorward. The name comes from an older one, "aurora borealis," Latin for "northern dawn," given because an aurora near the northern horizon (its usual location when seen in most of Europe) looks like the glow of the sky preceding sunrise. Also known as "northern lights," although it occurs both north and south of the equator.

Auroral oval

The region in which aurora can be seen at any single time, as observed (for instance) by satellite cameras. It resembles a circle centred a few hundred kilometres nightward of the magnetic pole, and its size varies with magnetic activity. During large magnetic storms it expands greatly, making auroras visible at regions far from the pole, where they are rarely seen.

Auto quench recovery (aqr)

A computer programme residing in the refrigerator micro-p which automatically performs cooldown after a quench.

Auto-gradient

Feature where the Linac RF gradients are controlled by computer through the Amplitude Control Module. Normally engaged.

Average velocity

Total displacement divided by elapsed time.

Avogadro number

The number of molecules in a gram molecular weight of a substance, it is equal to 6.02×10^{23}.

Avogadro's law

Under the same conditions of temperature and pressure, equal volumes of all gases contain equal number of molecules.

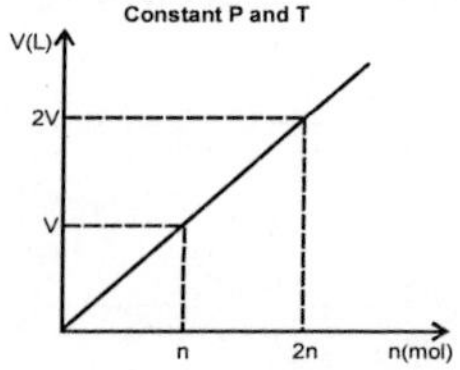

B

B clock

Obsolete. A frequency that was transmitted to a module in the MAC-A PDC crate which was proportional to the change in the Main Ring current. The dI/dT was measured in the magnet cage and transmitted over the Main Ring B-clock link via CC42 cards.

B0

A reference point on the Main Ring at which the Collider Detector at Fermilab is located (pronounced "B zero"). Other significant reference points include the D0 collision region, and C0, E0, and F0 regions used for specialized experiments.

B0 collision hall

Also referred to as the Collision Hall. CDF detector at B0 resides in this hall during collider operation.

Back emf

An induced emf in the armature of a motor that opposes the applied voltage.

Back racks

Electronics racks behind the primary working region of the Main Control Room; consists of patch panels, link modules, highpotters, and much more.

Background

Whatever devices are used to make a measurement in an experiment, the measurement is a superposition of events from the target and events from all other sources (background). The background therefore sets a lower limit on the detection of small signals. More generally, background is any unwanted signal.

Balmer lines

Lines in the spectrum of hydrogen atom in visible range, produced by transition between n 2 and n = 2, n is the principal quantum no.

Band spectrum

An emission spectrum consisting of fluted bands of colour. The spectrum of a substance in the molecular state.

Bao

Batavia Area Office of the DOE

Bar

A unit of pressure, equal to 105 Pascals.

Barn

A unit for measuring nuclear cross sections. 1 barn = 10^{-24} square centimetres. The units appropriate in high energy physics are usually the millibarn (10^{-3} barn), the microbarn (10^{-6}), or the nanobarn (10^{-9} barn).

Barometre

A device used to measure the pressure of the atmosphere.

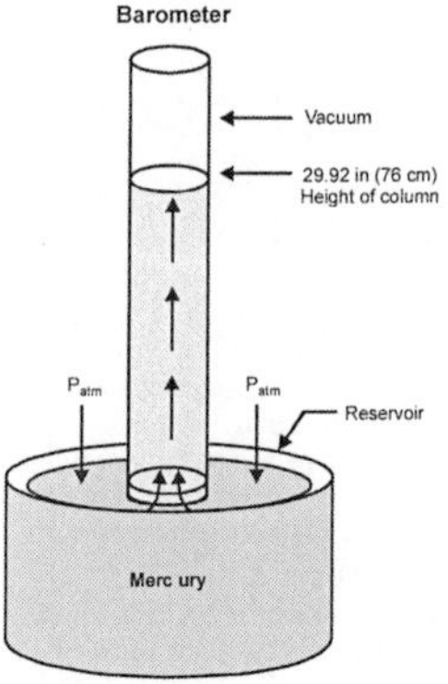

Baryon
A subatomic particle with a large rest mass, e.g., the proton.

Basic control
The ability to change the digital status of a device by interrupting on a parameter page. This function is supported by the database.

Basic equation
An equation that relates the unknown quantity with known quantities in a problem.

Basic law of electrostatics
Similarly charged objects repel each other. Oppositely charged objects attract each other.

Batch
A unit of beam corresponding to the output of one Booster cycle. Up to 12 batches of beam can be injected into Main Ring each cycle.

Baud
A unit of signalling speed; defined as the number of code elements (i.e. bits) per second.

Bayonet
A low heat conduction, longitudinally extended connector for cryogenic piping. see Transfer Line.

BCS theory
This is the successful theory of superconductivity developed in the 1950's and eventually resulting in the Nobel prize for the authors, J. Bardeen, L.N. Cooper, and J.R. Schrieffer, Phys. Rev. 108, 1175 (1957). This is the classic exposition of the BCS theory.

Beacon
Message on Linac serial data link flashed by a secondary microprocessor when the link repeater upstream of it fails.

Beam damper
A device for applying a force on the circulating beam in an accelerator to reduce either the excursions from the equilibrium orbit (betatron oscillations) or from equilibrium phase (synchrotron oscillations)

Beam dump
A massive object used to absorb an unwanted beam and dissipate the resulting heat. Dumps for high intensity beams are usually composed of large water cooled metal blocks. They must be shielded from the surrounding environment due to the extreme radioactivity induced by the absorbed beam.

Beam inhibit light link module
Linac Module through which the H- and I- secondary microprocessors can pull the beam inhibit line.

Beam intensity
The average number of particles in a beam passing a given point during a certain time interval, given, for example, as the number of protons per pulse or protons per second.

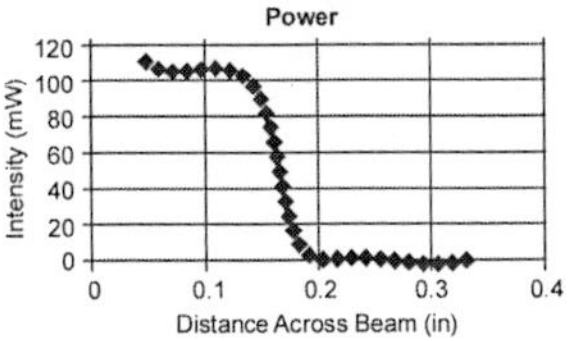

Beam line
Beam line is a collective term referring to all the devices used to control, monitor, and produce a beam having particular characteristics. The common elements of a beam line are magnets, intensity monitors, beam position monitors, and collimators.

Beam loading
Phenomenon whereby beam being accelerated by an RF cavity changes the gradient and phase of the RF in the cavity.

Beam loss
Loss of protons from the beam chamber.

Beam roll
A periodic change in horizontal and/or vertical positions during spill. This doesn't include changes caused by humans.

Beam sample pulse (bsp)
Obsolete. A pulse originated in a module of the MAC-A PDC crate which sent a signal around the ring by way of CC42 cards. It was a two-way communication, with each CC42 card echoing back a response to the BSP controller in the PDC crate. The pulse was used in generating the Main Ring sample time, as well as taking voltage-to-ground snapshots if a ramp current fault occured.

Beam stacking
A form of multi-turn injection in which a single turn is injected and then moved by acceleration or deceleration to make room for additional turns. This process, also called momentum space stacking, often appears in storage ring applications.

Beam stop
Linac primary critical device in the 750 keV line that blocks the beam path to prohibit beam in Linac. Controlled by CARESS and the pulse shifter.

Beam switch
Toggle switch to inhibit beam to a particular area of the accelerator on HEP pulses according to the logic in the Beam Switch Sum Box. Eight modules of these switches are found in the MCR.

Beam sync clock
The clocks MRBS and TVBS, for which the basic frequency is directly related to the revolution frequency of the beam. They are derived from their respective LLRF systems. They operate at frequencies of about 7.5 MHz and produce a clock "tick" every 7 bunches. Beam sync clocks are used for all critical timing of beam transfers between accelerators.

Beam toroid
A device used for measuring beam intensities by measuring the magnetic field fluctuations produced by the passing beam. The magnetic field fluctuations produce a current in a coil which is wound around a closed circular ring (torus) through which the beam passes.

Beam turns
The width of the beam pulse going to Booster divided by the revolution period of the Booster at injection.

Beam valve
A pneumatically operated gate valve that closes across the beam pipe to physically isolate one section of beam line from another. Beam valves are commonly used to isolate vacuum allowing the beamline in one sector or house to be brought up to atmosphere for maintenance while keeping adjacent sections under vacuum. In the event of a vacuum burst beam valves are closed automatically to

isolate sectors in order to localize the vacuum problem.

Beamline (transport line)

A series of magnets and vacuum pipe which carry the proton beam from one portion of the accelerator to another.

Beamline microcomputer

An NTF computer that monitors beamline devices, dose rates, and communicates with the NTF medical microcomputer as well as the local Linac secondary.

Beat

A phenomenon of the periodic variation in the intensity of sound due to superposition of waves differing slightly in frequency.

Becquerel

The rate of radioactivity equal to one disintegration per second.

Belly pan

A design feature of the Linac tanks that allows leaks in the tank welds to be put under vacuum.

Benelex

A substance similar to G-10 used to hold NTF neutron collimators in position.

Berm

Earth shielding over the top of a radiation enclosure.

Bernoulli's theorem

The total energy per unit volume of a non-viscous, incompressible fluid in a streamline flow remains constant.

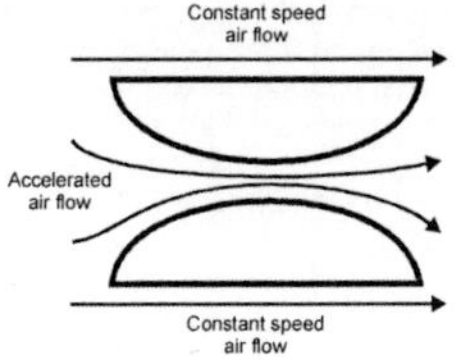

Beta (β) particle

An electron or positron emitted from a radioactive source.

Beta function

A measure of beam width. The beta function details how the beam changes around the accelerator. There are separate Beta functions for the x and y planes. The square root of bx is proportional to the beam's x-axis extent in phase space.

Beta matching

Matching of the beam size to the radius of the receiving beam pipe.

Betatron

A device that accelerates electrons by means of the transformer principle.

Betatron oscillations

Stable oscillations about the equilibrium orbit in the horizontal and vertical planes; these oscillations were the first studied in betatron oscillators, hence the name.

Bevatron

A high-energy synchrotron.

Bias pulser

A Linac module that drives the grid of the 7651 tube in the Buncher RF system.

Bias supply

Programmable power supply used to power the ferrite tuners of RF cavities in the Booster and Main Ring.

Bimodal ramp

The Main Ring magnets are pulsed to create two flattops to allow extraction at two different energies.

Binding energy

Energy that must be applied to a nucleus to break it up.

Bipolar supply

A power supply that has an operating voltage range of positive to minus. A unipolar supply has an operating range from zero to some positive value.

Birkeland currents
Electric currents linking the Earth's ionosphere with more distant regions, flowing along magnetic field lines. Named for Kristian Birkeland, a pioneer of auroral research who first proposed such currents around 1900, these currents are often associated with the polar aurora.

Bit
This stands for Binary digit. It may have a value of zero or one and is the smallest unit of measure. See byte and word.

Black body
An ideal body which would absorb all incident radiation and reflect none.

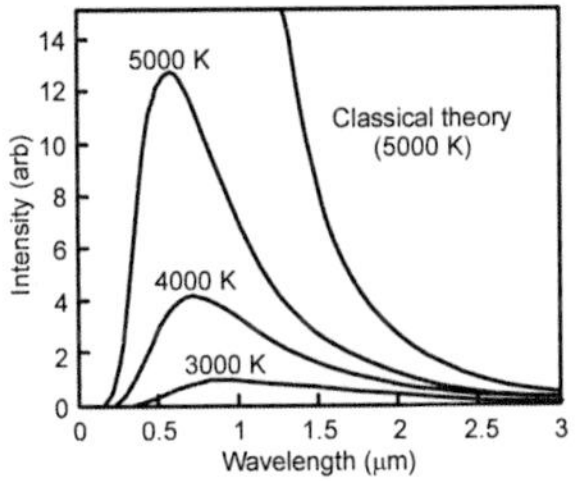

Black hole
The remaining core of a supernova that is so dense that even light cannot escape.

Bleeder resistors
In the Linac application, the resistors placed between the High-Voltage supply for the purpose of discharging energy when the power supply is turned off.

Blind scaler
A scaler made without a display for computer readout only.

BLM
A device used to measure beam loss from the accelerator. The detectors are sealed ionization chambers. BLM stands for Beam Loss Monitor.

Block transfer (BTR)
An option for data transfer in the CAMAC links. Although data is transmitted serially, it arrives at the MAC or front-end in a continuous stream rather than in discrete units. The BTR link is on a separate cable from the CAMAC serial link. It is able to transfer information at a 10 Mbit/sec rate in blocks 196 Kbytes in length.

Blow up
A relatively sudden and usually catastrophic increase in beam size generally caused by some magnetic field error driving the beam to resonance.

Blowing up emittances
To try to keep down beam-beam tune shifts the emittances of the proton bunches are increased. This is known as "blowing up the emittances". Emittances will also blow up unintentionally when the machine is tuned wrong.

Boiling point
Any point on a vapour pressure curve.

Boiling Water

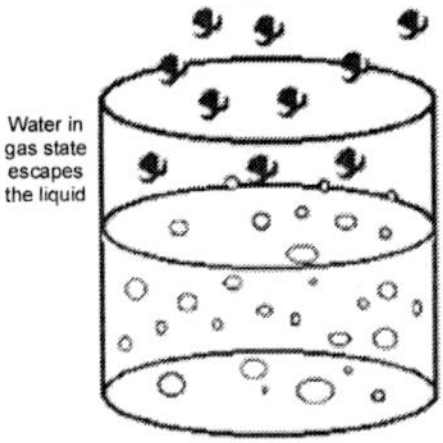

Bubbles contain water in gas state
Vapor pressure is equal or greater
than atmospheric pressure

Booster

The ring directly behind the south side of Wilson Hall surrounding the cooling pond. Protons are accelerated here to 8 GeV for injection into the Main Ring.

Booster clock

The booster clock was a continuous pulse train of 1 microsecond pulses that was synchronized to the power line. A signal marking a specific time like T1, T4 T8, was indicated by a missing pulse or gap in this continuous pulse train. These times initiated actions which carried the booster through its cycle. It was the primary time standard for all accelerator systems.

Booster pulse

That portion of the beam in the Main Ring resulting from the injection of one booster load, viz., about 1/ 13 of the Main Ring azimuth.

Booster serial link

This is the CAMAC link to which all Booster CAMAC crates are connected and through which control cards communicate with the Booster Serial (DEC BS) front-end.

Bouncer circuit

Haefely-designed system used to boost Dome voltage to compensate for charge leaving the Dome during the beam pulse. Not installed at FNAL.

Bow shock

A sharp front formed in the solar wind ahead of the magnetosphere, marked with a sudden slowing-down of the flow near Earth. It is quite similar to the shock forming ahead of the wing of a supersonic airplace. After passing near Earth, the slowed-down flow gains speed again, to the same value as the surrounding solar wind.

Boyle's law

The volume of a dry gas varies inversely with the pressure exerted upon it, provided the temperature is constant.

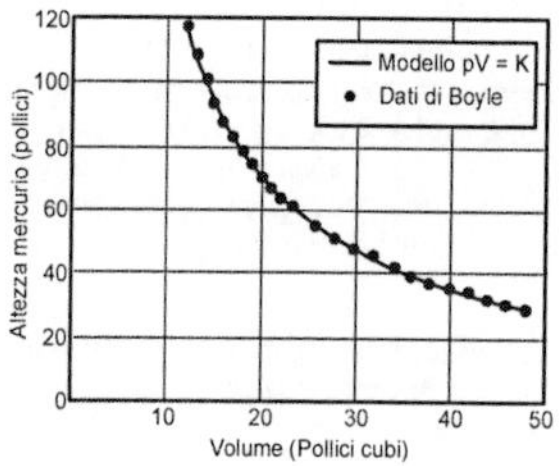

BPM

A diagnostic device used to measure beam positions. BPM stands for Beam Position Monitor.

Breakover

When a Main Ring or Tevatron power supply SCR shorts and conducts continuously (i.e., while in bypass, etc.).

Breeder reactor

A nuclear reactor in which a fissionable material is produced at a greater rate than the fuel is consumed.

Bremsstrahlung

Radiation that is emitted when a free electron is deflected by an ion, but the free electron is not captured by the ion. Generally, it is a type of radiation emitted when high energy electrons are accelerated. (German for braking radiation).

Bremsstrahlung radiation

Electromagnetic radiation, usually in the x-ray region of the spectrum produced by electrons in a collision with the nucleus of an atom. Bremsstrahlung is German for breaking. Bremsstrahlung radiation is produced in regions of high electric potential such as areas surrounding electrostatic septa and RF cavities.

Brewster's law

States that the refractive index of a material is equal

to the tangent of the polarizing angle for the material.

Brownian motion
The continuous random motion of solid microscopic particles when suspended in a fluid medium due to the consequence of ongoing bombardment by atoms and molecules.

Brownian movement
The irregular and random movement of small particles suspended in a fluid, known to be a consequence of the thermal motion of fluid molecules.

BSP link
Obsolete. In a hardware context the link was the physical cable between and including the Main Ring CC42 repeaters. In a software context it was the electrical path which carried the beam sample pulse around the ring.

Bubble chamber
Instrument used for making the paths of ionizing particles visible as a trail of tiny bubbles in a liquid.

Bucker
An air core quadrupole magnet used in the Tevatron to eliminate 4-400 Hz structure in the extracted spill.

Bucket
Stable phase space area where beam may be captured and accelerated.

Bucket (R.F.)
A bucket is the stable region in longitudinal phase space. The bucket width gives the maximum phase error or timing error at the R.F. cavity which a particle may have and still complete the whole acceleration cycle. The bucket height is the corresponding limit on momentum error.

Bulk tuner
A long copper bar, D-shaped in cross section, that runs the length of a Linac RF cavity and roughly determines the correct cavity volume.

Bulk's modulus of elasticity
The ratio of normal stress to the volumetric strain produced in a body.

Bump
A localized orbit displacement created by vertical or horizontal correction element dipoles used to steer beam through available aperture or around obstacles.

Bunch
A group of particles captured in a phase space bucket.

Bunch satellites
When a bunch is coalesced it is more than likely that the bunch is not ideally coalesced. There are often secondary bunches in buckets to either side of the coalesced bunch. These are known as satellites and are undesireable.

Buoyant force
upward force on an object immersed in fluid.

Bus
A rigid electrical conductor generally for carrying high currents and for power distribution to several devices.

Byte
A byte consists of 8 bits. It may have a signed value of -128 to + 127.

C

Calorie
The quantity of heat equal to 4.19 joules.

Calorimeter
A heat-measuring device consisting of nested metal cups separated by an air space.

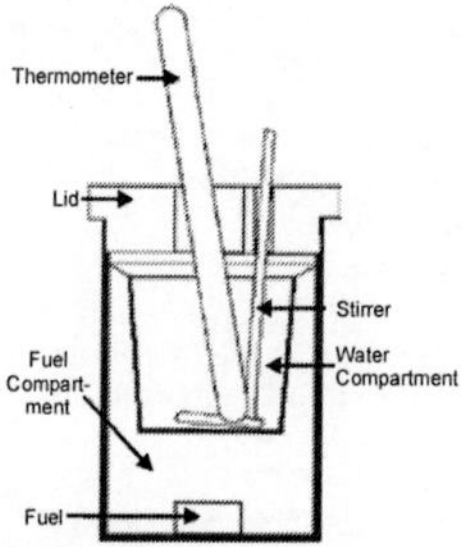

Camac module
A "control" card plugged into a CAMAC system for a specific input or output function.

Candela
The S.I. unit of luminous intensity defined as the luminous intensity in a given direction of a source that emits monochromatic photons of frequency 540 x 10^{12} Hz & has a radiant intensity in that direction of 1/683 watt per steradian.

Candle
The unit of luminous intensity of a light source.

Canned magnet
Magnets which are completely encased in their own vacuum jackets.

Capacitance
The ratio of charge stored per increase in potential difference.

Capacitor
Electrical device used to store charge and energy in the electrical field.

Capillarity
The elevation or depression of liquids in small-diameter tubes.

Capture
The process of putting the beam into RF buckets.

Carbon resistor thermometer
A carbon resistor whose temperature sensitivity provides good temperature resolution, especially below <= 10ºK.

Card
Modular piece of electronics housed in a crate. Cards are typically used to interface a hardware device with a computer system.

Card (printed circuits)
An insulating substrate to which an electronic circuit is bonded and discrete components are attached. Often used as a synonym for a CAMAC module.

Caress
Acronym for Central Accelerator Radiation and Electrical Safety System. Hardware dedicated to monitoring and controlling the accelerator safety systems and critical devices. Independent of any other control system. Located in and below the MCR.

Carnot's theorem
No engine operating between two temperatures can be more efficient than a reversible engine working between the same two temperatures.

Cathode
(1) The negative electrode of an electric cell.
(2) The electron-emitting electrode of an electronic tube.
(3) The electron-rich electrode.

Cathode rays
Particles emanating from a cathode; electrons.

Diagram of Cathode Ray

Cavity short
A grounded metal rod that goes in and out of the body of an RF cavity. When a station is off it is still a resonant cavity and can remove energy from the beam. By grounding the cavity it is kept from resonating.

CBA
Colliding Beams Adrastus. Dave Herrup of the MAD group is responsible for this term. It is the name of a colliding beams tune & chromaticity feedback control system that Dave is involved in.

CC130 card
Obsolete. MADC controller for the Main Ring. It was capable of storing a limited amount of data from the MADC and transmitting it back to MAC-A and eventually to MR DEC.

CC27 card
Obsolete. Was the Main Ring abort module. It accepted up to 8 inputs; if any of these sensed an abort condition the abort loop was broken and the abort kickers were fired.

CC48 card
Obsolete. Monitored crate voltages and temperatures in the utility crate. It can also acted as an F-slot controller, a secondary crate controller which talked to modules for beam loss monitors, a Johnson controller, and a vacuum ion pump readback.

CCI console
Obsolete. A computer console that was manufactured by Computer Communications, Inc. consisting of a colour TV display, keyboard, and supporting hardware. CCI Consoles were used at Fermilab in the Main Control Room and the switchyard experimental area control centres for monitoring and control of various accelerator and beam line parametres. CCI consoles in the Main Control Room interacted with devices they controlled through the Xerox 530 and MAC-16 computers, which are also ancient history. In the experimental areas, this linkage was usually through a PDP-11 and MAC-16 computer system.

CDF
Collider Detector Facility. A huge colliding beam detector located at B0 experimental facility.

CEA quads
Six large aperture quadrupole magnets in the N1 line used for focusing the muon beam. These quads were originally used at the Cambridge Electron Accelerator (CEA).

Cell
A unit of the Main Ring and Tevatron lattices. A cell runs from one F-quad to the next F-quad.

Celsius scale
The temperature scale using the ice point as 0° and the steam point as 100°, with 100 equal divisions, or degrees, between; formerly the centigrade scale.

Centre of curvature
The centre of the sphere of which the mirror or lens surface forms a part.

Centre of gravity
The point at which all of the weight of a body can be considered to be concentrated.

Centrifugal force
An outward pseudo force acting on a body in circular motion.

Centripetal acceleration
Acceleration directed toward the centre of a circular path.

Centripetal force
The unward force that produces centripetal acceleration.

Centroid
Technically, the centre of mass. Used here to describe the centre of a beam profile.

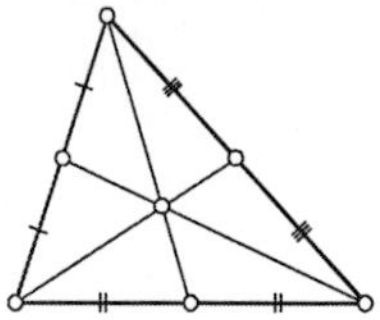

Cerenkov counter
A detector for charged particles which consists essentially of a transparent medium such as a gas which emits Cerenkov radiation when a charged particle passes through at a velocity greater than the velocity of light in the medium. The mass of a particle in a beam of known momentum can be determined with such a counter by measuring the characteristic angle at which the Cerenkov radiation is emitted.

Cerenkov radiation
Light emitted when a charged particle traverses a medium with a velocity greater than the velocity of light in the medium. The Cerenkov light is emitted in a cone centred on the particle trajectory. The opening angle of this cone depends on the velocity of the particle and on the velocity of light in the medium. The phenomenon involved is that of an electromagnetic shock wave and is the optical analogue of sonic boom. Cerenkov radiation provides an important tool for particle detection.

Cesium boiler
Electrically-heated crucible in the Pre-Acc dome used to vaporize Cesium used to coat the source cathode.

CGS
Centimetre-Gram-Second (abbrevi- ated *cm-gm-sec* or *cm-g-s*). The system of measurement that uses these units for distance, mass, and time.

Chain reaction
A reaction in which the material or energy that starts the reaction is also one of the products and can cause similar reactions.

Channel 13
This is a lab-wide closed circuit TV channel used for displaying accelerator data. The data displayed may consist of machine intensities, experimental area intensity requests, measured experimental area intensities, Main Ring and Tevatron ramp waveforms. For colliding beams the batch intensities, store number, Pbar stacking rate, stack size, etc. are displayed.

Charles' law

The volume of a dry gas is directly proportional to its Kelvin temperature, providing the pressure is constant.

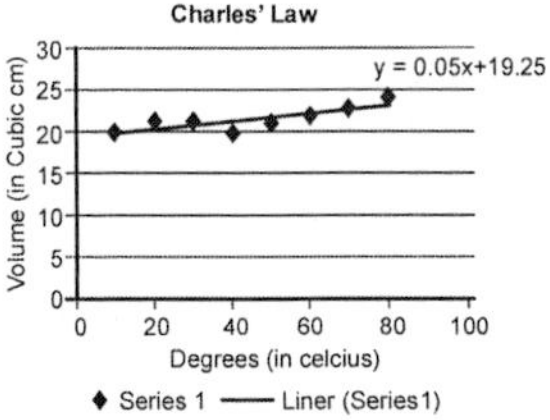

Charm

A physical property (quantum number, degree of freedom) carried by a fourth quark. In the original quark model, three quarks ("up", "down", "strange") are variously combined to produce the known hadrons. The addition of a fourth quark, the "charmed" quark, gives rise to several new hadron states called charmed particles. Proposed to account for an apparent lack of symmetry in the behaviour of hadrons relative to that of leptons, to explain why certain reactions of elementary particles do not occur.

Chemical change

A change in which new substances with new properties are formed.

Chemical equivalent

The quantity of an element, expressed in grams, equal to the ratio of its atomic weight to its valence.

Chemical screening

The screening of an applied magnetic field experienced by a nucleus due to the electron cloud around an atom or molecule.

Chemical shift

A variation in the resonance frequency of a nuclear spin due to the chemical environment around the nucleus. Chemical shift is reported in ppm.

CHL

The refrigeration plant which supplies liquid helium and liquid nitrogen to the Tevatron and Switchyard. CHL stands for Central Helium Liquefier.

Chop time selector

Module in the preacc control room that selects times generated by predets and sends them on to the 750 keV choppers.

Chopper

Electrostatic device that selectively deflects a portion of the beam pulse to control intensity in the linac or beam turns in booster. Two are found in the 750 keV lines, and one in the 200 MeV area.

Chromatic aberration

Beam spreading out due to different momentum particles being bent by the quadrupole fields at different angles.

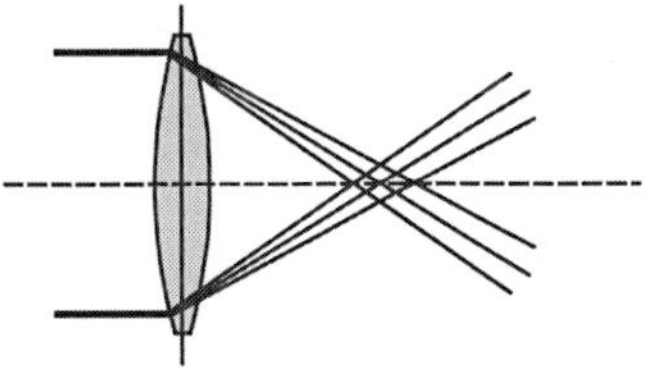

Chromatic Aberration

Chromosphere

A reddish layer in the Sun's atmosphere, the transition between the photosphere and the corona

Chute

Passageway leading from the 200 MeV area to the booster radiation enclosure. The 200 MeV transport line to the booster travels through this.

Circular motion
Motion of a body along a circular path.

Clausius' statement of second law of Thermodynamics
It is not possible that at the end of a cycle of changes heat has been transferred from a colder body to a hotter body without producing some other effect.

Clib
Acronym for Console object LIBrary. It is a collection of commonly used or convenient routines kept on the Development VAX which can be called upon by applications programmers.

Clock
A series of digital pulses generated at regular intervals used to mark time. Clocks at Fermilab generally operate at either 15 Hz or in the MHz range, and can be encoded with timing information to be sent around the accelerator.

Clock decoder
Any card, such as a 177 or 279, which recognizes a clock event and acts on it. Most of the decoder modules in the accelerator are based on a custom made Fermilab chip built specifically for decoding TCLK. The 177 modules decode TCLK only; the 279 modules can decode MRBS and TVBS as well.

Clock encoder
A card, such as a 175 module, which stamps a bit pattern (clock event) onto a clock signal for recognition by a device.

Clock event
A bit pattern superimposed on the clock frequency at a certain time in the accelerator cycle which is broadcast through the accelerator for decoding and action by a set of devices. Since they are eight bits long there can be a total of 256 unique events.

Clock generator
Modules in the preacc control room (one for H- , one for I-) that take the 1 MHz clock and convert it to light pulses to send to the domes via fibre optic cables.

Clock module
Module in the preacc control room that converts all the phase reversals on the booster clock to 1-gaps, as well as providing backup 15 Hz and 1MHz clocks for the linac in case the booster clock fails.

Clock, (main ring)
Most Main Ring events are controlled from TCLK. There is a 1 MHz phase reversal clock dedicated to Main Ring which translates TCLK events into phase reversal events for use by MAC-A, DEC B, and DEC C.

Clock, (tevatron)
Also known as TCLK. Although the name implies it is only used for the Tevatron, it is essentially the master clock for the accelerator. It operates at a 10 MHz rate and is able to transmit encoded events at about a 1 MHz rate. There are 256 possible events (displayed in 2-digit hexadecimal numbers) which the clock can send out.

Clockodile
A console applications programme which monitors the clock events actually being sent out on the link. It currently resides on D33.

Closed orbit
The ideal orbit of particles in the accelerator. Betatron oscillations are superimposed on this orbit.

Closed system
The system which cannot exchange heat or matter with the surroundings.

Cloud chamber
A chamber in which charged subatomic particles appear as trails of liquid droplets.

CNSCOM
CoNSole COMmon. An area in console memory via which information flows between APM, PLD, DPM, and the applications programmes (See APM, PLD, and DPM.)

Coasting beam safety system
Part of the radiation safety system that protects

personnel from circulating beam in Main Ring, Tevatron, and the Accelerator/Debuncher. This system controls beam valves that are inserted into the beam tube to dissipate circulating beam when an unsafe situation is detected.

Coasting beam valve

Special beam line valves that close in order to stop circulating beam in the Main Ring, Tevatron, and Accumulator/Debuncher. These devices are part of the Coasting Beam Radiation Safety Systems.

Cockcroft-walton accelerator

A high-voltage DC accelerator, especially for the acceleration of protons. The DC voltage is produced from a circuit of rectifiers and capacitors to which a low AC voltage is applied. The PreAcc accelerator at Fermilab is a Cockcroft-Walton design.

Cockroft walton

The electrostatic generator used to create the negative hydrogen ions which are accelerated in the Linac and eventually stripped down to protons on their way into the Booster ring.

Coefficient of area expansion

The change in area per unit area of a solid per degree change in temperature.

Coefficient of cubic expansion

The change in volume per unit volume of a solid or liquid per degree change in temperature.

Coefficient of linear expansion

The change in length per unit length of a solid per degree change in temperature.

Coefficient of sliding friction

The ratio of the force needed to overcome sliding friction to the normal force pressing the surfaces together.

Coefficient of superficial expansion

The increase in area per unit original area per degree rise in temperature.

Coefficient of volumetric expansion

The increase in volume per unit original volume per degree rise in temperature.

Cogging

The process of spacing bunches of protons or antiprotons in the Main Ring or Tevatron so that they will collide at the proper points in the ring. It is used only in colliding beams mode.

Coherence

The property of two wave trains with identical wavelengths and a constant phase relationship.

Coherent source

A source in which there is a constant phase difference between waves emitted from different parts of the source.

Cohesion

The force of attraction between like molecules.

Coil

One or more loops of a conductor used to create a magnetic field. In NMR, the term generally refers to the radiofrequency coil.

Coincidence

(1) A coincidence or logic unit generates an exactly timed output signal whenever the time overlap of input signals satisfies a preselected coincidence requirement.

(2) Occurring or existing at the same time.

Cold box

Usually low pressure vessel providing vacuum insulation for cryogenic heat exchangers. Often, loosely, synonymous with refrigerator box.

Cold cathode gauge

An ionization vacuum gauge with no hot filament which uses electrons spiralling in a magnetic field to ionize any gas present. The ions produced are drawn to electrostatic plates. The current produced in this way is interpreted as a pressure. This type of gauge operates down to about 1 E-5 torr.

Cold valve

A valve with I zero heat leak. Usually pneumatically activated by a noncondensable gas through long connecting tubes.

Collider
A mode of running beam in which two counter-circulating beams of similiar energy are made to collide at an interaction point around which detectors can be placed. The centre of mass energy available for creating new particles is best in this mode since it is always the same order of magnitude as the beam energy. Fermilab runs in collider mode and fixed target mode seperately. The luminosity is an issue though since the beam is not as dense as a solid target.

Collider Detector at Fermilab (CDF)
The apparatus used for experiments designed to measure the results of colliding beams of protons and antiprotons. CDF experiments study the highest energy collisions ever produced in a laboratory. This allows physicists to probe much deeper into the structure of matter than heretofore possible.

Collimator
A collimator is generally a large block of steel or iron, sometimes having an adjustable aperture, that enables one to choose the beam cross section or angular divergence. It is also used to absorb the beam halo and if closed further it can be used to control the intensity.

Collision
A close approach of two or more particles, photons, atoms or nuclei during which quantities such as energy, momentum, and charge may be exchanged.

Colour
The visual perception of light associated with its frequency or wave length.

Com
COMputable. A process scheduling state on the VAX meaning that a given process is ready to use the cpu.

Commutator
A split ring in a d-c generator, each segment of which is connected to an end of a corresponding armature loop.

Compiler
A programme which converts programmes from problem oriented language (Fortran, BASIC, COBOL, etc.) into machine language.

Complementary colours
Two colours that combine to form white light.

Complete vibration
Back-and-forth motion of an object describing simple harmonic motion.

Complex data
Numerical data with a real and an imaginary component.

Component
One of the several vectors that can be combined geometrically to find a resultant vector.

Composition of forces
The combining of two or more component forces into a single resultant force.

Compression
The region of a longitudinal wave in which the distance separating the vibrating particles is less than their equilibrium distance.

Compressor building
A building located at each zero location of the Main Ring that contains several Mycom Helium compressors. The compressors draw low pressure Helium from the suction header in the Main Ring tunnel and send high pressure Helium along the discharge line atop the Main Ring berm to each of the satellite refrigerator buildings.

Computing counter
A device that measures pulse frequencies with great accuracy. Used for the display of the linac master oscillator frequency.

Concave
Surface with centre of curvature on the same side as the observer.

Concave lens
A lens that diverges parallel light rays (assuming

the outside refractive index to be smaller).

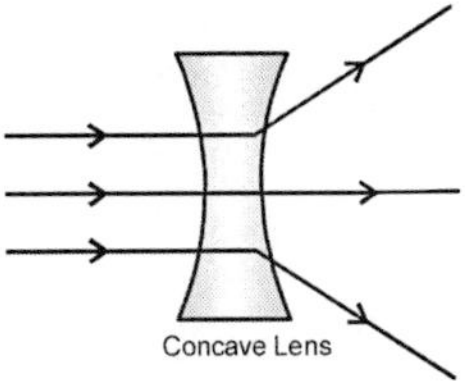

Concave Lens

Concave mirror

A mirror that converges parallel light rays incident on its surface.

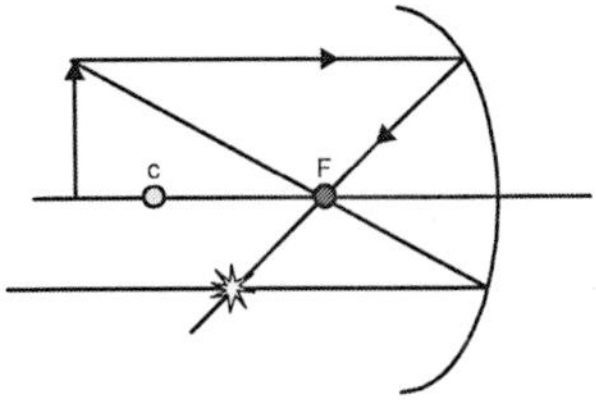

Concurrent forces

Forces with lines of action that pass through the same point.

Condensation

The change of phase from a gas or vapour to a liquid.

Condensation point

The temperature at which a gas or vapour changes back to liquid.

Condenser

An extended surface heat exchanger for the purpose of extracting the heat of vaporization of fluid.

Conductance

The reciprocal of the ohmic resistance.

Conduction

The transfer of heat from a region of higher temperature to a region of lower temperature by increased kinetic energy moving from molecule to molecule.

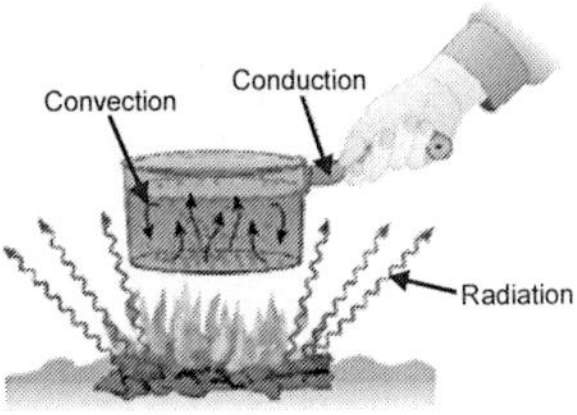

Conduction, thermal

Solid heat flow. Similar to electrical conduction.

Conductor

A material through which an electric charge is readily transferred.

Conservative forces

Forces for which the law of conservation of mechanical energy holds true; gravitational forces and electrostatic forces.

Console

A standard set of screens and other devices from which an operator or systems specialist controls and monitors devices in the accelerator complex. Each console includes a colour TV monitor, a colour Lexidata screen, a 613 storage scope, a touch panel and an alarm screen. Each console station is supported by a PDP-11 computer. There are currently 7 consoles in the MCR, and numerous others at locations such as AP-10, Booster West Gallery, CHL, and CDF.

Console crate

A CAMAC crate which acts as the interface between the console PDP-11/34 processor and the console hardware. It holds the video generator modules (CC130's), the Lexidata interface (134), the 613 interface, and the TSCC crate controller cards which accept serial data coming from the TSCC link driver in the computer room.

Console disk

There are two RL02 disks for each console. The top, or "0" disk, contains the operating system and other management programmes which are a permanent part of the console. The bottom, or "1" disk, holds the applications programmes which usually claim only a temporary residence on the console.

Console users guide

This is an Accelerator Division publication, Software Documentation Memo No. 62.3, which describes the ACNET consoles and contains useful information for writing applications programmes for the consoles.

Continuous spectrum

A spectrum without dark lines or bands or in which there is an uninterrupted change from one colour to another.

Continuous wave (cw)

A form of spectroscopy in which a constant amplitude electromagnetic wave is applied.

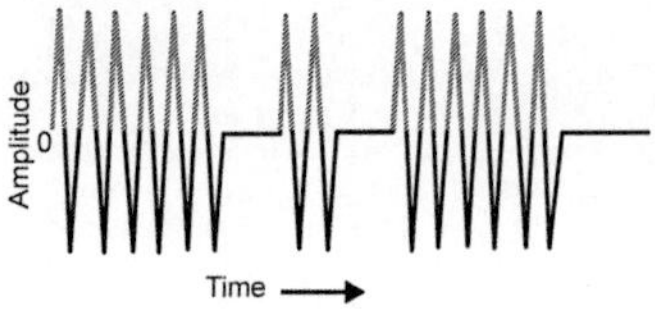

Contour map

A map showing the intensity of radiation as a function of position. Each contour line corresponds to a specific intensity of radiation, with inner contours corresponding to higher intensities than outer contours. Therefore, a closed contour encircles a region where the intensity of the emitted radiation is greater than or equal to the intensity on the contour line. The contours outline the shape of the emitting source.

Controlled access

Method used to enter an accelerator enclosure when three conditions have not been met: (1) A radiation survey has been performed in the enclosure. (2) The proper power supplies to the devices in the enclosure have been padlocked off. (3) The safety system has been broken requiring a search and secure.

Controls hardware release (HDWREL)

A type of document published by the Accelerator Division Controls group and distributed within the Division (including the Operations group) which details the operation of new control cards and other hardware built by the Controls group.

Controls software release (SFTREL)

A document also published by the Controls Group which includes detailed information on new applications programmes and other software paraphernalia.

Controls software update (SFTUPD)

New versions of Software Releases which update information on applications programmes, etc. This type of document is currently being phased out in favor of multiple versions (xx.1, xx.2, etc.) of the Software Release.

Convection

The transfer of heat by the actual transfer of matter.

Convection zone

A layer in a star in which convection currents are the main mechanism by which energy is transported outward. In the Sun, a convection zone extends from just below the photosphere to about seventy percent of the solar radius.

Convection, forced
A transfer of heat by a stream driven by external means between a region and itself, or between regions, of different temperature.

Convection, natural
A transfer of heat by a stream driven by density differences that result from distinct heating and cooling regions.

Converging lens
A lens that is thicker in the middle than it is at the edge and bends incident parallel rays toward a common point.

Converter
A thin piece of material used to generate electron-positron pairs from incident photons via the process of pair production.

Convex
Surface with centre of curvature on the opposite side from the observer.

Convex lens
A lens that converges parallel light rays (assuming the outside refractive index to be smaller). convex mirror. A mirror that diverges parallel light rays incident on its surface.

Convolution
A mathematical operation between two functions.

Cooper luminosity
A measure of integrated luminosity when CDF is up and data collecting. Accelerator division integrated luminosity continues to integrate when beam is in the machine even though CDF is down. Cooper luminosity is named after John Cooper of CDF who suggested the measure.

Coordinate transformation
A change in the axes used to represent some spatial quantity.

Core
The active memory section of a computer system in which stored data may be most readily accessed by the CPU. Generally when programme execution is complete, data stored in core is lost.

Corona
The outermost layer of the solar atmosphere. The corona consists of a highly rarefied gas with a low density and a temperature greater than one million degrees Kelvin. It is visible to the naked eye during a solar eclipse.

Corona rings
Curved metal surfaces shielding the outside of high-voltage devices to forestall the ionization of air by electric discharges. Used in the HV sources for the preaccelerators.

Coronal mass ejection (CME)
a huge cloud of hot plasma, expelled sometimes from the Sun. It may accelerate ions and electrons, and may travel through interplanetary space as far as the Earth's orbit and beyond it, often preceded by a shock front. When the shock reaches Earth, a magnetic storm may result.

Correction element
Additional magnet inserted in an accelerator's lattice to correct for manufacturing defects, variations in power supplies and magnets, obstacles in the beam path, etc.

Cosmic rays
High-energy nuclear particles apparently originating from outer space.

Cosmology
Branch of astrophysics dealing with explaining the origins of the universe.

Cosmotron
A high-energy synchrotron.

Coulomb
The quantity of electricity equal to the charge on 6.25×10^{18} electrons.

Coulomb's law
The force between any two charges is directly proportional to the product of charges and inversely proportional to the square of the distance between the charges.

Coulomb's law of electrostatics
The force between two point charges is directly proportional to the product of their magnitudes and inversely proportional ta the square of the distance between them.

Coulomb's law of magnetism
The force between two magnetic poles is directly proportional to the strengths of the poles and inversely proportional to the square of their distance apart.

Couple
Two forces of equal magnitude acting in opposite directions in the same plane, but not along the same line.

Coupling
A generally undesirable situation in which motions in the transverse plane (or transverse-longitudinal) planes are not independent, but are related in some way.

Coupling capacitor
A capacitor used to couple AC voltages to parts of an electrical circuit while blocking DC voltages.

CPLD
Central Programme LoaDer. A programme on the VAX which loads applications programmes onto the console disk. When a programme is called by a console computer it works in conjunction with PLD to assure that the console has the newest version of the programme.

CPU (central processor unit)
The main "thinking" component of a computer system. All arithmetic and logical functions are performed by the CPU of a system. In addition, the CPU is in control of all data acquisition and storage.

Crash cord
A yellow and black rope in the Transfer Hall and in some of the experimental target halls. Its purpose is to protect individuals from radiation caused from the beam. If an individual is inside one of these areas and realizes beam is about to be turned on, he pulls the crash cord which immediately turns off the accelerator.

Crate
A repository for control cards. Each type of crate has a different protocol for accessing and distributing information which must be recognized by the respective front-end. There are CAMAC, NIM, Multibus, Unibus, and several less important types of crates. The cards for each of these crates are not interchangeable.

Crate (camac crate)
A standardized receptacle for electronic circuit modules providing a common set of data, control, and power lines.

Crate controller
The card(s) in a given crate which decodes address information arriving on the link and distributes messages to the appropriate cards in that crate. These cards also arbitrate the data and messages to and from each card in the crate, as they all share the same data lines.

Crate save/restore
Using the D1 save/restore programme to save/ restore parameter values of all devices controlled by a particular crate.

Crates and slots page
An applications programme which allows the user to examine the types of microprocessors residing in a given building and its status. There is an individual applications programme for each of the serial front-ends (B59, T96, P66, and S54).

Crest
A region of upward displacement in a transverse wave.

Critical angle
The angle of incidence in a denser medium for which angle of refraction.

Critical device
A device that can prevent beam from entering a

specific accelerator area. Generally critical devices are designed for fail safe operation. The Radiation Safety System provides permits for critical devices.

Critical device failure

A safety system condition where the Radiation Safety System (RSS) for an area drops before the critical device for that area has been turned off to remove beam from the area. Results in a pulse shifter inhibit and must be reset at the CARESS racks.

Critical magnetic field

This is the maximum magnetic field that a superconductor can tolerate before abruptly returning to the normal resistive state.

Critical mass

The amount of a particular fissionable material required to make a fission reaction self-sustaining.

Critical point

The point on the vapour pressure curve at which the heat of vaporization is zero and the temperature and pressure exhibit a maximum.

Critical pressure

The pressure needed to liquefy a gas at its critical temperature.

Critical temperature

The temperature to which a gas must be cooled before it can be liquefied by pressure.

Critical temperature, pressure

The temperature and pressure at the critical point.

Critical velocity

Velocity below which an object moving in a vertical circle will not describe a circular path.

Cross section

The effective area a target presents to a high energy particle (measured in barns = 10^{-24} centimetres). It is used as a standard unit of measure to compare the probability of a certain type of interaction to occur as opposed to a different type when the same type of particles collide. Multiplying the luminosity by the cross section results in the event rate which is the what is directly measured.

Crowbar

Electronic safety circuits which turn off power when current and/or voltage goes to a dangerous level.

Crowbar compare circuit

Modulator and PA protection circuit that shuts down the RF system if the current from the modulator to the PA anode exceeds certain limits.

Cryogen

A refrigerant to be used in a refrigerator for producing low temperatures. To reach superconducting temperatures, liquid gases such as Nitrogen are used in succession with liquid helium to reach the lowest temperatures.

Cryogenic

Cryogenics is the study of the production of very low temperature (below -150 °C, -238 °F or 123 K) and the behaviour of materials at those temperatures. A person who studies elements under extremely cold temperature is called a cryogenicist. Rather than the relative temperature scales of Celsius and Fahrenheit, cryogenicists use the absolute temperature scales. These are Kelvin (SI units) or Rankine scale (Imperial & US units)

Cryopumping

The condensation of air onto a surface cooled by a cryogenic liquid .

Cryostat

A vacuum insulated vessel for cryogenic fluids.

C-seal

A metal vacuum seal, usually coated with lead or indium, with a c-shaped cross-section. It is used in high radiation environments where O-ring seals would deteriorate.

CTF

Cancer Therapy Facility. Now called Neutron Treatment Facility (NTF). A small area in the Linac Gallery devoted to cancer treatment using neutrons produced on a beryllium target by 66 MeV protons diverted from between the fifth and sixth tanks of the linac during periods when it is not needed to fill the Booster. The facility consists basically of the neutron beam line, a treatment enclosure with patient positioning apparatus, a few offices, patient preparation rooms, etc.

CUB
Central Utility Building. This facility provides LCW for accelerator cooling as well as chilled water for air conditioning systems. It is located directly behind the Booster pond.

CUR
CURrent. A process scheduling state on the VAX indicating that a given process is currently operating.

Curie
The quantity of any radioactive nuclide that has a disintegration rate of 3.7×10^{10} becquerels.

Current sensitivity
Current per unit scale division of an electric metre. cut-off bias. The smallest negative grid voltage, for a given plate voltage, that causes a vacuum tube to cease to conduct.

Cursor
A visible marker on the screen which indicates where on the screen a user may be interacting with the programme.

Curves mac
Obsolete. This was a MAC-16 computer located in the Mac Room and used for calculation of the ramps for the Main Ring RF high and low level systems.

CUSPS (of the magnetosphere)
Two regions of weak magnetic field, on the sunward boundary of the magnetosphere, one on each side of the equator. They separate magnetic field lines closing on the front from those swept into the earth's magnetotail.

Cut-off frequency
A characteristic threshold frequency of incident light below which, for a given material, the photoelectric emission of electrons ceases.

Cut-off potential
A negative potential on the collector of a photoelectric cell that reduces the photoelectric current to zero.

CVT
Stands for Constant Voltage Transformer. It provides proper voltage for Main Ring and Tevatron power supply SCR firing circuits.

Cycle
A series of changes produced in sequence that recur periodically.

Cyclotron
A particle accelerator in which the particles move in a constant magnetic field in a spiral orbit, the energy of the particles begin increased by the application of an alternating electric field at constant frequency. Authors side note. In college we actually made one of these in a coffee can being blissfully unaware of the X-ray or Radiation hazard we had created. It was demonstrated for a professor and promptly confiscated to disappear into the low level radiation storage locker never to be seen again.

Cyclotron magnet, chicago
The large magnet from the synchrocyclotron used by Fermi and his colleagues at the University of Chicago now used not as an accelerator, but as a particle-momentum analyzing device (spectrometer) in the N1 muon beam of the Neutrino Area. It is located in the Muon Lab Enclosure. The magnet is so massive that it was moved in several pieces, assembled and the building then built around it.

D

D to A Line

The transport line joining the Debuncher and Accumulator. Extraction/injection is realized by means of sets of pulsed magnetic septa and kicker magnets all oriented to displace the beam horizontally. The Accumulator injection kicker is unique in that a physical shutter moves into the aperture when the kicker is fired to shield the already circulating stack from the magnetic field if the kicker (only the injected beam is perturbed).

D/a

Digital to Analogue converter (hardware) or a setting value for a device (software). The hardware is a unit which accepts a number from the control system (binary encoded) and converts it to a corresponding output voltage. Such a device is the complement of an A/D converter. In many instances the output is used to programme the output of a power supply. In such a situation the transfer function of the power supply is assumed to be a constant. A user should be aware of this potential problem. Most D/As in the accelerator control system output voltages in the range of -10 to 10 volts and have a resolution of 12 bits (including the sign bit).

D0 collision hall

Collider Detector at D0 interaction region.

Dabble

An interactive programme on the Operational VAX which implements changes in the system database.

DAC

Digital-to-Analogue converter. It is an electronic circuit which takes a digital message, usually transmitted on a link, and converts it to an analogue voltage for use by a device. This usually means that the circuit has many input lines (generally 8, 12, or 14) corresponding to the number of bits in the digital word and a single output line whose voltage represents the sign and magnitude of the digital word.

Damper

Device used to damp out coherent transverse beam oscillations.

Damping

The reduction in amplitude of a wave due to the dissipation of wave energy.

Dark current

Current that flows from a photomultiplier tube in the absence of light. The main sources of dark current are ohmic leakage due to imperfect insulation and thermionic emission.

Data selector

Part of the monitor/control module for the Haefely power supply which selects either the voltage readback or the command voltage for display on the front of the module.

Database

A list of properties for each device on the ACNET

system, kept on the Operational VAX. These properties include mnemonics, alarm limits, descriptor texts, and scaling information.

Datalogger

A programme residing on the VAX which allows for the automatic and regular acquisition of data from a given set of devices, each with its own frequency. The limit is about 900 devices.

DBM

This acronym stands for Data Base Manager. This is a process on the VAX which maintains the database. All accesses to the information in the database must be through routines which interface with this database manager.

Dbpeeker

A programme on the operational VAX which allows the user to look at the database of a particular device or set of devices.

Debuncher

A radio frequency cavity phased so that particles at the leading edge of a bunch of beam particles (higher momentum particles) are decelerated while the trailing particles are accelerated, thereby reducing the range of momenta in the beam. Such a device may be placed between two stages of acceleration to increase the efficiency of capturing the beam in the second stage as, for example, with the 200 MHz debuncher cavity installed between the Linac and Booster at Fermilab.

Debuncher; booster

Something of a misnomer. The debuncher is used to reduce the momentum spread of the Linac beam by decelerating particles with higher than nominal energy and accelerating those with lower energy.

DEC

Digital Equipment Corporation, manufacturers of the PDP and VAX series computers and perpetrators of the UNIBUS.

Decay

A transformation in which an atom, nucleus, or subatomic particle changes into two or more objects whose total rest energy is less than the rest energy of the original object.

Decay constant

The ratio between the number of nuclei decaying per second and the total number of nuclei.

Decay length

The average distance a species of a particle at a given energy travels before decaying.

Decay muon

A muon produced via pion or kaon decay.

Decay pipe

The 400 metre long beam pipe downstream of the Neutrino Area target train. The p and K particles produced at the target decay in flight through the decay pipe into the muons and neutrinos used by the experiments. The length of the decay pipe is determined by the decay half-life of the p and K particles and their velocity.

Dec-B

This is a PDP-11/55 computer located in the Mac Room. It is used for Main Ring power supply calculations.

Dec-BS

This is the Booster Serial front-end, a PDP-11/44, located in the Computer Room. It is used to interface and control devices on the Booster Serial Camac Link.

Dec-C

This is a PDP-11/55 computer located in the Mac Room. It is used for Main Ring Power Supply ramp control.

Deceleration

The process of decelerating the antiproton stack to a set momentum for the E760 experiment located at AP50 in the Antiproton Source

Decibel

A unit of sound intensity level. The smallest change of sound intensity that the normal human ear can detect.

Declination
The angle between magnetic north and the true north from any surface location; also called variation.

Decnet
A system developed by the Digital Equipment Corporation which links the DEC computers together. Just about any DEC computer system (worldwide) may be connected to DECnet so that a communication link may be established between computer systems. Decnet is the largest single computer network in the United States.

Dec-P
This is the Antiproton front-end, a PDP-11/44, located in the Computer Room. It is used to interface and control devices on the Antiproton Serial Camac Link.

Dec-S
This is the Switchyard front-end, a PDP-11/44, located in the Computer Room. It is used to interface and control devices on the Switchyard Serial Camac Link. These devices include all Switchyard devices, most 8-Gev devices, and TCLK.

Dec-T
This is the Tevatron front-end, a PDP-11/44, located in the Computer Room. It is used to interface and control devices on the Tevatron Serial Camac Link.

Decwriter
A hardcopy terminal located in the computer room. There are dedicated Decwriters which interface with each of the VAX computers and other Decwriters that can be connected to the PDP-11's.

Dees
The electrodes of a cyclotron.

Defocussing quadrupole magnet
A quadrupole magnet that focuses beam in the vertical plane and defocuses in the horizontal plane.

Density
The amount of mass or number of particles per unit volume. In cgs units mass density has units of gm cm^{-3}. Number density has units cm^{-3}.

Dephasing gradient
A magnetic field gradient used to dephase transverse magnetization.

Derived unit
A unit of measure that consists of combinations of fundamental units

Detector building
The airplane hanger shaped building in the Meson Area providing weather protection, crane coverage, and utility connections for the "upstream" end of the experiments in that area. Beam line monitoring and tuning is also conducted from the operations area on the mezzanine floor of the Detector Building. Also called Meson Hall.

Deuteron
The nucleus of the deuterium atom (an isotope of the hydrogen) consisting of a proton and a neutron.

Development VAX
This is a VAX-11/785 used for software development. It is located in the Computer Room.

Device index (DI)
This is a number assigned by DBM to all devices entered into the database. This number is then used by software routines to access information about a device from the database.

Dew point
The temperature at which a given amount of water vapou r will exert equilibrium vapour pressure.

Dewar
A dewar is a vacuum insulated container for keeping material, chiefly liquids, cold or hot. The common thermos bottle is an example of a dewar. In the accelerator business dewars are often used to store large quantities of cryogenic liquids. In Pbar the nitrogen dewars are used to submerge the

stochastic cooling electronics in order to reduce the amount of thermally induced electronic noise.

DFG

Acronym for Dipole Function Generator. It is the card which controls and provides the output waveform for the Tevatron correction dipole regulators. These are also known as 160 modules.

Diamagnetism

The property of a substance whereby it is feebly repelled by a strong magnet.

Dichroism

A property of certain crystalline substances in which one polarized component of incident light is absorbed and the other is transmitted.

Dielectric

An electric insulator. A nonconducting medium.

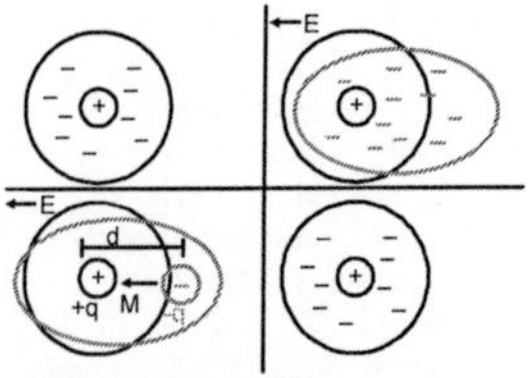

Dielectric constant

The ratio of the capacitance with a particular material separating the plates of a capacitor to the capacitance with a vacuum between the plates.

Diffracted beam

Particles exhibit wave like characteristics in their passage through matter. In striking a target the incident beam scatters off nucleons. The scattered waves then combine according to the superposition principle and the peak of this scattered wave is called the diffracted beam. Diffraction takes place when the wavelength of the incident beam is short compared to the interaction distance.

Diffraction

The spreading of a wave disturbance into a region behind an obstruction.

Diffraction angle

The angle that a diffracted wavefront forms with the grating plane.

Diffraction grating

An optical surface, either transmitting or reflecting, with several thousand equally spaced and parallel grooves ruled in it.

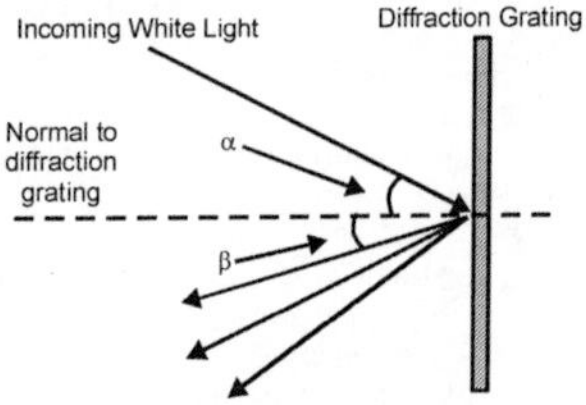

Diffuse aurora

A spread-out glow often covering much of the *auroral oval*. It is not seen by the eye but can be observed well by satellite cameras.

Diffusion

(1) The penetration of one type of particle into a mass of a second type of particle.

(2) The scattering of light by irregular reflection.

Diffusion pump

After a mechanical (roughing) pump is used to remove about 99.99% of the air in the beam tube, the remaining air can then be removed by a diffusion pump, down to about 1E-5 torr.

Digital filtering

A feature found on may newer spectrometres which eliminates wraparound artifacts by filtering out the higher frequency components in the time domain spectrum.

Digital status

Indicates whether a given device is on or off, and whether or not it has been reset. Usually there are also digital bits which signify interlock status, etc.

Digital voltmeter (DVM)

A modern solid state device capable of measuring voltage and displaying the value in digitized form. The term is also used loosely for the digital multimeter which can measure current and resistance as well.

Dimensional analysis

The performance of indicated mathematical operations in a problem with the measurement units alone.

Diode

A two-terminal device that will conduct electric current more easily in one direction than in the other.

Dioptre

Unit of power of a lens.

Dipole

A compact source of magnetic force, with two magnetic poles. A bar magnet, coil or current loop, if their size is small, create a dipole field. The Earth's field, as a crude approximation, also resembles that of a dipole.

Direct current

An essentially constant value current in which the movement of charge is in only one direction.

Direct muon

A muon produced by the direct interaction of a proton with a target rather than produced as a decay product.

Direct proportion

The relation between two quantities whose graph is a straight line.

Discrete aurora

(Or "auroral arcs") are the typical ribbon-like structures of aurora observed from the ground. From space they may appear as brighter spots in the diffuse aurora.

Discriminator

A discriminator is a circuit that accepts signals of various shapes and amplitudes, and for each input signal that is above threshold, it outputs a standardized logic pulse. The outputs are of standard amplitude and duration, completely independent of all characteristics of the input except time of occurrence.

Diskette

Also known as a "floppy disk". A small device which carries magnetically encoded information readable by a computer or microprocessor.

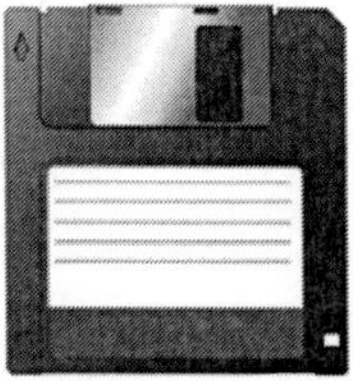

Dispersion
Quality of a beam transport system at a given point that defines the variation of the transverse position of the beam with variations in beam momentum. Usually expressed in metres.

Displacement
(1) A change of position in a particular direction.
(2) Distance of a vibrating particle from the midpoint of its vibration.

Dissipative forces
Forces for which the law of conservation of mechanical energy does not hold true; frictional forces.

Distance
The actual path length covered by a body. It is a scalar quantity.

Distillation
The evaporation of volatile materials from a liquid or solid mixture and their condensation in a separate vessel.

Divergence
The angle that the trajectory of each particle makes with the beam axis. Accelerator systems always try to reduce beam divergence.

Diverging lens
A lens that is thicker at the edge than it is in the middle and bends incident parallel rays so that they appear to come from a common point.

DL0 disk drive
The upper disk drive on a console PDP-11/34. It contains the console operating system management programmes and system common block areas.

DL1 disk drive
The lower disk drive on a console PDP-11/34. It contains images of the most used applications programmes on that console.

Dogleg
A shifting of the beam axis by a pair of dipole magnets, such that the initial and final beam axes are parallel.

Domain
A microscopic magnetic region composed of a group of atoms whose magnetic fields are aligned in a common direction.

Dome (pre-accelerator)
The -750 kilovolt direct current terminal of the Cockcroft Walton preaccelerator containing, among other things, the proton source for the accelerator.

Donor
A substance with five valence electrons per atom which when added to a semiconductor crystal provides free electrons in the lattice structure of the crystal.

Doppler effect
The change observed in the frequency with which a wave from a given source reaches an observer when the source and the observer are in relative motion.

Dosimeter
An instrument used for measuring or evaluating the absorbed dose of radiation. It may depend on the measurement of ionization for its operation or may simply involve the darkening of a piece of photographic film ("film badge").

Dosyl
DOcument SYstem Locator. A documentation system residing on the Development VAX which is used to reference Operations Bulletins, Technical Memos, Software Releases, etc. It contains information which can be accessed by keyword, date, author, or subject concerning major documents released by the Accelerator Division or the Publications Office.

Double refraction
The separation of a beam of unpolarized light into two refracted plane-polarized beams by certain crystals such as quartz and calcite.

Doublet (quadrupole)
A beam optical system consisting of two quadrupoles of opposite sign which provides net particle focusing in all planes.

Doubly balanced mixer
An electrical device, often referred to as a product detector, which is used in NMR to convert signals from the laboratory frame of reference to the rotating frame of reference.

Doughnut club
The group of Physicist, Specialist, and Techs that gathers each morning to read the bulletin board in the west entrance MCR while eating doughnuts and spilling coffee.

Download
To write an operating programme from one machine to another. Often the programmes are stored in one machine and written onto the second if problems develop during operation.

Downstream
A relative term which corresponds to the direction that the protons travel in that portion of the accelerator.

DPM
Data Pool Manager. A task on the console computer which accesses the database in the VAX in order to organize request lists for setting and reading data.

Drift chamber
A series of drift chambers are used to detect particle trajectories. They are similar to multi-wire proportional chambers, except the wire spacing is increased. The correlation between the position of an ionized track produced by a charged particle and the time of appearance of an electric pulse at the wire is used to measure the distance of the trajectory from the wires.

Drift tube
In Linac a long copper torus, containing a quadrupole magnet, through which beam passes during acceleration in a linac RF cavity. The beam is shielded from the electric field in the cavity while in the drift tube, and is accelerated by the field while passing between drift tubes.

Drive loop
Termination of the Linac coaxial transmission line leading from the PA to the RF cavity which couples the energy in the transmission line to the magnetic fields in the cavity.

Driver
The 4616 power amplifier tube (200 kw output) used in linac to drive the 5 MW PA.

Dry engine
Cryogenic device which cools the helium by allowing it to do work against a piston. It is used to cool the shell side of the heat exchangers.

Ductility
The property of a metal that enables it to be drawn through a die to form a wire.

Dugan
Pbar term. Unofficially used to describe the rate of stacking pbars. 1 Dugan = 1 mA/Hr. Named in honour of Dr. G.Dugan who used to be head of pbar.

Dumb module
A relative term designating any card or module which does no on-board data processing or error checking. For dumb modules these functions are usually performed by the front- end.

Dump resistor
Resistor which is switched into the Tevatron magnet circuit in order to dissipate the stored energy in the magnets in the event of a ramp trip.

Duoplasmatron
A type of ion-producing source that develops protons by extracting positive ions from an arc struck in hydrogen gas. The I- source in the PreAcc used to be a duoplasmatron. Both sources are now magnetrons.

Duplex

Simultaneous two-way independent transmission in both directions. This may also be referred to as full duplex.

Dynamics

The study of the motion of particles under the influence of forces. Dynamics deals with the causes of motion, as opposed to kinematics which deals with its geometric description.

Dynamo process

the generation of an electric currents by the flow of an electrically conducting fluid through a magnetic field. For instance, the magnetic field originating inside the Earth is believed to come from a dynamo process involving the flow of molten iron in the Earth's hot core. The energy required by the current is obtained from the motion of the flow.

E

E17 kicker

The kicker magnet responsible for moving Main Ring beam from the circulating orbit to the extraction orbit for injection into the Tevatron. The misfiring of this magnet can result in severe quenches in E and F sectors.

Earth radius (RE)

the average radius of the Earth, a convenient unit of distance in describing phenomena and orbits in the Earth's neighborhood in space. 1 RE = 6371 km = 3960 miles, approximately.

East (west) anode supply

The high voltage d.c. power supply for the anodes of the power amplifiers located under the east (west) gallery of the booster.

Echo

A form of magnetic resonance signal from the refocusing of transverse magnetization.

Echo time (TE)

The time between the 90 degree pulse and the maximum in the echo in a spin-echo sequence.

Echoing

The returning of information from a computer or some part of the control system to insure that the information was received correctly.

Eddy currents

Closed loops of induced current set up in a piece of metal when there is relative motion between the metal and a magnetic field. The eddy currents are in such direction that the resulting magnetic forces oppose the relative motion.

Edison effect

The flow of an electric current through a laboratory vacuum, between two metal wires, one of which is heated. The current flows only when the heated wire is more negative, because it is carried by free electrons released from the wire by its heat. The Edison effect was the principle behind "vacuum tubes" used in radio and television receivers and transmitters before the invention of the transistor.

Efficiency

The ratio of the useful work output of a machine to total work input.

Einstein mass energy relation

E = mc2, E is the energy released, m is the mass defect and c is the speed of light.

Elastic collision

A collision in which objects rebound from each other without a loss of kinetic energy.

Elastic limit

The condition in which a substance is on the verge of becoming permanently deformed.

Elastic potential energy

The potential energy in a stretched or compressed elastic object.

Elasticity
The ability of an object to return to its original size or shape when the external forces producing distortion are removed.

Electric charge
That which causes electrons and ions to attract each other, and the repel particles of the same kind. The electric charge of electron is called "negative" (-) and that of ions "positive" (+). Materials such as glass, fur and cloth acquire and electric charge by rubbing them egains each other, a process which tears electrons off one substance and attaches it to the other. Electric charges (+) and (-) may also be separated by a chemical process, as in an electric battery.

Electric current
The rate of flow of charge past a given point in an electric circuit.

Electric field
The region in which a force acts on an electric charge brought into the region.

Electric field intensity
The force per unit positive charge at a given point in an electric field.

Electric field line
An imaginary curve tangent to which at a point gives the direction of electric field at that point.

Electric ground
(1) A conductor connected with the earth to establish zero (ground) potential.
(2) A common return to an arbitrary zero potential.

Electric potential energy
The energy due to the position of a charge near other charges.

Electrical conductors
The materials that have free electrons and allow current to flow through them.

Electrical insulators
The materials which do not allow current to flow through them.

Electrical resistance
The property to oppose the flow of current.

Electrification
The process of charging a body by adding or removing electrons.

Electrochemical cell
A cell in which chemical energy is converted to electric energy by a spontaneous electron transfer reaction.

Electrochemical equivalent
The mass of an element, in grams, deposited by one coulomb of electric charge.

Electrode
A conducting element in an electric cell, electronic tube, or semiconductor device.

Electrolysis
The conduction of electricity through a solution of an electrolyte or through a fused ionic compound, together with the resulting chemical changes.

Electrolyte
A substance whose solution conducts an electric current.

Electrolytic cell
A cell in which electric energy is converted to chemical energy by means of an electron-transfer reaction.

Electromagnetic field (EM field)
the regions of space near electric currents, magnets, broadcasting antennas etc., regions in which electric and magnetic forces may act. Generally the EM field is regarded as a modification of space itself, enabling it to store and transmit energy.

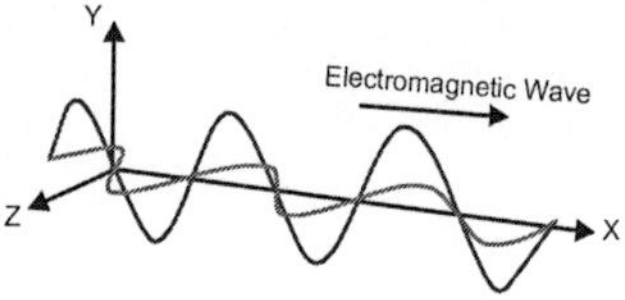

Electromagnetic induction

The process by which an emf is set up in a conducting circuit by a changing magnetic flux linked by the circuit.

Electromagnetic interaction

The interaction that keeps electrons in orbit and forms bonds between atoms and molecules.

Electromagnetic spectrum

The entire range of all the various kinds or wavelengths of electromagnetic radiation, including (from short to long wavelengths) gamma rays, x-rays, ultraviolet, optical (visible), infrared, and radio waves.

Electromagnetic wave

an electric field spreading in wavelike-fashion through space at a speed of about 300000 km/sec, with its direction and intensity at any point in space oscillating rapidly back and forth. James Clerk's Maxwell's theory in 1864 suggested that light was such a wave, and today we know that such waves include all forms of light—also infra-red and ultra-violet, as well as radio waves, microwaves, x-rays and gamma rays.

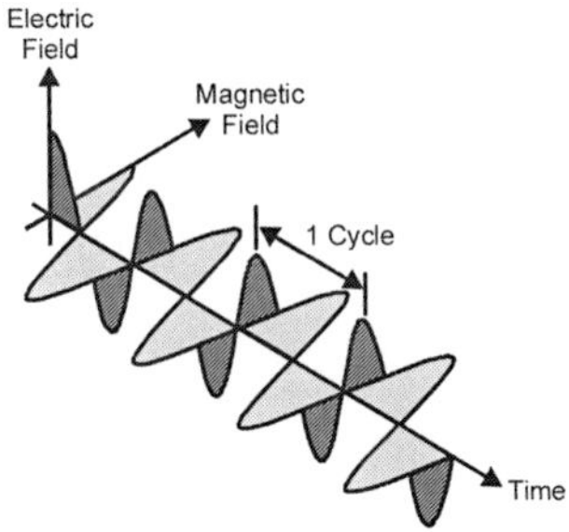

Electron

A stable, elementary, negatively charged particle. Electrons have the smallest amount of mass of all the subatomic particles. Electrons may be in bound states around nuclei where they determine chemical properties of elements, may radiate through space as electron beams or g-rays or through conductors to form an electrical current. Electrons are spin 1/2 fermions and interact via the electro-magnetic and weak forces.

Electron flux

The rate of flow of electrons through a reference surface. In cgs units, measured in electrons s^{-1}, or simply s^{-1}.

Electron shell

A region about the nucleus of an atom in which electrons move and which is made up of electron orbitals.

Electron shower

These are usually called electron-photon showers and are made by high energy electrons or photons passing through a medium. A parent electron radiates photons in traversing a medium, and the photons convert to electron-positron pairs, which again radiate. The number of electrons and photons therefore increase exponentially until ionization loss becomes important and no further radiation is possible.

Electron volt (EV)

A convenient unit of energy applied to ions and electrons, equal to the energy gains when such particles "fall" across a voltage difference of 1 volt. Gas molecules at room temperature have about 0.03 ev, on the Sun about 0.6 ev, typical electrons of the aurora 5000 ev, typical protons in the inner radiation belt 20,000,000 ev, typical cosmic ray protons near Earth 10,000,000,000 ev, and the highest energies of cosmic rays may reach up to 1,000,000,000 times more.

Electronics

The branch of physics concerned with the emission, behaviour, and effects of electrons.

Electroscope
A device used to observe the presence of an electrostatic charge.

Electrostatic septum
The septum is the principal component of a beam splitting system. Static electric charges produce a different field on opposite sides of the septum. Segments of beam on opposite sides of the septum will be deflected opposite directions, thus cutting the beam into two parts, or "splitting the beam".

Elementary colours
The six regions of colour in the solar spectrum observed by the dispersion of sunlight: red, orange, yellow, green, blue, indigo, and violet.

Elongation strain
The ratio of the increase in length to the unstretched length.

EMC
Event Message Code. A list of alarms assembled by the appropriate front-end. This list is eventually given to AEOLUS, which organizes the data for display on the alarm screens.

Emergency loop
System of microswitches which when opened (by pulling on a crash cord on the tunnel wall) will disable the radiation and electrical safety systems for that particular enclosure.

EMF
The energy per unit charge supplied by a source of electric current.

EMI
The EMI (External Muon Identifier) is a set of muon detectors (proportional wire chambers) attached to the outer shell of the 15-foot bubble chamber. In conjunction with the chamber it aids in the interpretation of neutrino and antineutrino interactions by positively identifying muon tracks in the chamber. Note that the 15-foot bubble chamber is no longer used.

Emission spectrum
A spectrum formed by the dispersion of light from an incandescent solid, liquid, and gas.

Emittance
The area in phase space occupied by a particle beam. The units are mm-milliradians for transverse emittance and eV-sec for longitudinal emittance.

Emittance probe
Linac device used to measure the size of the phase space ellipse occupied by the beam, done by measuring the divergence of the beam at a number of points across the beam axis.

Emulsion (nuclear)
A photographic substance designed for the detection of ionizing particles. When high speed charged particles traverse the emulsion, they cause ionization tracks which show up when the emulsion is developed. The charge, energy, and momenta of the particles may be deduced from their range in the emulsion, from the grain density of their tracks, and from their curvature in a magnetic field.

Enable
A request for beam sent to the prom module in the preacc control room. Three types of enables exist: HEP, NTF, and P-bar.

Enclosure
A portion of the accelerator tunnel.

End pulse
Pulsing of the QXR magnets at the end of flat top to extract the final fast spill. An attempt is made to extract all the beam remaining in the Tevatron during that pulse.

Endothermic
Referring to a process that absorbs energy.

Endothermic process
The process in which heat is absorbed.

Energy
Loosely, anything that can cause a machine to

move. For example, energy is contained by moving water, water raised to a high place, heat or magnetic fields. The energy of fast ions and electrons (measured in "electron volts") is a measure of their speed, and it enables them (for instance) to penetrate matter.

Energy doubler/saver

The name originally given to the Tevatron. It is an "energy doubler" because it permits acceleration of protons to about 1000 GeV which is twice the energy attainable in the Main Ring. It is an "energy saver" because the superconducting magnets permit the acceleration of beam using less electrical energy than the Main Ring uses to reach the same energy.

Energy flux

The rate of flow of energy through a reference surface. In cgs units, measured in erg s^{-1}. Also measured in watts, where 1 watt = 1×10^7 erg s^{-1}. Flux density, the flux measured per unit area, is also often referred to as "flux".

Energy level

One of a series of discrete energy values that characterize a physical system governed by quantum rules.

Enthalpy

The sum H of the internal energy U and the work energy PV of a fluid at a given temperature and pressure. H = U + PV. (J/g)

Entropy

(1) The internal energy of a system that cannot be converted to mechanical work.

(2) The property that describes the disorder of a system.

EPB

Extracted Proton Beam. This term refers to 5 and 10 foot dipoles and quadrupoles originally designed for use in the Switchyard.

Equilibrant force

The force that produces equilibrium.

Equilibrium

The state of a body in which there is no change in its motion.

Equilibrium position

Midpoint of the path of an object describing simple harmonic motion.

Equilibrium vapour pressure

The pressure exerted by vapour molecules in equilibrium with a liquid.

ERG

A cgs unit of energy equal to work done by a force of 1 dyne acting over a distance of 1 cm. 10 (ten million) erg/sec erg s^{-1} (ergs per second) = 1 watt. Also, 1 Calorie = 4.2×10^{10} (42 billion) ergs.

ERM

Event Request Modules. These are the CAMAC 175 Modules which encode events onto the Tevatron clock. They are located in the MAC room.

Error codes

Messages which appear in red on the TV or Lexidata screens which carry information about the controls system pertinent to the fact that you have no data. These messages can be deciphered from D11 or using the error help facility under the utility window on the consoles.

Es1, Es2

Electrostatic Septa 1 and 2 responsible for guiding Tevatron beam to the extraction orbit for delivery to switchyard. ES1 and ES2 are located at D0.

Escape velocity

The minimum velocity with which an object must be thrown upwards so as to overcome the gravitational pull, it is equal to, where M is the mass of the planet and R is the radius of the planet.

ESEP

Vertical splitting septa in the proton line. It is called ESEP because it is located in enclosure E in Switchyard.

Ethernet
The link and communication protocol which is generally used between computer systems. It is a half-duplex link which transmits data serially (both directions) at a 10 Mbyte rate. The primary use in the Accelerator Division is for the link between the Linac front-end (a PDP-11) and the Linac Primary Station (a 68000 microprocessor). This type of link is also used on site for the DECnet link between the AD VAXCluster and the FNAL VAX Cluster.

Ethernet controller board
Board found in the linac primary microcomputer that handles communication with the Ethernet link.

Eurobus crate
One of two small crates in the preacc control room containing cards used to interface the local microcomputer to the Haefely power supply controls.

Evaporation
The change of phase from a liquid to a gas or vapour.

Exchange, chemical
The interchange of chemically equivalent components on a molecule.

Exchange, spin
The interchange of spin state between two nuclei.

Exclusion principle
No two electrons in an atom can have the same set of quantum numbers.

Exothermic
Referring to a process that liberates energy.

Exothermic process
The process in which heat is evolved.

Expansion
To make the volume in which a given mass, or mass flow, resides suddenly larger as in Joule-Thomson and engine expansion.

Expansion engine, turbine
Devices that are driven by gases, extract work, and lower.the temperature of the gas.

Extended stem
Modifier for valves with long stems for cryogenic service.

External combustion engine
A heat engine in which the fuel burns outside the cylinder or turbine chamber.

External interrupt panel
This 16 input panel (with on/off switches for each input) is used to interface external interrupt signals, which may be clock events, to the computer processor interface cards. These panels are located behind the PDP-11 Status Display Units and are also behind the Mac computers.

Extraction
The process of taking the protons out of the accelerator in a controlled fashion once acceleration has been accomplished. Extraction from the Tevatron takes place during the flattop of the ramp.

Extractor
An electrostatic device used to extract ions from the magnetron ion source in PreeAcc. It consist of a pair of plates mounted beneath the source connected to a pulsed power supply.

E-z writer
Applications programmes which store commonly used plot information for convenient display on the Lexidata or storage scope. Currently residing on D77, B67, M77, M78, T102, T107, S67, and P77.

F

F slot controller
The CC48 card in the F0-slot which controls cards in the succeeding slots (F1-F4) in a modified CAMAC crate.

F slots
A set of five slots in the modified CAMAC crates for Main Ring (Utility Crates) which are denoted by F0, F1, F2, F3, F4. The last four slots may only be addressed by a card residing in the F0 slot. These slots are said to have subaddresses. Only the card in the F0 slot may be addressed by the crate controller. This slot is currently filled by a CC48 card.

Factory (antiproton)
An installation where Antiprotons are produced and accumulated. Fermilab's Antiproton source, consisting of the Target station, Debuncher and Accumulator rings, and the associated transport lines, is a good example of an Antiproton factory. It is hoped that this factory will eventually produce 5 X 1011 p-'s every 8 hours. The best so far has been 1.2 X 1010 per hour.

Fail safe mode
A situation in which the failure of a component results in a safe condition. The critical devices of the safety system are designed to be fail safe, ie. they will not allow the transmission of beam pass the critical device.

Fan-in
A board or other device which gathers signals from a variety of devices and consolidates them for processing (as with an MADC).

Fan-in and Fan-out
A fan-in is a module that performs the function of linearly adding either analogue or logic signals. A fan-in is often used to perform high-order majority logic decision. (e.g., any 6 out of 32) by attenuating each input and discriminating on the summed output. (Many inputs, few outputs.) A fan-out is a module used to distribute a fast signal to several 50W loads with no loss in signal amplitude.

Fan-out
A board or other device which receives a signal, replicates it, and sends it out to a number of devices.

Farad
The unit of capacitance; one coulomb per volt.

Faraday
The quantity of electricity (96,500 coulombs) required to deposit one chemical equivalent of an element.

Faraday's first law
The mass of an element deposited during electrolysis is proportional to the quantity of charge that passes through the electrolytic cell.

Faraday's second law

The mass of an element deposited during electrolysis is proportional to the chemical equivalent of that element.

Fast spill

The resonant extraction of intense pulses of protons using the QXR system. These pulses last only a few milliseconds. This is sometimes referred to as a Fast pulse.

Fast time plot

The standard plot generated on a Lexidata or Storage Scope. The sample rate is usually generated automatically, but the range and length of time are selected by the user.

Fast trip

The switching off of a power supply or supplies (e.g. Main Ring or Tevatron power supplies) in response to a signal from an overcurrent, overvoltage, or ground fault detection circuit.

Feed can

Device which connects the satellite refrigerators to the magnet strings. At every '1' and '4' building there is a normal feed can, and at every '2' and '3' building there is a power feed can. The power feed cans are the points where the power supply bus enter the cryogenic system.

Feeder

A 13.8 kV electrical power distribution cable running between the Master Substation and a unit substation near the location at which the power is used.

Fermat's principle

An electromagnetic wave takes a path that involves the least time when propagating between two points.

Fermilab clock decoder

A custom-made integrated circuit which decodes TCLK for internal use on a board.

Fermion

A generic term for half integral spin particles to which Fermi-Dirac statistics apply (total wave function antisymmetric under identical fermion exchange). The Pauli Exclusion Principle applies for such particles (two fermions cannot simultaneously occupy the same quantum state). Examples are electrons, protons, neutrons, muons and hyperons.

Ferromagnetism

The property of a substance by which it is strongly attracted by a magnet.

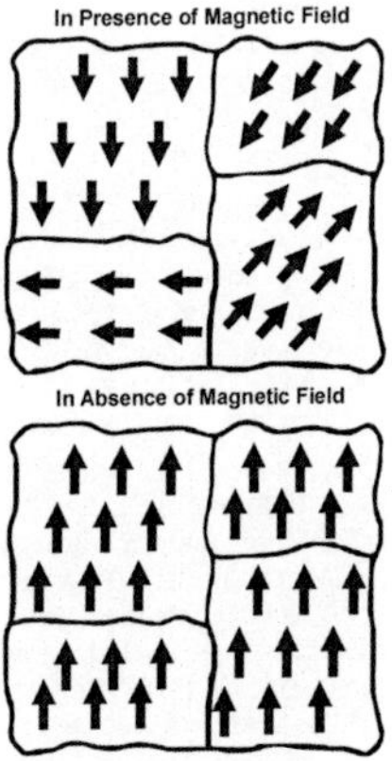

Ferromagnetism

Feynman diagram

A diagram showing the production and exchange of particles during a subatomic interaction.

Fibre-optic link repeater

Chassis associated with Linac primary and all

Linac secondary microcomputers that maintain continuity of the serial data link and control the microcomputers' interfacing with it.

Fiducial volume

The volume of a detector or spectrometer system within which events are accepted as measurable.

Fiducials

In general, reference marks to which particle trajectories are compared; may apply to wire spark chambers, optical spark chambers, bubble chambers, etc. In particular, permanent reference markings in SWIC displays to facilitate the referencing of beam trajectories in beam lines.

Field lamp

Light source between the NTF primary and main collimators designed to duplicate the profile of the neutron beam with any given collimator insert. Used in patient set-up.

Filemaster

This is a user account on the Operational VAX which coordinates the creation, deletion and modification of all filesharing files on the AD OPER VAX. This also keeps track of all files on a master list.

Filesharing

This refers to a type of file access system established on the OPER VAX. This system allows shared access to files from any connected node. This means that any console, front-end, OPER VAX process, or DEV VAX process may read from or write to a filesharing file.

Film badge

A device worn by those who work in radiation areas to record the amount of exposure the individual has received over a one month period.

Finite state machine (FSM)

An applications programme currently residing on T13 which controls the refrigerators during automatic quench recovery or automatic cooldown.

First law of photoelectric emission

The rate of emission of photoelectrons is directly proportional to the intensity of the incident light.

First law of thermodynamics

When heat is converted to another form of energy, or when another form of energy is converted to heat, there is no loss of energy.

Firus

Acronym for FIRe and Utility System. A site-wide alarm system which reports alleged fires, power failures, pump alarms, etc. The FIRUS screen in the MCR is edited to report only those problems relevant to the Accelerator Division.

Fission

The splitting of a heavy nucleus into nuclei of intermediate mass.

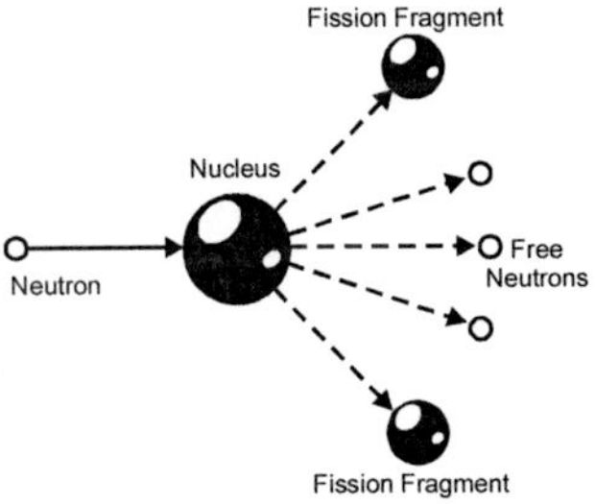

Fixed target

A mode of running beam in which a beam is pointed at a target material such as a metal block which is at rest. The centre of mass energy obtainable using this method for creating new particles is much less as beam energies get larger since it scales as the square root of the beam energy. Fermilab runs in collider mode and fixed target mode seperately.

Fixed target lines
The beamlines extend straight from an intersection with the Tevatron very close to Wilson Hall out to the fixed target experiments which steer the 1 TeV beams into targets creating hosts of secondary particles. After a switchyard, 3 seperate beamlines (Proton, Neutrino, and Meson) extend to the experiments.

Flare (or "solar flare")
an rapid outburst on the Sun, usually in the vicinity of active sunspots. A sudden brightening (usually seen only through special filters) may be followed by the signatures of particle acceleration to high energies—x-rays, radio noise and often, a bit later, the arrival of high-energy ions from the Sun.

Flare (solar)
Rapid release of energy from a localized region on the Sun in the form of electromagnetic radiation, energetic particles, and mass motions.

Flare star
A member of a class of stars that show occasional, sudden, unpredicted increases in light. The total energy released in a flare on a flare star can be much greater that the energy released in a solar flare.

Flash tube
The ionization tube that emits the light in a chemical laser.

Fleming valve
The first vacuum-tube diode.

Flow orifice
A carefully constructed hole used to measure flow by the small pressure difference across it. Temperature and Pressure dependant.

Fluid
The gas, liquid, or mixed phase of a cryogen.

Fluorescence
The emission of light during the absorption of radiation from another source.

Flying wire
A single wire that is rapidly passed through the beam. The wire in the beam causes beam loss which can be plotted as downstream BLM vs. wire position. This gives a profile of the beam. Flying wires are passed through the beam horizontally or vertically for horizontal or vertical beam profiles. Flying wires are used in the Main Ring, Tevatron, Booster and Pbar.

F-number
The ratio of the focal length of a lens to the effective aperture.

Focal length
The distance from the centre plane of the lens at which an input beam, parallel to the axis and displaced from the axis, crosses the axis after passing through the lens. The point where the beam crosses the axis is known as the principal point of the lens.

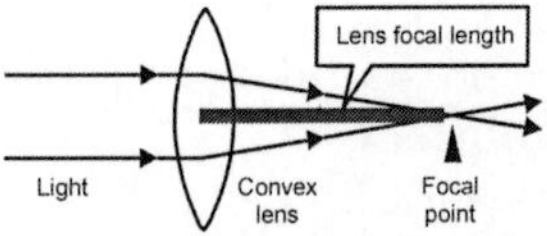

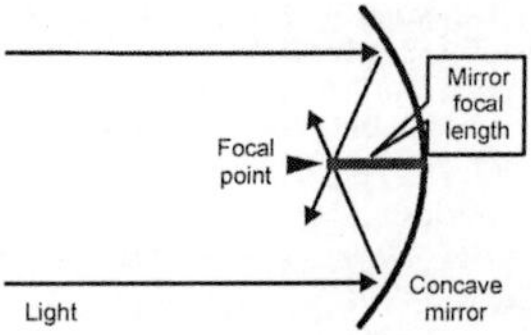

Focal plane
The plane perpendicular to the principal axis of a converging lens or mirror and containing the principal focus.

Focus
The point to which rays that are initially parallel to the axis of a lens or mirror are converged or from which they appear to diverge.

Focussing quadrupole magnet
A quadrupole magnet that focuses beam in the horizontal plane and defocuses beam in the vertical plane.

Footpoint
The intersection of magnetic loops with the photosphere.

Force
(1) A physical quantity that can affect the motion of an object.
(2) A measure of the momentum gained per second by an accelerating body.

Forced vibration
Vibration that is due to the application of a periodic force, and not to the natural vibrations of the system.

Foreline
A vacuum line leading from a vacuum pump to the device or devices to be pumped.

Fortran 77
This is the version of Fortran supported by the VAX and PDP compilers.

Forward bias
Voltage applied to a semiconductor P-N junction that increases the electron current across the junction.

Forward power
The power transmitted from one stage of an RF system to the next, which may not represent the full power of the first stage due to power reflected from the second (reverse power).

Fourier transform (FT)
A mathematical technique capable of converting a time domain signal to a frequency domain signal and vice versa.

Four-momentum
The relativistic generalization of momentum which describes the energy and momentum. It is a Lorentz 4-vector whose time like component is the energy and whose space like components are the momentum components. The four-momentum is easily transformed from one coordinate system to another (Lorentz transformation) and its product (Lorentz product) with any other 4-vector is independent of the particular coordinate system used.

FPS-164
This is a Floating Point Systems 64-bit processor attached to the ADCALC VAX. This is typically used for accelerator calculations where the increased accuracy and high performance is needed. It is different from a computer as it contains only disks and no other peripheral or I/O equipment, so that it requires the services of the ADCALC VAX to load and execute user programmes.

Fractional distillation
The process of separating the components of a liquid mixture by means of differences in their boiling points.

Frame of reference
Any system for specifying the precise location of objects in space.

Fraunhoffer lines
The dark lines in the spectrum of sun.

Free electron
An electron that has broken free of it's atomic bond and is therefore not bound to an atom.

Free fall
The motion of a body under the effect of gravity alone.

Free induction decay (FID)
A form of magnetic resonance signal from the decay of transverse magnetization.

Freezing point
The temperature at which a liquid changes to a solid.

Frequency

the number of back-and-forth cycles per second, in a wave or wave like process. Expressed this way, the frequency is said to be given in units of Hertz (Hz), named after the discoverer of radio waves. Alternating current in homes in the US goes through 60 cycles each second, hence its frequency is 60 Hz; in Europe it is 50 cycles and 50 Hz.

Frequency Control and Phase Lock Module

Linac module in the low-level RF system that provides RF input to the amplifier chain at the correct phase.

Frequency control module

Linac module in the low-level RF system that commands the tuning slug controller in response to error signals that represent the difference between the transmission line RF phase and the cavity RF phase.

Friction

A force that resists the relative motion of objects that are in contact with each other.

Front end

A PDP-11 which gathers and transmits data for a given accelerator subsystem. The front-ends are interfaced to the MAC's or CAMAC crates on one side, and to the consoles or the VAX on the other. Examples include DEC-T for Tevatron devices, MR DEC for the Main Ring, etc.

Front porch

Portion of Tevatron ramp before flat top where bend field is held constant for a period of time.

Fsep

Splitting septa in the meson line. It is called FSEP because it is located in the F1 manhole in switchyard.

Fshare

File SHARE. This is a process on the OPER VAX which coordinates and manages access to the Filesharing files for console and front-end programmes.

Fuel cell

An electrochemical cell in which the chemical energy of continuously supplied fuel is converted into electric energy.

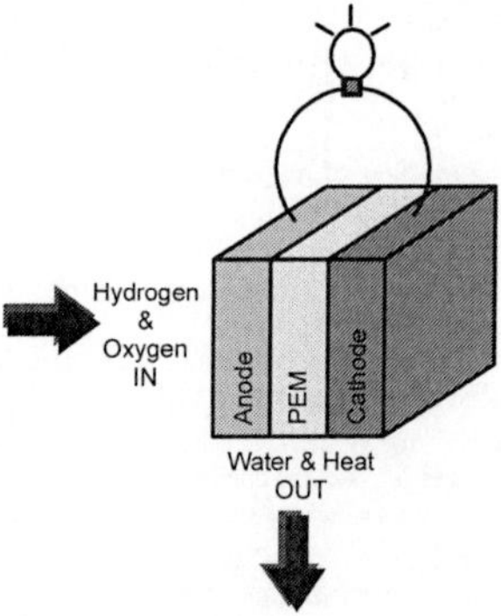

Fundamental

The lowest frequency produced by a musical tone source. That harmonic component of a wave which has the lowest frequency.

Fundamental frequency

The lowest frequency at which a system vibrates freely.

Fundamental unit

Any one of seven basic units of measure.

Fusion

(1) The change of phase from a solid to a liquid; melting.

(2) A reaction in which light nuclei combine, forming a nucleus with a larger mass number.

G

G-10
A green glass-epoxy electrical insulator material used throughout the laboratory.

Galvanometer
An instrument used to measure minute electric currents.

Gamma ray
The highest energy (shortest wavelength) photons in the electromagnetic spectrum. Gamma rays are often defined to begin at 10 keV, although radiation from around 10 keV to several hundred keV is also referred to as hard x-rays.

Gamma ray bursts
brief bursts of gamma rays from the distant universe, observed by satellites.

Gannon box
Another name for the NTF interlock module, built by Jeff Gannon.

Gas
A fluid with zero heat of vapourization (devoid of liquid). Denoted GHe, GH2, GN2, etc. 4

Gas barrier
A ceramic insulator in the Linac 9-3/16" transmission line that isolates RF cavity vacuum from the nitrogen that pressurizes the transmission line.

Gate
An electronic circuit capable of turning a device

(usually a counter) on at a particular time and for a specified interval. It is usually used with fast logic devices to insure that certain conditions are met before counting can begin.

Gate valve controller

A module in the preacc control room which shows the status of the 750 keV line vacuum valves and permits local control of those valves. Also the module at each cavity that monitors the ion pump power supply status and controls the vacuum valves at each end of the cavity.

Gateway mode

One of three modes of Linac control system operation where data requests and commands from the front end are serviced by the secondary microcomputers.

Gauss

A unit of measure for magnetic fields. At 900 GeV, the Tevatron magnets produce a field of 39,600 gauss or 39 kilogauss.

Geiger tube

Ion sensitive instrument used for the detection of subatomic particles.

General relativity

Theory used to describe how space-time is not flat near objects of large mass such as black holes. It is responsible for the force of gravity experienced between two objects with mass.

Geomagnetic storm

A worldwide disturbance of the Earth's magnetic field, associated with solar activity.

Geosynchronous orbit

The orbit of a satellite that travels above the Earth's equator from west to east so that it has a speed matching that of the Earth's rotation and remains stationary in relation to the Earth (also called geostationary). Such an orbit has an altitude of about 35,900 km (22,300 miles).

Getter

Material used to absorb residual molecules in vacuum spaces. Sometimes used in transfer lines.

Gev/c or GEV/C

A unit of momentum appropriate to high energy particle physics. At kinetic energies much larger than the rest energy, the momentum of a particle in GeV/c is slightly less than the total energy in GeV.

Ghasp

General Host And Subsystem Protocol. A software protocol used for communication between a CAMAC front-end processor and intelligent subsystems, such as the microprocessors distributed around the accelerator.

Glitch

A sharp increase/decrease and then immediate restoration of electrical power, often times causing devices to trip off.

Global mode

One of three modes of linac control system operation were data requests and commands from secondary microcomputers are serviced by other secondaries.

Glueball

A bound state of only gluons thought to exist and predicted by an intensive lattice gauge theory computation. The lowest mass glueball should is predicted to be near 1500 MeV/c^2.

Gluon

The force carrier for the strong nuclear force between quarks. There are 8 varieties resulting from the SU(3) symmetry.

GPIB interface

General Purpose Interface Board. An interface between a hardware device and ACNET. The interface is available commercially from Hewlett-Packard. Examples include spectrum analyzers and the DCCT current monitors for the antiproton source.

Gradient (G)

A variation in some quantity with respect to another.

In the context of NMR, a magnetic field gradient is a variation in the magnetic field with respect to distance.

Gradient magnet power supply (GMPS)

The power supply for the main Booster magnets.

Gradient regulator

Module in the modulator pulse-forming circuitry that acts to keep RF cavity gradient at the desired level.

Graham's law of diffusion

The rate of diffusion of a gas is inversely proportional to the square root of its density.

Gravitational constant (G)

The constant of proportionality in Newton's law of gravitation, $G = 6.67 \times 10^{-11}\ Nm^2/kg^2$

Gravitational field

Region of space in which each point is associated with a value of gravitational acceleration.

Gravitational force

The mutual force of attraction between particles of matter.

Gravitational interaction

The interaction between particles of matter that has no known distance limitations, but is the weakest interaction of all.

Gravitational potential at a point

The amount of work done against the gravitational forces to move a particle of unit mass from infinity to that point.

Gravitational potential energy

Potential energy acquired by an object when it is moved against gravity.

Graviton

The carrier for the gravitational interaction.

Gravity

The force of gravitation on an object on or near the surface of a celestial body.

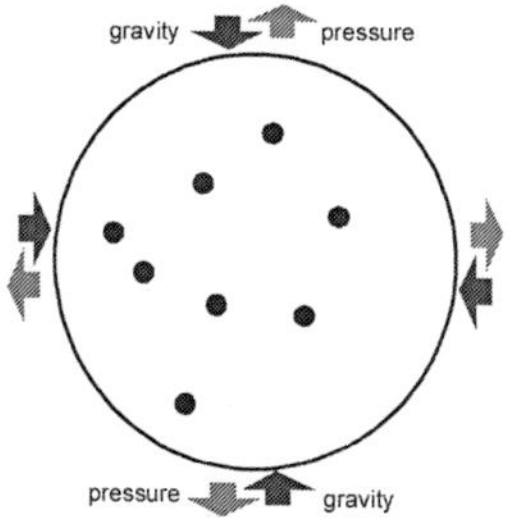

Grid

An element of an electronic tube. An electrode used to control the flow of electrons from the cathode to the plate.

Grid bias

The grid-to-cathode voltage.

Ground fault

A ground fault is the shorting of an electrical device or circuit to ground.

Ground state

The lowest energy state of an atom.

Guiding centre

The centre point of the gyration of ion and electrons in a magnetic field. The guiding centre of radiation belt particles bounces back and forth between mirror points and also undergoes a slow drift from one field line to the next.

Gyration

A term used in plasma research for the circular motion of ions and electrons around magnetic field lines.

Gyromagnetic ratio

The ratio of the resonance frequency to the magnetic field strength for a given nucleus.

H

Hadron

A particle which interacts via the strong force, either a meson or a baryon.

Haefely

Trade name for a Swiss company that manufactures high-voltage equip- ment. In this application the high- voltage power supply that maintains the preaccelerator dome at -750 kV.

Half-duplex

This is a data transmission scheme which is characterized by transmission in both directions in an alternate one-way-at-a-time fashion.

Half-high NIM

A small NIM crate at each of the console stations in the MCR which contains hardcopy buttons, beam switches, console abort buttons, etc. Half-high NIM's are also used in other places.

Half-life

The average time required for the amount of a particular radionuclide (radioactive substance) to be reduced to half its value as a consequence of radioactive decay. Like wise, the average time to decay for an unstable particle. The time during which half the number of atoms in the element disintegrate.

Hall probe

A hall probe is used to measure the strength of magnetic fields. When a magnetic field is perpendicular to a conductor carrying current, a potential difference is observed between points on opposite sides of the bar. A measurement of this potential difference gives the value of the magnetic field.

Halon

A gas (CBrf3) used principally in computer fire protection systems. It can extinguish a fire by chemical decomposition at the combustion site without damaging the computer or injuring personnel.

Hard line

A term that generally refers to a physical cable connecting two devices such as computers, control modules, repeaters, etc.

Hardcopy

A paper copy of the image from the TV screen, Lexidata, Alarm screen, Storage scope, or Touch screen. A hardcopy can be either colour or black and white.

Hardwire loop

Monitors the status of all interlocked doors and gates in an accelerator enclosure. If one is opened, the loop drops.

Harmonic(s)

An integer multiple of some fundamental frequency. Also, something expressible as a combination of sine and cosine terms. In Ham Radio parlance a

Harmonic is known as a son or daughter of a Ham operator, as in "getting a lot of noise from harmonics"

Harmonic number

The number of times the RF voltage oscillates during the time the beam makes one revolution around a circular accelerator. It also equals the number of RF buckets in the machine.

Head

The pressure in length units (pressure/density) exerted by a fluid column or developed by a pump.

Heat

Thermal energy in the process of being added to or removed from, a substance.

Heat capacity

The quantity of heat needed to raise the temperature of a body one degree.

Heat engine

Any device that converts heat energy into mechanical work.

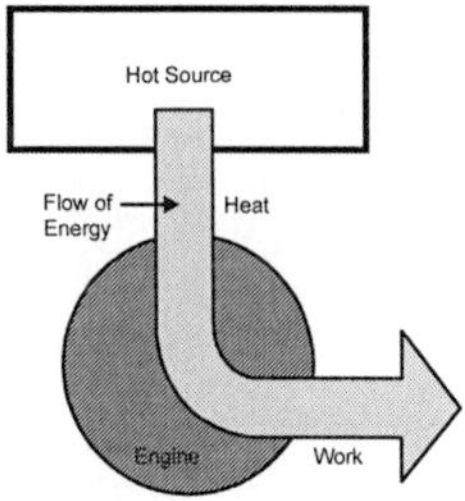

Heat exchanger

A device for passing heat from a working fluid (e.g. Main Ring magnet cooling water) to a reservoir or heat sink (e.g. Main Ring cooling ponds). Heat exchangers are also found in the satellite refrigerator buildings. These devices have an enormous range of forms and sizes depending on the application.

Heat leak

The enemy of things cryogenic. The inability to thermally isolate a given cryogenic system due to conduction, convection or radiation.

Heat of Conversion

Heat required (or released) to change an equilibrium state. Ortho to Para Hydrogen for instance releases heat.

Heat of fusion

The heat required per unit mass to change a substance from solid to liquid at its melting point.

Heat of vapourization

The heat required per unit mass to change a substance from liquid to vapour at its boiling point.

Heat pump

A device that absorbs heat from a cool environment and gives it off to a region of higher temperature.

Heat sink

A reservoir that absorbs heat without a significant increase in temperature.

Heavy water

Water in which Deuterium replaces Hydrogen, $D_2 0$. The source which yields gaseous Deuterium under electrolysis.

Heisenberg uncertainty principle

It is impossible to have a particle that has an arbitrarily well-defined position and momentum at the same time.

HELP facility

Information which is readily available at a console on how to use a given applications programme. The VAX cluster computers also have a help facility on many topics.

Hemorrhoid

Beam Switch Sum Box chassis in MCR. So called because when it breaks down it can can be a real pain.

Henry

The unit of inductance; one henry of inductance is present in a circuit when a change in the current of 1 ampere per second induces an emf of 1 volt.

HEP

High Energy Physics. Means particle physics research where the particles involved have extremely high energy. It's the real reason we're all here.

Hermes

The process on the vax which displays messages on Channel 13.

Hertz (hz)

A unit of frequency equal to one cycle (repetition) per second (cps).

HFU

Heater Firing Unit. Device which dumps current into the Tevatron magnet heater elements in the event of a quench. This action serves to spread the quench quickly which also spreads out the energy deposition.

HIB

HIBernate. A process scheduling state on the VAX. It signifies that a particular process is inactive. The process is present on the system and just waiting for a "wake up" call to start doing its thing. This is a very similar state to LEF.

High rise

Alternative name for Wilson Hall used among accelerator personnel

Hlu link

A single continuous loop circling the Main Ring in a clockwise direction which transmits information from the House Logic Units. The signal originates in the PDC crate of MAC A and returns to the same card.

Hodoscope

A group of particle detectors (usually scintillation counters) arranged to give accurate positional or directional information.

Hog

Higher Order Generator. Device which controls and provides the output waveform for the power supplies which power the Tevatron quadrupole, sextupole, and octupole correction elements.

Hooke's law

Below the elastic limit, strain is directly proportional to stress.

HOPS

Higher Order Power Supply. Power supply for Tevatron quadrupole, sextupole, and octupole correction elements.

Horn

A magnetic focusing device used to produce a more intense beam of neutrinos. Charged mesons from the target are focused by these horn shaped pulsed current sheets before they decay into neutrinos and muons, resulting in a more intense neutrino beam. Unlike a standard magnet focusing system, the horns can efficiently focus the meson beam over a wide momentum range.

Horsepower

Unit of power, 1H.P. = 746 Watts.

Hourly

Periodic tune measurements of a store done by the operators. The upper and lower tunes are measured. A data logger existence proof is run, and the T48 scheduler is checked to see if the flying wires were run.

Huygens'principle

Each point on a light wavefront can be regarded as a source of secondary waves, the envelope of these secondary waves determining the position of the wavefront at a later time.

Hydrogen

The element from which protons are extracted for acceleration.

Hydrogen pump

A centrifugal pump used to circulate liquid hydrogen (LH2).

Hyperbola
Graph of an inverse proportion.

Hypercharge
A property of some baryons and leptons that is conserved in strong and electromagnetic interactions but not in weak interactions.

Hyperon
Heavy unstable (short-lived) particles. Hyperons all have half-integral spin (hyperons are fermions), are more massive than either a proton or neutron, include protons or neutrons as final decay products (hyperons are baryons), interact via the strong and electromagnetic interactions (hyperons are hadrons). Examples are the lambda, sigma, xi, and omega particles.

Hypothesis
A plausible solution to a problem.

Hysteresis
The phenomenon where the magnetization induced in iron or steel which is made to vary over time lags behind the magnetic field. This term is also used in general to indicate that changes in a system are dependent upon its past history.

I

Ice point
It is the melting point of pure melting ice under 1 atm pressure. the ice point is taken as the lower fixed point (0 deg C or 32 deg F) for temperature scales.

Ideal gas
A theoretical gas consisting of infinitely small molecules that exert no forces on each other; also called perfect gas.

Ideal gas equation
PV = nRT

Ideal-lens equation
1/p + 1/q = 1/f, where p is the distance from object to lens, q is the distance from lens to image, and f is the focal length of the lens. This equation has important limitations, being only valid for thin lenses, and for paraxial rays. Thin lenses have thickness small compared to p, q, and f. Paraxial rays are those which make angles small enough with the optic axis that the approximation (angle in radian measure = sin (angle)) may be used.

Ignitron
Device found in modulators used to dump the capacitor bank voltage in the event of a PA crowbar. An ignitron passes electrical current to a pool of liquid mercury at ground potential.

Ilamb
Injection LAMBertson from 8 Gev line to Main Ring.

Illumination
The luminous flux per unit area of a surface.

Image
A place where an object appears to be, because the rays diffusely reflected from any given point on the object have been bent so that they come back together and then spread out again from the image point, or spread apart as if they had originated from the image

Imaginary component
The component of a signal perpendicular to the real signal.

Imaging sequence
A specific set of RF pulses and magnetic field gradients used to produce an image.

Imaging sequence
A specific set of RF pulses and magnetic field gradients used to produce an image.

Impedance
(1) The ratio of applied wave-producing force to resulting displacement velocity of a wave-transmitting medium.

(2) The ratio of sound pressure to volume displacement at a given surface in a sound-

transmitting medium.

(3) The ratio of the effective voltage to the effective current in an a-c circuit.

Impedance matching

A technique used to ensure maximum transfer of energy from the output of one circuit to the input of another.

Impulse

The impulse acting on a body is equal to the product of the force acting on the body and the time for which it acts. If the force is variable, the impulse is the integral of Fdt from t0 to t1. The impulse of a force acting for a given time interval is equal to change in momentum produced over that interval. J = m(v - u), assuming that the mass m remains constant while the velocity changes from v to u. The SI units of impulse are kg m/s.

Impulsive force

The force which acts on a body for a very short time but produces a large change in the momentum of the body is called an impulsive force.

Incandescent

Matter emitting visible light as a result of high temperature for example, a light bulb, a flame from any burning source, and the sun are all incandescent sources because of high temperature.

Incident ray

Line representing the direction of motion of incoming light approaching a boundary.

Inclusive reaction

A reaction in which measurements are conducted on a specific subspace of the final state of particles and information on the remaining complementary components of the final state is disregarded. (e.g. p + p → p + "anything".)

Independence

The lack of any relationship between two random events.

Index of refraction

The ratio of the speed of light in a vacuum to its speed in a given matter medium.

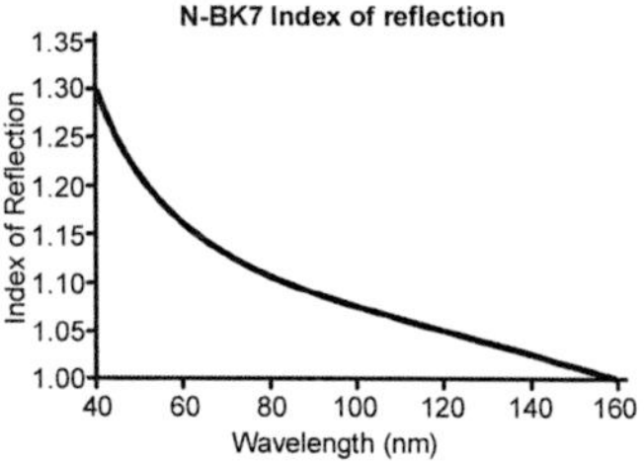

Index of refraction (scalar)

An intrinsic property of a transparent substance, which measures the speed of light in the material compared to the speed of light in a vacuum.

Index page

A list of applications programmes available at a console. Each major accelerator system has a representative console programme which displays this list. If no specific applications programme is requested, the index page is displayed by default. Any programme displayed on the list may be executed by interrupting under the programme name or number.

Induced magnetism

Magnetism produced in a ferromagnetic substance by the influence of a magnetic field.

Inductance

The Property of an electric circuit by which a varying current induces a back emf in that circuit or a neighboring circuit.

Inductance

A property of a circuit that is the proportionality constant between the rate of change of the current in that circuit and the emf that this changing current produces.

Induction
The process of charging one body by bringing it into the electric field of another charged body.

Inductive reactance
Reactance in an a-c circuit containing inductance, which causes a lagging current.

Inductrol
Voltage regulator for the Linac PA filament supply that compensates for variations in line voltage due to other large loads at the laboratory.

Inelastic collision
A collision between objects in which the kinetic energy changes, for example, due to deformation or frictional loss.

Inertia
A descriptive term for that property of a body which resists change in its motion. Two kinds of changes of motion are recognized: changes in translational motion, and changes in rotational motion. In modern usage, the measure of translational inertia is mass. Newton's first law of motion is sometimes called the "Law of Inertia", a label which adds nothing to the meaning of the first law. Newton's first and second laws together are required for a full description of the consequences of a body's inertia. The measure of a body's resistance to rotation is its Moment of Inertia.

Inertial frame
A frame of reference that is not accelerating, one in which Newton's first law is true.

Inertial frame of reference
A nonaccelerating frame of reference in which Newton's first law holds true.

Inflector
A magnetic or electrostatic device to apply a transverse force to a beam. Most often the term is applied to the pulsed septa which bend the injected beam onto the equilibrium orbit of a circular accelerator.

Infrared light
Electromagnetic waves longer than those of visible light and shorter than radio waves.

Infrasonic
Sound waves having too low a frequency to be heard by the human ear; sound having a frequency of less than 20 Hz.

Infrasonic range
Vibrations in matter below 20 cycles/second.

Injection
The process of putting a beam of particles into an accelerator.

Injector
Usually depends on context of system being discussed. When talking about Booster, it is the 200 Mev line. When talking about Main Ring it is the 8 Gev line or collectivly Pre-Acc, Linac, and Booster. With the plan to move Main Ring to its own enclosure the term injector has also come to mean the new Main Ring in its own enclosure which will be called the Main Injector.

Instantaneous current
The magnitude of a varying current at any instant of time.

Instantaneous velocity
Short displacement divided by elapsed time. Slope of the line that is tangent to a velocity graph at a given point.

Instantaneous voltage
The magnitude of a varying voltage at any instant of time.

Insulating vacuum
A vacuum provided for the express purpose of reducing gaseous conduction, usually <10-4mm Hg.

Insulation
A means to reduce heat transfer. Conductive, radiated, or convected.

Insulator
A material through which an electric charge is not readily transferred.

Integrated luminosity
The total number of collisions (collisions per second times the number of seconds).

Intensity
A measure of the energy carried by a wave.

Intensity level
The logarithm of the ratio of the intensity of a sound to the intensity of the threshold of hearing.

Intensity map
A colour-coded map of radiation intensity as a function of position. Different colours or shades represent different intensities of observed radiation.

Intensive variable
A measurable property of a thermodynamic system is intensive if when two identical systems are combined into one, the variable of the combined system is the same as the original value in each system. Examples: temperature, pressure.

Interaction
Any change in the amount or quantum numbers of particles that are near each other.

Interaction length
The interaction length is the mean distance a particle travels through a medium before it interacts with one of the target particles. Interaction as taken here is any effect of interest to the observer.

Interface
A surface that forms the boundary between two phases or systems.

Interference
(1) The superposing of one wave on another.
(2) The mutual effect of two beams of light, resulting in a reduction of energy in certain areas and an increase of energy in others.

Interlock
Something which constrains or inhibits a device, generally for the purpose of safety. There are temperature interlocks, electrical interlocks, radiation interlocks, etc.

Intermediate cylinder
Cylinder inside of Main Ring RF cavity between the drift tube and outer wall. It is biased with a dedicated power supply.

Intermolecular forces
Forces of interaction between molecules.

Internal combustion engine
A heat engine in which the fuel burns inside the cylinder or turbine chamber.

Internal energy
Total potential and kinetic energy of the molecules and atomic particles of a substance.

Internal target area
Obsolete term. Originally meant a long straight section in the Main Ring at CO where high energy physics experiments were performed. The Main Ring and Tevatron abort dumps are now located at C0. There is also an experimental detector area known as the Spectrometer Room adjacent to the CO straight section.

Interplanetary magnetic field (IMF)

The weak magnetic field filling interplanetary space, with field lines usually connected to the Sun. The IMF is kept out of the Earth's magnetosphere, but the interaction of the two plays a major role in the flow of energy from the solar wind to the Earth's environment.

Interplanetary sector

A region of interplanetary space in which all magnetic field lines point either away from the Sun (away sector) or towards the Sun (towards sector). Typically the interplanetary magnetic field consists of 4 sectors, but 2 or 6 are not unusual.

Interplanetary shock

the abrupt boundary formed at the front of a plasma cloud (e.g. from a coronal mass ejection) moving much faster than the rest of the solar wind, as it pushes its way through interplanetary space.

Interrupt

In an operational context it is usually the point at which a change is made or verified in the operation of a device or programme. It is required for changes in the D/A of a device, to change pages on a console, etc. In a computer context it is a temporary break in the sequencing of a programme initiated by events in the outside world.

Interrupt button

A button next to the keyboard at each ACNET console which provides interrupt capability in conjunction with the selected applications programme. The function is duplicated with the RETURN key on the keyboard.

Intersecting storage ring

An accelerator in which particles collide as they move in opposite directions.

Intertank phase

A signal that represents the difference in phase of two adjacent RF cavities in the linac.

Invariant

A quantity that does not change when transformed.

Inverse photoelectric effect

The emission of photons of radiation from a material when bombarded with high speed electrons.

Inverse proportion

The relationship in which the value of one variable increases while the value of the second variable decreases at the same rate (in the same ratio).

Inversion recovery sequence

A pulse sequence producing signals which represent the longitudinal magnetization present after the application of a 180° inversion RF pulse.

Inversion time

The time between the inversion pulse and the sampling pulse(s) in an inversion recovery sequence.

Invert

To invert a power supply is to reverse its polarity at the end of a ramp to reduce the current at a rate exceeding the natural fall rate of the circuit. Only certain ramped power supplies such as the Main Ring supplies are designed to be inverted.

IOMAC

MAC Input/Output. A process that resides in the MR.BaRF front-end which is used for MAC to DEC communication. Operators usually see the term as an error message on the TV screen when there are communications problems with a given MAC.

Ion

An ion is an atom or molecule which has lost or gained one or more electrons, making it positively or negatively charged. A negatively charged ion, which has more electrons in its electron shells than it has protons in its nuclei, is known as an anion, due to its attraction to anodes. Conversely, a positively-charged ion, which has fewer electrons than protons, is known as a cation.

Ion gauge

A vacuum-measuring gauge that works by ionizing gas molecules with electrons and measuring the amount of ion current drawn to an anode.

Ion pump
Usually means sputter-ion pump. A vacuum pump in which pumping is achieved by ionizing gas molecules through collisions with high speed electrons. The ions are then captured on electrostatic plates. Permanent magnets around the pump increase the electrons' path length into a spiral and hence produce more ionization. This pump usually cannot be used at pressures much above 1 E-04 torr.

Ion source
The source of the protons to be accelerated, which is an electrical arc in hydrogen gas located in the high voltage electrode (dome) of the Cockcroft-Walton preaccelerator.

Ionization
the process by which a neutral atom, or a cluster of such atoms, becomes an *ion*. This may occur, for instance, by absorbtion of light ("photoionization") or by a collision with a fast particle ("impact ionization"). Also, certain molecules (such as table salt or sodium chloride, NaCl) are formed by natural ions (like Na+ and Cl-) held together by their electric attraction, and they may fall apart when dissolved in water (which weakens the attraction), enabling the solution to conduct electricity.

Ionization chamber
A particle passing through the gas in a small chamber forms ions. A voltage will cause the ions to be attracted to the collection plate, depending on their charge. As a result a pulse of current will flow for each particle that forms ions. Each pulse is proportional to the ionization energy delivered by the particle.

Ionization energy
The ionization energy of a chemical species, i.e. an atom or molecule, is the energy required to remove 1 mole of electrons from 1 mole of gaseous atoms or ions. Large atoms or molecules have a low ionization energy, while small molecules tend to have higher ionization energies.

Ionization gauge controller
One of two ion gauges in the preacc control room that monitor column vacuum and control the vacuum valves leading to the columns, as well as being interlocked inputs to the 750 keV chopper supply controllers.

Ionized
An atom or a particle that has a net charge because it has gained or lost electrons.

Ionosphere
A region covering the highest layers in the Earth's atmosphere, containing an appreciable population of ions and free electrons. The ions are created by sunlight ranging from the ultra-violet to x-rays. In the lowest and least rarefied layer of the ionosphere, the D-layer (around 70 km or 45 miles), as soon as the Sun sets the ions and electrons recombine, but in the higher layers, collisions are so few that its ion layers last throughout the night.

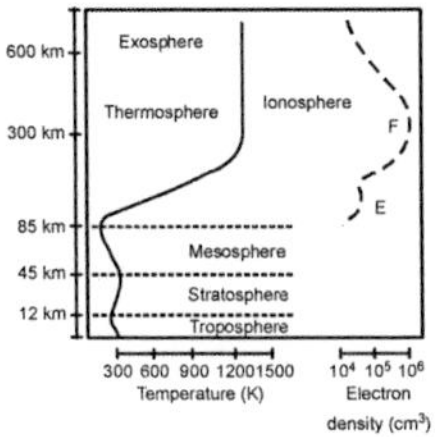

IPA
Intermediate Power Amplifier. An intermediate level of amplification in the Linac high-level RF system. The 400 W solid- state amplifier is the first IPA, and the 7651 tube is the second IPA.

IPE
Index Page Editor. A programme for enabling the programmer to make an applications programme available from a console index page. Included is the capability of assigning a page number and title to the programme.

Irregular reflection
Scattering. Reflection in many different directions from an irregular surface.

Isobaric
At constant pressure.

Isobaric process
In which pressure remains constant.

Isocentre
One of two points in space defined by alignment fixtures in the NTF set-up and treatment rooms. Patient set-up is usually done on the premise that the area to be treated will lie at the isocentre.

Isochoric process
In which volume remains constant.

Isoplane
An imaginary plane perpendicular to the neutron beam axis and containing the isocentre. Used in NTF patient setup.

Isothermal process
An isothermal process is a change of a system, in which the temperature remains constant: DT = 0. This typically occurs when a system is in contact with an outside thermal reservoir (heat bath), and the change occurs slowly enough to allow the system to continually adjust to the temperature of the reservoir through heat exchange.

Isotope
One of two or more atoms having the same number of protons in its nucleus, but a different number of neutrons and, therefore, a different mass.

J

Jacketed
Cryogenic devices that contain an outer covering to hold an insulating vacuum.

Jets
Narrow clusters of subatomic particles resulting from collisions of quarks and antiquarks. The particles in jets are the objects actually observed in experiments such as those in the Collider Detector at Fermilab.

Johnson controller
Pneumatically controlled regulation system located next to the lcw heat exchanger in Main Ring service buildings which controls valves affecting the flow of lcw through the heat exchanger.

Joule
Metric unit used to measure work and energy; can also be used to measure heat; equivalent to newton-metre.

Joule thomson coefficient
The Joule thomson coefficient, m, is defined as m = -Cp-1 (oH/oP)T = (oT/oP)H. The sign of m indicates weather a gas expansion will cause an increase or decrease in the temperature. If m is positive, the expanding gas will be cooled. The locus of points where m = 0 is called the Joule Thomson inversion curve.

Joule's law
The heat developed in a conductor is directly proportional to the resistance of the conductor, the square of the current, and the time the current is maintained.

Joule's law of heating
The heat produced when a current 'I' flows through a resistor 'R' for a given time 't' is given by $Q = I^2Rt$ joules.

Jt
Joule-Thomson expansion valve.

JT valve
A cryogenic valve which cools the helium and nitrogen by allowing it to expand. They also serve to control helium flow. JT stands for Joule-Thompson.

Junction detector
A solid-state device based on the transistor principle that is used to detect the passage of charged particles.

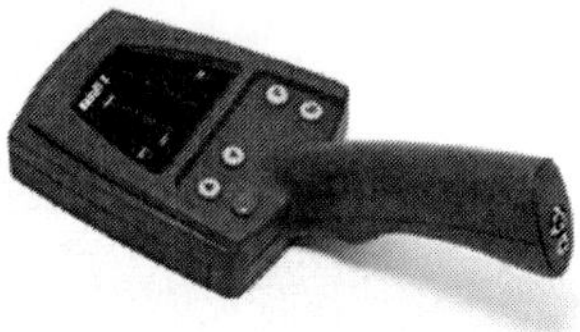

K

Kaon

K-Meson. An elementary particle of spin 0 having a rest mass about 970 times that of the electron. It occurs in neutral, positive, and negative charge states.

Kautzky valve

Cryogenic relief valve for Tevatron style magnets and spool pieces. They are kept closed under normal conditions by a constant pressure of helium gas.

Kelvin

The kelvin is a unit of measurement for temperature. It is one of the seven base units in the International System of Units (SI) and is assigned the unit symbol K. The Kelvin scale is an absolute, thermodynamic temperature scale using as its null point absolute zero, the temperature at which all thermal motion ceases in the classical description of thermodynamics. The kelvin is defined as the fraction 1/273.16 of the thermodynamic temperature of the triple point of water (273.16 K (0.01 °C; 32.02 °F)

Kelvin scale

The scale of temperature having a single fixed point, the temperature of the triple point of water, which is assigned the value 273.16 °K.

Kelvin scale of temperature

On this scale, the ice-point (the lower fixed point) is taken as 273.15K and the (the upper fixed point) is taken as 373.15K. The interval between these two points is divided into 100 equal parts. Each division is equal to 1K.

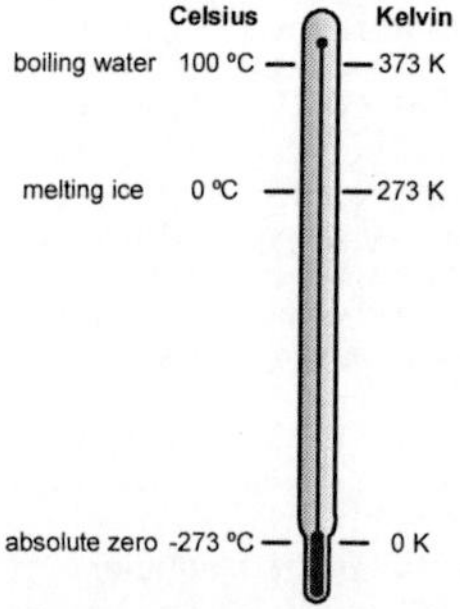

Kepler's first law

The first law of Kepler states that a planet moves in an elliptical orbit around the Sun that is located at one of the two foci of the ellipse. An ellipse is one of the conic curves originally studied by Greek geometres.

Kepler's second law
Relationship in planetary motion that an imaginary line between the sun and a planet moves over equal areas of the ellipse during equal time intervals.

Kepler's third law
Relationship in planetary motion that the square of the period of an orbit is directly proportional to the cube of the radius of the major axis of the orbit.
Kepler's first law of planetary motion
Each planet moves in an elliptical orbit, with the sun located at one of the foci.

Kepler's second law of planetary motion
The radius vector joining the planet to the sun covers equal areas in equal intervals of time.

Kepler's third law of planetary motion
The square of the period of a planet is directly proportional to the cube of the radius of the semi major axis of the orbit.

Kev
One thousand electron volts.

Keyer
A solid-state device providing the first stage of amplification in a linac modulator. The light-pipe input to the modulator is amplified to about 1 kV by the keyer.

Keylock valves
Beam line vacuum valves that are manually opened and closed to isolate beam pipe for maintenance.

Keyswitch module
Also known as the Pulse Shifter Controller Module. This module produces an HEP enable to be sent to the Pre- Acc prom module. Keyswitches on the front of the module selectively bypass beam switches in the MCR, as well as other inputs to the module.

Kicker magnet
Very fast rise time magnet used to divert the entire beam at once. Typical uses are Booster extraction, Main Ring extraction, Main Ring and Tevatron abort.

Kilocalorie
The amount of energy required to raise the temperature of one kilogram of water by 1°C, 1 Kcal = 1000 calories.

Kilogram
A unit of mass in the metric system; one of the seven fundamental units.

Kilometre
Abbreviated *km*. 1 km = 1000 metres = 10^5 cm = 0.62 mile.

Kilowatt hour
A unit of electric energy equal to 3.6×10^6 joules.

Kinematics
The description of the motion of particles and bodies without reference to the forces associated with that motion.

Kinetic energy
The energy possessed by a body due to its motion, it is equal to $\frac{1}{2}mv^2$, where m is the mass and v is the speed of the body

Kinetic friction
A friction force between surfaces that are slipping past each other.

Kinetic theory
The molecules of matter are continuously in motion and the collisions between molecules are perfectly elastic.

Kinetic theory of gases
A model of an ideal gas that treats it as a collection of molecules undergoing motion according to Newton's laws of classical mechanics and predicts macroscopic quantities such as pressure and temperature in terms of molecular properties, such as the velocity of the molecules.

Kirchhoff's first law
The algebraic sum of the currents at any circuit junction is equal to zero.

Kirchhoff's second law
The algebraic sum of all changes in potential occurring around any loop in a circuit equals zero.

Kirk keys

Any keys that are captured by the lock they reside in. They are used in situations where a degree of safety is desired. Some are used to prevent a mechanical linkage from being manipulated unless the key is present in the lock. An example of this use is the Booster Brentford breaker switch arms. Others require another keys presence before they can be removed and used for access in another part of the system. An example of this use is accessing the Tev power supply DC breaker cabinet. The name Kirk comes from the company that makes the captured locksets.

Klixon

A temperature-sensitive electrical switch used in interlock circuits of power supplies and magnets that opens when a certain temperature is exceeded.

K-Meson

An elementary particle of spin 0 having a rest mass about 970 times that of the electron. It occurs in neutral, positive, and negative charge states.

Knife switches

Single pole switches that connect individual Main Ring and Tevatron power supplies to their respective power buses. These knife switches are located in a cabinet on top of each Main Ring power supply. The Tev knife switches are located over the Tev dump switch. The knife switches have to be manipulated locally. The knife switches can be put in any of three states. They can be placed so that the power supply is racked in to the bus. They can also be placed so that the bus is shorted in the power supply effectively bypassing the supply from the bus. In the last state the knife switches are manipulated so that the bus is broke open at the power supply. This is done to facilitate high potting a section of the bus in order to track down a ground fault.

Knob

A wheel connected to a shaft encoder in the MCR capable of making a continuous change in the D/A of a device. This is generally located in the half-high NIM, bin on the right-hand side of the console.

Ko regeneration

A neutral kaon beam consists of two states, KL ("K-long") and KS ("K-short") particles. The KS component decays rapidly, but can be "regenerated" when the remaining KL component is retargeted.

K-space

That image space represented by the time and phase raw data. The Fourier transform of k-space is the magnetic resonance image.

L

Ladder control

Obsolete: A method of controlling quadrupole power supplies whereby the settings of a few supplies determined the settings for a number of others.

Lagrangian point

in a system dominated by two attracting bodies (such as Sun and Earth), a point at which a third, much smaller body (such as a satellite) keeps the same position relative to the other two. Theoretically, the Sun-Earth system has 5 Lagrangian points, but only two are important: L1 (L-one), on the sunward side of Earth, about 4 times the distance of the Moon, and L2 at approximately the same distance on the midnight side.

Lam

Look At Me. It is a flag used by many accelerator control cards to indicate a state. In other words, the device has information to be passed to the front-end and uses the flag to indicate to the front-end that it should read its information.

Lambda particle

A neutral elementary particle just slightly more massive than the proton. A hyperon member of the baryon family.

Lambda supply

A power supply which provides +5, -5, +15,and -15 volts. They are used to power Main Ring electronics in the service buildings.

Lambertson (magnetic septum)

A special type of magnet having two vacuum chambers with one having a magnetic field and the other being field-free. They are usually found downstream of electrostatic septa.

Lambertson magnet

A special magnet used to separate two adjacent beams by providing a bending field for one beam and a field-free region for the other beam. A beam is usually separated into two adjacent beams upstream of a Lambertson magnet by a septum. The Lambertson magnet was designed at Fermilab and is named for its designer.

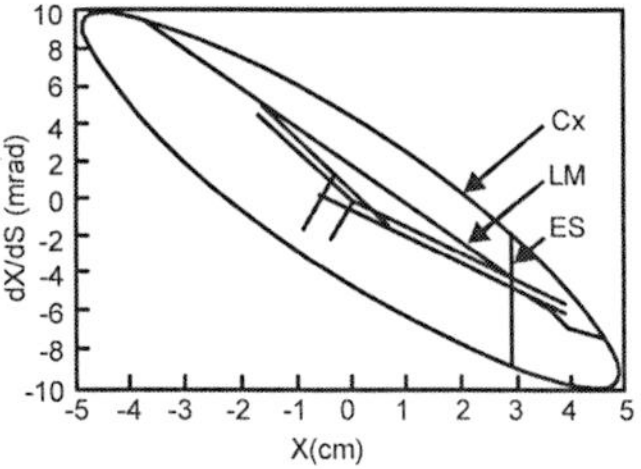

Larmor frequency

The resonance frequency of a spin in a magnetic field. The rate of precession of a spin packet in a magnetic field. The frequency which will cause a transition between the two spin energy levels of a nucleus.

Laser

A device that produces coherent light by stimulated emission of radiation.

Laser printer

Otherwise known as the Talaris T2400. One of the printing options residing in the computer room, accessible through the Development VAX. It is used for high quality prints. It has 300 dots/inch resolution and can produce up to 24 pages/min.

Latent heat

In thermochemistry, latent heat is the amount of energy in the form of heat released or absorbed by a substance during a change of phase (i.e. solid, liquid, or gas), – also called a phase transition. A typical example is a change of state of matter, meaning a phase transition such as the melting of ice or the boiling of water

Latent heat of evaporization

The heat absorbed when one gram of a substance changes from the liquid phase to the gaseous phase, or the heat released when one gram of gas changes from the gaseous phase to the liquid phase.

Latent heat of fusion

The quantity of heat required to convert one unit mass of a substance from solid to the liquid state at its melting point (without any change in its temperature) is called its latent heat of fusion (L). The SI unit of latent heat of fusion is J/kg.

Latent heat of sublimation

The quantity of heat required to convert one unit mass of a substance from solid to gaseous state without any change in its temperature.

Latent heat of vapourization

The quantity of heat required to convert one unit mass of a substance from liquid to gaseous state at its boiling point without any change in its temperature.

Lattice

The periodic relative arrangement of quadrupoles and drift spaces in an accelerator.

Law

A statement, usually mathematical, which describes some physical phenomena.

Law of conservation of baryons

When a baryon decays or reacts with another particle, the number of baryons is the same on both sides of the equation.

Law of conservation of energy

The change of one form of energy into another is called transformation of energy. For example, when a body falls its potential energy is converted to kinetic energy. The total energy of a group of objects remains constant.

Law of conservation of hypercharge

Hypercharge is conserved in strong and electromagnetic interactions, but not in weak interactions.

Law of conservation of leptons

In a reaction involving leptons, the arithmetic sum of the lepton numbers is the same on each side of the equation.

Law of conservation of mass

Same as law of conservation of matter; mass, including single atoms, is neither created nor destroyed in a chemical reaction.

Law of conservation of matter

Matter is neither created nor destroyed in a chemical reaction.

Law of conservation of mechanical energy

The sum of the potential and kinetic energies of an ideal energy system is constant.

Law of conservation of momentum

When no net external forces are acting on an object, the total vector momentum of the object remains constant.

Law of entropy

A natural process always takes place in such a direction as to increase the entropy of the universe.

Law of heat exchange

In any heat transfer system, the heat lost by hot materials equals the heat gained by cold materials.

LCW

Low Conductivity Water. Water that has had the free ions removed in order to increase the resistivity of the water to 9 MW/cm or greater. Found in the 55R and 95R systems used to cool linac components.

Lead flows

Cryogenic cooling at the point where the warm Tevatron bus enters the cryostat. Liquid helium is allowed to flow from the single phase system out the feed can or power spool and around the bus to cool it down. When the Tev is at 90 Gev or 150 Gev the low energy lead flows are on leaking out a low rate of flow of single phase helium. When the Tev is ramped up to 800 Gev for fixed target or 900 Gev for collider operation the high energy lead flows are on leaking out a high rate of flow. When the Tev is not powered there is no need for cooling. If there is more lead flow cooling than is needed (having the high energy lead flows on when at 150 Gev) there is a possibility of ice balls forming around the leads. This can cause the LCW in the Tevatron bus to freeze and crack the LCW insulators.

Lead glass counter

A Cerenkov Counter using dense lead glass as the Cerenkov radiator. It is sensitive down to very low velocities and therefore may be used as a total absorption shower counter for identifying electrons.

Leak detector

A device for finding leaks in a vacuum system. The standard type for use in high vacuum systems is a mass spectrometer which can detect minute quantities of helium which is released outside the system at a suspected leak. The sensitivity of the leak detectors used in leak checking Tevatron components is one part in 10 billion.

Led

Light Emitting Diode. A light-emitting diode (LED) is a semiconductor light source. LEDs are used as indicator lamps in many devices and are increasingly used for other lighting. Introduced as a practical electronic component in 1962, early LEDs emitted low-intensity red light, but modern versions are available across the visible, ultraviolet, and infrared wavelengths, with very high brightness.

LEF

Local Event Flag. A process scheduling state of activity for a given process on the VAX. It means that the process is waiting for a flag to be set before resuming activity.

Left bends

A set of large bending magnets that initially direct the beam toward the Meson Area. Also known as the MH-200's.

Lens

A transparent object with two refracting surfaces. Usually the surfaces are flat or spherical (spherical lenses). Sometimes, to improve image quality. Lenses are deliberately made with surfaces which depart slightly from spherical (aspheric lenses).

Lenz's law

An induced current is in such a direction that its magnetic property opposes the change by which the current is induced.

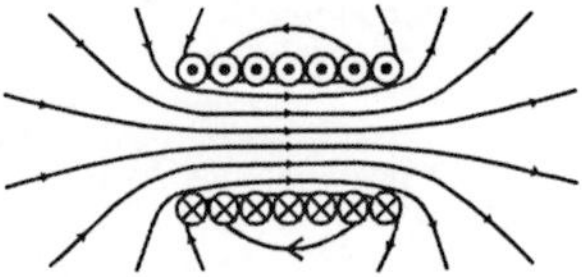

Lepton

A collective term for those spin 1/2 particles (Fermions) which do not undergo strong interactions. The word Lepton was coined from Greek root to indicate that these are light particles. The known leptons (e;, m;, ne, nm) are all lighter than the mesons and baryons.

Lexidata

The commercial name for a colour display screen available at all ACNET consoles. It is a medium performance display unit which generates a 640(H) by 512(V) pixel display refreshed at a non-interlaced 60 Hz rate to minimize flickering. There are eight colours which may be displayed on a pixel by pixel basis. These may be displayed directly or combined through one of three logical functions (AND, OR, XOR).

Light

Anything that can travel from one place to another through empty space and can influence matter, but is not affected by gravity.

Light link

A light link is a light modulator/receiver combination used to carry control signals along a path across which a large electrical potential difference exists. The encoded control information crosses this high voltage region on either an optical fibre bundle or an air path.

Light-year

A light-year, also light year or lightyear (symbol: ly) is a unit of length, equal to just under 10 trillion kilometres (10×10^{15} metres, 10 petametres or about 6 trillion miles). As defined by the International Astronomical Union (IAU), a light-year is the distance that light travels in a vacuum in one Julian year.

Linac

Hydrogen ions are accelerated using radio frequency cavities from the exit of the Cockroft Walton generators up to 200 mev for injection into the Booster ring where the negative ions are stripped of both electrons to become bare protons.

Linac 68k mp beam inhibit module

Module in the preacc control room that sends the beam/no beam status to the linac secondaries, and causes a beam inhibit if one of the secondaries or the primary pulls the beam inhibit line.

Linac front-end

A DEC PDP-11/34 which serves as the central node for the Linac controls system.

Linac primary

An Motorola 68000 microprocessor which initiates requests and gathers data on behalf of the Linac front-end. It is located behind Linac Station 6.

Linac secondary

Any of sixteen Motorola 68000 micro- processors which serve as local control stations in the Linac. There are separate secondaries for each of the nine Linac stations, one for each of the Haefelys a ground station for the Haefelys, and one each for the Buncher, Debuncher, 200 Mev equipment, and Station 10. The secondaries gather data and change the parametres of their associated equipment.

Linac steering

Procedure whereby beam is aligned at the head of the 200 MeV transport line by steering dipoles between tanks 6-7 and 7-8. Can be performed automatically by ACNET page L36.

Line of force

A line of force in Faraday's extended sense is synonymous with Maxwell's line of induction. A line so drawn that a tangent to it at any point indicates the direction of the electric field.

Line spectrum

A spectrum consisting of monochromatic slit images having wavelengths characteristic of the atoms present in the source.

Linear accelerator

A device for accelerating particles in a straight line through many stages of small potential difference.

Linear magnification

Is the ratio of the size of the object to the size of the image.

Linear voltage differential transformer

LVDT. Also called Linear Variable Differential Transformer. Detects small position changes along an axis. They are used to detect position changes of Septa and Tevatron cryo valves among other places.

Lines of force

Lines drawn to make an electric field strength map, with each line originating on a positive charge and ending on a negative charge; each line represents a path on which a charge would experience a constant force and lines closer together mean a stronger electric field.

Link

At Fermilab, links are the the systems of cables and repeaters which carry information to and from distant points in the accelerator.

Link driver

A device which organizes and transmits digital information on a link. In the context of the link drivers for the console and front-end computers this device performs a parallel to serial conversion on data to be transmitted on the link. It also acts as a receiver of data from the link and performs the reverse conversion.

Linlock line

Linac vacuum valve status input to the prom module and pulse shifter, powered by a small 5 volt supply at RF station 9. Vacuum valve controllers at each station short out the line whenever a valve closes, inhibiting beam.

Liouville's theorem

A theorem from classical mechanics which states that for a beam with constant total energy, the area occupying a spatial coordinate and its conjugate momentum (q and p phase space) for each particle in the beam is conserved over time, although the shape and position of this region may vary.

Liquefaction

The change to the liquid phase. The condensation of a gas to a liquid.

Liquid

The fluid phase with finite heat of vaporization and density greater than the gas phase. Denoted by LH2, LD2, LHe, LN2, etc.

Liquid helium

This is the coldest substance that is still a liquid and thus the only refrigerant at temperatures of a few degrees Kelvin and atmospheric pressure.

Litre

A metric system unit of volume, usually used for liquids.

Lithium lens

A device located directly downstream of the antiproton production target which acts to collect the secondary particles by reducing the solid angle of particles coming off of the target. The lithium lens could be looked at as a high gradient bi-planar quadrupole magnet. The lenses at Fermilab typically run at currents of hundreds of kiloamperes.

LLPA

Low Level Power Amplifier. Linac 5-watt solid-state amplifier in the rear of the A5 racks that is the first step in the high-level RF system.

LLRF
Low Level Radio Frequency. This refers to the electronics that provide the proper phase and frequency for the RF voltage. The LLRF controls the High Level RF Power Amplifiers which in turn control the electric fields in the RF acceleration cavities.

Local mode
One of three secondary modes in Linac where the secondary microcomputer satisfies data requests and commands from the local console.

Lock out
The process of placing locks on power supplies or power distribution panels so that the supplies can not be turned on or energized. This is a safety measure allowing maintenance to be performed on individual devices. It is also done to power supplies that feed electrical devices in the tunnel, such as magnets and correction elements, as part of the conditions for an open access.

Logic loop
An electrical relay loop that protects an accelerator enclosure by ensuring that no one can enter the area and reset the loop once inside. Once the logic loop has been dropped the interlocks must be reset in a specified manner on a search and secure.

Longitudinal magnetization
The Z component of magnetization.

Longitudinal strain
The ratio of change in length of a body to its initial length.

Longitudinal transit time factor
Ratio of the energy gain of particle traversing a cell with a constant electric field to the energy gain of a particle traversing a cell with a sinusoidally varying electric field.

Longitudinal wave
Longitudinal waves, as known as "l-waves", are waves that have the same direction of vibration as their direction of travel, which means that the movement of the medium is in the same direction as or the opposite direction to the motion of the wave. Mechanical longitudinal waves have been also referred to as compressional waves or compression waves.

Loop
A midpoint of a vibrating segment of a standing wave.

Lorentz contraction
The effect that an observer moving with respect to a given object will find the object to be shortened compared with the measurement by an observer at rest relative to the object.

Lorentzian lineshape
A function obtained from the Fourier transform of an exponential function.

Loss monitor
Diagnostic device which is used to measure the amount of beam lost from the vacuum chamber.

Loudness
Loudness is the quality of a sound that is primarily a psychological correlate of physical strength (amplitude). More formally, it is defined as "that attribute of auditory sensation in terms of which sounds can be ordered on a scale extending from quiet to loud."

Low beta magnets
Magnets used to focus the beam to create collisions of high luminosity. Low beta magnets are installed at both ends of the Collider Detector in the accelerator at B0 and D0.

Low beta squeeze
After injecting protons and pbars into the Tevatron for collider operation a special set of quadrupoles are turned on at B0 to reduce the size of the beam and increase luminosity.

Lumen
The unit of luminous flux; the luminous flux on a unit surface all points of which are at unit distance from a point source of one candle:

Luminosity

A measure of the potential number of particle interactions for colliding beams. The luminosity depends on the intensity and phase space density of the interacting beams. The higher the luminosity is, the better it is for quark and Higgs hunters. The design peak luminosity of the TeVatron I project is 1030 sq.cm/sec. Integrated luminosity is measured in inverse nanobarns.

Luminous

An object or objects that produce visible light; for example, the sun, stars, light bulbs, and burning materials are all luminous.

Luminous ether

Ether is the medium on which light waves were once presumed to propagate. The luminous ether does not exist.

Luminous flux

The part of the total energy radiated per unit of time from a luminous source that is capable of producing the sensation of sight.

Lust

Leaking underground storage tank.

Lxcent

A process on the OPER VAX which saves Lexidata images in circular buffer files for recall at a later time.

Lxprnt

A process on the OPER VAX that interfaces the colour printer to the controls system to allow printing of Lexidata images.

Lyman series

A group of lines in the ultraviolet region in the spectrum of hydrogen.

M

Mac
A Lockheed Electronics 16-bit minicomputer used for remote monitoring and control.

Mac room
A room under the MCR which houses a number of MAC-16 and DEC-11/55 computers which interface some of the front-ends to equipment in the accelerator. The MAC room also includes the most important clock generators and encoders as well as equipment for putting scope traces and intensities on Channel 13.

Mac-16
A parallel-processing 16-bit minicomputer once manufactured by Lockheed. They are used in some of the older systems, especially Main Ring, to interface between the front- ends and the equipment. All maintenance is performed by Accelerator Division personnel.

Machine
A machine manages power to accomplish a task, examples include, a mechanical system, a computing system, an electronic system, and a molecular machine. In common usage, the meaning is that of a device having parts that perform or assist in performing any type of work. A simple machine is a device that transforms the direction or magnitude of a force.

Machine cycle reset
A signal, or clock event, to any specific accelerator to begin a programmed sequence of events. The major signals originate in the Time-Line Generator and are clock events encoded onto the Tevatron clock.

Macro
The assembly language for the DEC's. It is rarely used in applications programmes.

Macroscopic
A physical entity or process of large scale, the scale of ordinary human experience. Specifically, any phenomena in which the individual molecules and atoms are neither measured, nor explicitly considered in the description of the phenomena.

MADC
Multiplexed Analogue-to-Digital Converter. At Fermilab, these are usually local stations capable of accepting up to 64 analogue inputs and converting each of them into a digital signal expressed in units of voltage. They consist of a single analogue to digital converter with an analogue input multiplexor to select one of the many possible input signals for conversion. Since only one channel may be digitized at a time, many commands are needed to digitize all possible input channels. This gives rise for the need of an MADC controller to coordinate its activities and issue the necessary commands. The Main Ring utility crates use a CC130 module while

the newer CAMAC design is the 190 module. If each input to the analogue mux is the output of a "sample and hold" circuit, then all the inputs may be sampled simultaneously even though the conversion must proceed sequentially.

MADC volts

The voltage output of an MADC, ranging from -10.24 V to +10.24 V. The least significant bit is 2.5 mV. The voltage represents a a twelve-digit bit pattern generated from an analogue signal. Conversion factors to engineering units are kept in the System Database.

Magnet cage

Caged-in area in the Transfer Gallery where a B1 dipole magnet, a B2 dipole magnet, an F-quadrupole magnet, and a D-quad are kept. These are electrically in series with their respective Main Ring buses and are used to monitor fields and currents.

A

B

Magnetic dipole

An object, such as a current loop, an atom, or a bar magnet, that experiences torques due to magnetic forces; the strength of magnetic dipoles is measured by comparison with a standard dipole consisting of a square loop of wire of a given size and carrying a given amount of current.

Magnetic domain

Tiny physical regions in permanent magnets, approximately 0.01 to 1 mm, that have magnetically aligned atoms, giving the domain an overall polarity.

Magnetic field

A field of force that is generated by electric currents. The Sun's average large-scale magnetic field, like that of the Earth, exhibits a north and a south pole linked by lines of magnetic force.

Magnetic field intensity

The force exerted by a magnetic field on a unit N pole situated in the field.

Magnetic field lines

Imaginary lines that indicate the strength and direction of a magnetic field. The orientation of the line and an arrow show the direction of the field. The lines are drawn closer together where the field is stronger. Charged particles move freely along magnetic field lines, but are inhibited by the magnetic force from moving across field lines.

Magnetic flux

Magnetic flux (most often denoted as Φm), is a measure of the amount of magnetic field passing through a given surface (such as a conducting coil). The SI unit of magnetic flux is the weber (Wb) (in derived units: volt-seconds).

Magnetic flux

The total sum of magnetic field vectors passing perpendicularly through a surface. According to faraday's law, the rate of change of the magnetic flux through a surface is proportional to electromotive force generated on the closed loop containing the surface.

Magnetic flux density

The magnetic flux through a unit area normal to the magnetic field; also called magnetic induction.

Magnetic force

A force associated with motion of electric charges.

Magnetic lines of force

Michael Faraday's original term for what is now widely called magnetic field lines.

Magnetic monopole

The magnetic monopole conjectured by Dirac is the counterpart of the electric charge. Analogous to electric monopoles, like magnetic monopoles would repel and oppositely charged magnetic monopoles would attract. As of this date there is no evidence supporting the existence of magnetic monopoles.

Magnetic poles

(1) the points on Earth towards which the compass needle points. (Several slightly different definitions exist, because the field is not exactly that of a dipole.) (2) A concentrated source of magnetic force, e.g. a bar magnet has two magnetic poles near its end.

Magnetic quantum number

From quantum mechanics model of the atom, one of four descriptions of the energy state of an electron wave; this quantum number describes the energy of an electron orbital as the orbital is oriented in space by an external magnetic field, a kind of energy sub-sublevel.

Magnetic reconnection

In a plasma, the process by which plasma particles riding along two different field lines find themselves sharing the same field line. For instance, solar wind particles on an interplanetary field line, and magnetospheric ones on a field line attached to Earth, finding themselves united on an "open" field line, which has one end anchored on Earth and the other in distant space.

Magnetic resonance imaging (MRI)

An imaging technique based on the principles of NMR.

Magnetic reversal

The changing of polarity of the earth's magnetic field as the north magnetic pole and the south magnetic pole exchange positions.

Magnetic storm

A large-scale disturbance of the magnetosphere, usually initiated by the arrival of an interplanetary shock, originating on the Sun. A magnetic storm is marked by the injection of an appreciable number of ions from the magnetotail into the ring current, a process accompanied by an auroral disturbance. The strengthened ring current causes a world-wide drop in the equatorial magnetic field, over perhaps 12 hours, followed by a more gradual recovery.

Magnetic tape

Magnetic tape is a medium for magnetic recording, made of a thin magnetizable coating on a long, narrow strip of plastic. Devices that record and play back audio and video using magnetic tape are tape recorders and video tape recorders. A device that stores computer data on magnetic tape is a tape drive (tape unit, streamer).

Magnetic Tape

Magnetic wave

The spread of magnetization from a small portion of a substance where an abrupt change in the magnetic field has taken place.

Magnetometer

intrument for measuring magnetic fields. Spacecraft often carry fluxgate magnetometres, which measure components of the magnetic field (3 of them are combined to give its strength and direction) but need to be calibrated. Rubidium-vapour and similar instruments measure only the strength, but their reading is absolute, related to atomic constants.

Magnetopause

The boundary of the magnetosphere, separating plasma attached to Earth from the one flowing with the solar wind.

Magnetosphere

The region around a planet such as the Earth within which the motion of charged particles is influenced by the planet's magnetic field. The Earth's magnetosphere consists of a dipole field, similar to that of a bar magnet, and a long tail on the night side produced by the interaction of the solar wind with the Earth's magnetic field.

Magnetotail

The region of the magnetosphere containing field lines stretched away from the Sun. It starts about 8 Earth radii (RE) nightward of the Earth and has been observed to distances of at least 22 RE.

Magnetron

Ion source that produces negative ions by extracting them from a plasma formed by an electric arc formed in hydrogen gas. Used in the Pre-Acc H- and I- sources at FNAL.

Magnification

The ratio of the image distance to the object distance; the ratio of the image size to the object size.

Magnitude

The length of a magnetization vector. In NMR, the square root of the sum of the squares of the Mx and My components, *i.e.* the magnitude of the transverse magnetization.

Main collimator

NTF collimator assembly following the primary collimator and containing inserts to shape the neutron beam to the desired size.

Main control room

The area at Fermilab located in the Cross Gallery where acceleration of the beam of protons is monitored and controlled.

Main injector

The newest accelerator to the Fermilab complex nearing completion of tunnel construction. The Main Injector is intended to replace the Main Ring and to significantly enhance the intensity of beams and thus the luminosity of the interactions at the colliders.

Main ring

The ring used to accelerate protons from the booster and antiprotons from the Accumulator from a beam energy of 8 GeV up to 120 GeV. The Main Ring will be replaced as the Main Injector becomes operational.

Main ring abort link

A hardwired link originating in the back racks of the MCR and sent around the ring via 200 modules in the utility crate of each service building. The signal is continuous until certain parametres go out of tolerance, at which point the link is broken and the abort sequence is initiated.

Main ring power supply (MRPS)

Power supplies for the Main Ring magnets. They are turned on sequentially to form the Main Ring ramp.

Main ring sample time

The time, once a cycle, during which the sample and hold modules are loaded before information is sent back to the MCR.

Mainframe

The cabinet or piece of equipment in a computer system which contains the cpu. The term also refers to the type of computer which requires a mainframe; i.e., a large computer.

Make up water

The process of replacing lost LCW or coolant for a particular cooling system.

Malleability

The property of a metal that enables it to be hammered or rolled into sheets.

Malus law

The intensity of the light transmitted from the analyzer varies directly as the square of the cosine of the angle between the plane of transmission of analyzer and polarizer.

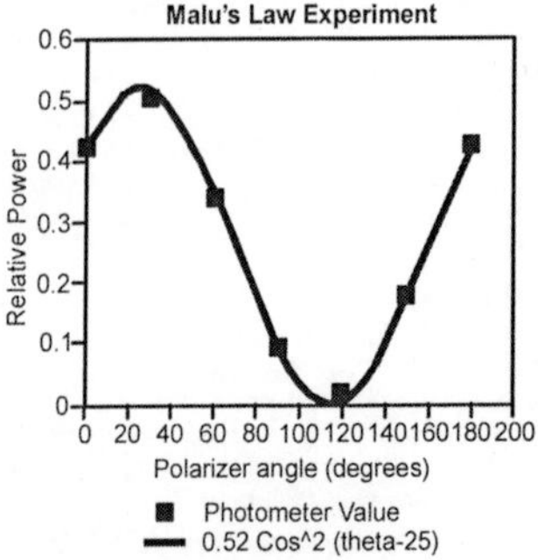

Manchester (encoding)

System of data encoding on a bipolar clock used in serial data link communications.

Manhole

A physically isolated section of accelerator tunnel.

Manual disconnect

Large switch on a power supply cubicle which can be used to disconnect the power supply (actually the primary of its transformer) from the feeder.

MARS

Main Ring Automated Ramp Start up. This is a computer programme currently found on page M10 that automatically starts the Main Ring ramp.

Maser

Microwave amplification by stimulated emission of radiation.

Mass

A numerical measure of how difficult it is to change an object's motion. (In the context of relativity, some books use the word "mass" to mean what we refer to as mass multiplied by gamma.)

Mass defect

The difference between the sum of the masses of the individual nucleons forming a nucleus and the actual mass of that nucleus.

Mass density

The mass density or density of a material is defined as its mass per unit volume. The symbol most often used for density is r (the Greek letter rho). The mass density of a material varies with temperature and pressure. (The variance is typically small for solids and liquids and much greater for gasses.) Increasing the pressure on an object decreases the volume of the object and therefore increase its density.

Mass number

(1) The sum of the number of protons and neutrons in the nucleus of an atom.

(2) The integer nearest to the atomic mass.

Mass spectrograph

Instrument used to determine the mass of ionized particles.

Master oscillator

Oscillator that provides the RF signal for all linac RF systems. Typically runs at 201.24 MHz.

Matching

The process of tailoring the emittance of a beam to the acceptance of a device.

Matter

The substance of which a physical object is composed. All materials in the universe have the same inner nature, that is, they are composed of atoms, arranged in different (and often complex) ways; the specific atoms and the specific arrangements identify the various materials.

Matter wave

A property of matter that is directly proportional to Planck's constant and inversely proportional to mass and velocity.

Maximum working pressure

Pressure beyond which a pressure container should not be operated.

MCCR

Main Control Room Relay Rack.

MCR

Main Control Room. The locus at which most of the information on the ACNET system is received and acted upon. A number of hardwired signals are available as well. The MCR does not control the experimental areas or the beam lines leading directly to them.

MDAT link

The link which communicates Tevatron ramp current information around the ring. MDAT stands for Machine DATa.

MDC

Multiplexed Data Channel. A MAC 16 option which allows communication with up to 16 external devices independent of programme instructions (Direct Memory Access) and is capable of transfer rates up to 330 K words/sec to or from memory. Communication is interleaved between processor execution of instructions and shares the PDC I/O lines. The programme must specify a device, destination in memory, and a transfer count before a transfer may begin. The processor is free to resume programme execution during the actual I/O. When the specified number of words has been transferred the MDC hardware interrupts the CPU.

MDC link

The link consists of two independent cables which perform block data transfers. Data may be transmitted in either direction, originating at MAC-A or any utility crate, but currently only the crate to MAC-A direction is implemented.

MDV

MoDulator View. RF abbreviation. This is the output voltage of the modulator that supplies anode voltage for the final tube of the power amplifier. There are two types of modulators. The originals that are calibrated for 1 V input equals 2,500 V output and some that have been modified for 1 V in equals 3,000 V out.

Mean life

The average time during which a system, such as an atom, nucleus, exists in a specified form.

Mechanical energy

The form of energy associated with machines, objects in motion, and objects having potential energy that results from gravity.

Mechanical equivalent of heat

The conversion factor that relates heat units to work units; 4.19 j/cal.

Mechanical phase shifter

Device strung between Linac RF cavities with inputs from each cavity which produces the intertank phase signal used for phase regulation.

Mechanical wave

The waves, which need a material medium for their propagation, are called mechanical waves. Mechanical waves are also called elastic waves. Sound waves, water waves are examples of mechanical waves.

Medical microcomputer

NTF computer that drives the NTF console and interfaces with the beamline microcomputer.

Medium

Any region through which a wave disturbance propagates. Mechanical waves require a matter medium. Electromagnetic waves propagate through a vacuum and various matter media.

Megahertz
Unit of frequency, equal to 10^6 hertz.

Megaton
An explosive force equal to one million metric tons of TNT. The energy released in the explosion of one megaton of TNT is equal to 4.2×10^{22} ergs.

Melting point
The temperature at which a phase change of solid to liquid takes place; the same temperature as the freezing point for a given substance.

Meniscus
The crescent-shaped surface at the edge of a liquid column.

Meshall
The large concrete pre-target enclosure in the Meson Area providing access to the target train for inspection and minor maintenance. Meshall also contains beam diagnostic equipment and beam line magnets. The primary Meson Area target is positioned in a heavily shielded tube just downstream of Meshall.

Meson
A member of the class of short lived, elementary particles having rest masses between that of the electron and the proton. Mesons are bosons, i.e., have integral intrinsic angular momentum. Examples: pi-mesons (pions) and K-mesons (kaons).

Metal
Matter having the physical properties of conductivity, malleability, ductility, and luster.

Metre
A unit of length in the metric system equivalent to 1,650,763.73 wave-lengths of the orange-red light emitted by krypton-86. One of the seven fundamental units of measure.

Metering resistor
Precision resistor-capacitor network used for measuring the voltage on the preaccelerator dome. 2125 MW.

Metric system
A system of measurement that is based on decimal multiples and subdivisions.

Mev
One million electron volts.

Microprocessor
A cpu contained on a single integrated circuit chip. Microprocessors commonly used at Fermilab include the Motorola 68000 and Zilog Z80 and Z8000.

Microscopic
A physical entity or process of small scale, too small to directly experience with our senses. Specifically, any phenomena on the molecular and atomic scale, or smaller.

Mil
Unit of measurement equal to .001. This is not to be confused with a millimetre.

Milliamp
A unit of current measurement. 1 thousandth of an amp. In the Antiproton Source it is used as a unit for quantifying beam intensity in the Accumulator.

Millibar
A measure of atmospheric pressure equivalent to 1000 dynes per cm^2.

Millirad
1/1000 of a rad. The rad (an acronym for Radiation Absorbed Dose) is defined as that quantity of radiation that delivers 100 ergs of energy to 1 gram of substance.

Milliradian
A unit of angular measurement. 1/1000 of a radian or about 0.057 degrees. Milliradians are often used when discussing the amount steering a magnet does to a particle beam for a given magnet current.

Millirem
1/1000 of a rem. The rem (an acronym for Roentgen Equivalent Man) is a biological rather than a

physical unit of radiation damage. It represents that quantity of radiation which produces the same biological damage as 1 rad of x-rays or gamma radiation.

Mil-std-1553b

Digital multiplex data bus standard used for interface between secondary.

Min/max

The limits of tolerance for a particular device. An alarm (and sometimes a beam inhibit or abort) is generated when the value of the device falls outside these limits.

Mini tube

Short beam pipe immediately downstream of a Main Ring quadrupole around which correction elements are located. This is also where the BPM detectors and other beam diagnostics are usually are located. The term mini-straight is sometimes used in place of mini-tube.

Minicomputer

A low-cost computer with a limited processing capability which is used for the more routine functions in a system. The PDP-11's are minicomputers used extensively at Fermilab.

Minimum ionizing

A charged particle traveling through matter near the velocity of light loses less energy per unit path to the atomic electron than a slower particle and is hence minimum ionizing. Above the velocity of minimum ionization there is a gradual (logarithmic) rise in ionization loss for extremely relativistic particles. Minimum ionization for protons is in the range from about 2-10 GeV.

Mirror point

For a particle spiraling around a field line of the magnetosphere, the point where the stronger field (of the Earth, usually) causes the spiral to flatten and then unwind again in the opposite directions. In the inner magnetosphere, ions and electrons are trapped between two mirror points, one north of the equator and one south of it; because of the "mirroring", ions and electrons are turned back before they reach the atmosphere, where they might have got lost.

Mixer

Final component in Linac low-level RF system that passes the RF signal to the amplifier chain when gate signal arrives from waveform generator/ sequencer.

MKSA

The system of physical units based on the fundamental metric units: metre kilogram, second and ampere.

Mod block

Premature termination of a Linac modulator pulse triggered by a modulator current of greater than 400 amps during the pulse.

Model

A mental or physical representation of something that cannot be observed directly that is usually used as an aid to understanding.

Modem

A device which translates computer signals into a format which can be transmitted over telephone lines. There are some controls personnel who have modems at home through which they can talk to Fermilab computers.

Moderator
A material that slows down neutrons.

Modern physics
The physics developed since about 1900, which includes relativity and quantum mechanics.

Modulator
High-voltage device connected to the anode of the PA that controls the RF output to the cavity.

Modulator regulator
Module that regulates modulator current to maintain constant RF cavity gradient.

Modulus of elasticity
The ratio of stress to the strain produced in a body.

Modulus of rigidity
The ratio of tangential stress to the shear strain produced in a body.

Mole
The amount of a substance that contains Avogadro's number of atoms, ions, molecules, or any other chemical unit; a mole is 6.02 x 1023 atoms, ions, or other chemical units.

Molecular mass
The molecular mass of something is the mass of one mole of it (in cgs units), or one kilomole of it (in MKS units). The units of molecular mass are gram and kilogram, respectively. The cgs and MKS values of molecular mass are numerically equal. The molecular mass is not the mass of one molecule. Some books still call this the molecular weight. One dictionary definition of molar is "Pertaining to a body of matter as a whole: contrasted with molecular and atomic." The mole is a measure appropriate for a macroscopic amount of material, as contrasted with a microscopic amount (a few atoms or molecules).

Molecule
The smallest chemical species of a substance that is capable of stable independent existence.

Momentum
The product of mass and velocity of a body, it is a measure of the quantity of motion in a body.

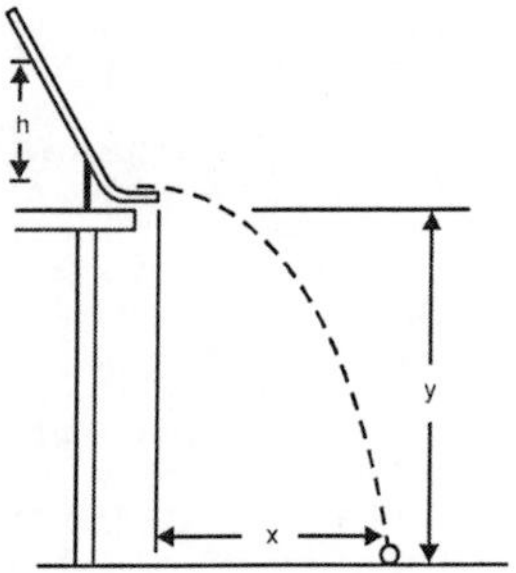

Momentum compaction
A function which describes the deviations from the equilibrium orbit due to momentum error in the beam.

Momentum dispersion
Spread in momentum due to the bending of particle of different momenta passing through a dipole.

Monitor unit
Artificially-derived unit used by NTF to define neutron dose rates.

Monitor/control module
Module in the preacc control room that monitors voltage on the preaccelerator dome, digitizes it, and sends it along with the command voltage to the regulator/oscillator module to complete the voltage regulation feedback loop.

Monitor/inhibitor module
Linac module that oversees a number of RF system interlocks and inhibits the modulator pulse if conditions warrant.

Monoatomic
Single atom molecules. Ex. He, A, Kr.

Monochromatic light
Light composed of a single colour.

Monte carlo calculation
Any method for obtaining a statistical estimate of a desired quantity by random sampling. The sampling is made from an artificial population that is in some sense a model of the physical system being investigated.

Mou
Memorandum of Understanding

Mountain range display
An oscilloscope plot, usually generated in the MRRF building, which displays bunch structure vs. time. The value of this type of display is that it can be triggered at some frequency to show information (such as bunch structure) for a set number of triggers, with each trigger having a different vertical offset. If the frequency is chosen to be the revolution frequency, one can watch the time evolution, within a window, of the same bunch as it circulates in the accelerator.

MRBS clock
Main Ring Beam Sync clock. It operates at about a 7.5 mhz rate, so that there are exactly 159 clock ticks per turn. It is used wherever synchronization to the beam has to be especially accurate.

MRRF mac
A MAC-16 computer located in the MRRF building which provides digital control of the RF stations.

MSDS
Material Safety Data Sheet.

Multibus
IEEE standard format for microcomputer systems hardware.

Multibus crate
A set of standard signal lines used to interconnect the modules of various microprocessors, such as the Z80 and Motorola 68000. Physically it is a backplane which the modules plug into. The Multibus crate is capable of supporting twenty address lines, sixteen bidirectional data lines, and eight parallel interrupt lines, as well as bus control signals, data control signals, and power distribution lines.

Multipactoring
An electron multiplication phenomenon observed in RF cavities when the fields between nearby metal surfaces is such that an electron originating on one surface can cross to the other surface in exactly one-half period of the RF. These electron beams can destroy parts of the cavities if not suppressed. Fortunately, there is a relatively narrow voltage range where multipactoring can occur, so the voltage can be stepped through this region rapidly.

Multiplex
A system where one output channel can be selected from among many input channels.

Multiplexing
A means of transmitting several independent signals over the same transmission line by separating them in time or frequency.

Multiplicity (special usage)
The number of particles produced from a single collision.

Multiturn injection
A technique of introducing beam into a circular accelerator over a time greater than the circulation period of the beam by moving the equilibrium orbit at the injection point so that the injected beam just misses the injection septum at the end of its first turn.

Multiwire
A device consisting of many thin wires stretched across an opening in a paddle. This paddle can be

rotated into the beam and each wire will produce an output signal proportional to the number of particles it intercepts. These signals are plotted by a computer to create a beam profile.

Muon

A charged elementary particle having a mass about 207 times that of the electron. It decays into an electron and two neutrinos.

Mutual inductance

The ratio of the induced emf in one circuit to the rate of change of current in the coil of another circuit.

Mux

Multiplexor. It is a device which receives inputs from a number of sources but outputs only the one selected by the user.

N

Narrowband train

One of the target train systems in the Neutrino Area. It provides a momentum selected dichromatic neutrino beam (neutrinos of mainly two energies) and is compatible with operation of the muon beam N-1. "Narrowband" refers to the peaking of the neutrino beam intensity at two energies as opposed to a neutrino beam composed of a wide range of energies ("broadband").

Natural frequency

The frequency, with which a system oscillates in the absence of external forces, it depends on the size, composition, and shape of the object.

NBP

Normal (atmospheric) Boiling Point. A fluid temperature.

NBS clock

National Bureau of Standards Clock. There are two of these clocks in the MCR. One of these arrives via a WWV signal broadcast from Boulder, Colorado. The other is transmitted via satellite.

NEC

National Electric Code.

Negative electric charge

One of the two types of electric charge; repels other negative charges and attracts positive charges.

Negative frequency artifact

The appearance of smaller in amplitude peaks in one half of the spectrum which are the mirror image of ones in the opposite half.

Negative ion

Atom or particle that has a surplus, or imbalance, of electrons and, thus, a negative charge.

NEPA

National Environmental Policy Act.

NERP

National Environmental Research Park.

Net force

The resulting force after all vector forces have been added; if a net force is zero, all the forces have canceled each other and there is not an unbalanced force.

Net magnetization vector

A vector representing the sum of the magnetization from a spin system.

Netprocess

NETwork Process. Another name for ACNET. It is a process on the VAX which manages communications between nodes.

Neuhall

A large concrete enclosure comprising the pre-target area of the Neutrino Area. The target trains may be pulled from the target tube into Neuhall for inspection and minor maintenance. Neuhall also contains beam diagnostic equipment, beam line magnets, and sometimes a small scale experiment.

Neutral current

The first evidence of neutral current interactions was the observation absence of a charged muon in the final state of the reaction nm + p -> nm + hadrons in which no muon appears in the final state. The theoretical necessity of neutral currents emerged as a result of the attempts to renormalize the theory of weak interactions so as to cure its divergence at high energies.

Neutral point or neutral line

A point or line along which the magnetic intensity is zero. Plays an important role in magnetic reconnection.

Neutral weak current

A subatomic reaction in which leptons collide without change in the charges of the colliding particles .

Neutrino

There are 3 generations of neutrinos corresponding to the electron, muon, and the tau lepton. Neutrinos interact very weakly with matter. Assumed massless for a long time, evidence is starting to indicate neutrinos have a mass and in fact oscillate between the different generations. Measuring neutrinos are important though in modelling what stage of development the sun is undergoing. Scientists believe their is a deficit in the amount of neutrinos seen from the sun for which one explanation is the oscillation of one flavour to another.

Neutron

An elementary particle with no charge and a rest mass slightly greater than the proton rest mass. The neutron is a spin 1/2 fermion. It is one of the basic constituents of the atomic nucleus. A free neutron decays with a half life of 12 minutes into a proton, an electron, and a neutrino (beta-decay). The neutron and proton are sometimes considered in nuclear physics to be differing charge states of the nucleon.

Newton

The unit of force; a derived unit having the dimensions kg m/s^2. The force required to accelerate a one-kilogram mass at a rate of one metre per second each second.

Newton's first law of motion

A body continues in a state of rest or of uniform motion in a straight line unless it is acted upon by an external (unbalanced) force.

Newton's law of gravitation

The gravitational force of attraction acting between any two particles is directly proportional to the product of their masses, and inversely proportional to the square of the distance between them. The force of attraction acts along the line joining the two particles. Real bodies having spherical symmetry act as point masses with their mass assumed to be concentrated at their centre of mass.

Newton's second laws of motion

$F = d(mv)/dt$. F is the net (total) force acting on the body of mass m. The individual forces acting on m must be summed vectorially. In the special case where the mass is constant, this becomes $F = ma$.

Newton's third law of motion

When body A exerts a force on body B, then B exerts an equal and opposite force on A. The two forces related by this law act on different bodies. The forces need not be net forces.

Newton's first law of motion

A body at rest or in uniform motion in a straight line will remain at rest or in the same uniform motion unless acted upon by an external force; also called the law of inertia.

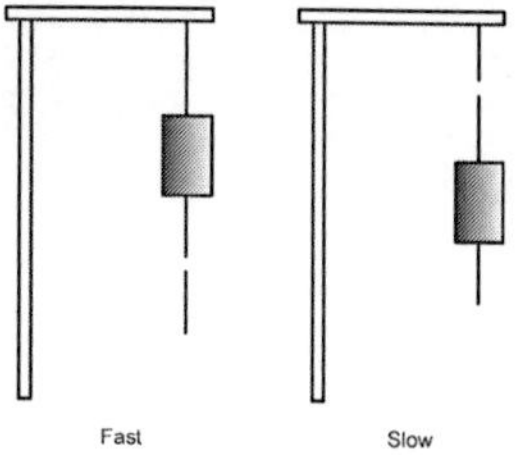

Newton's law of gravitation

The gravitational force of attraction acting between any two particles is directly proportional to the product of their masses, and inversely proportional to the square of the distance between them. The force of attraction acts along the line joining the two particles.

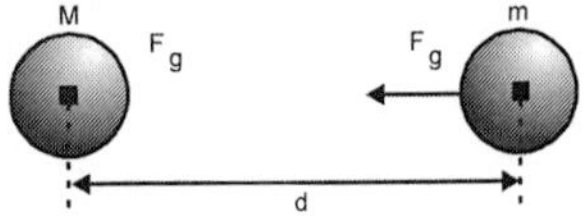

$$F_g = \frac{GMm}{d^2}$$

Newton's law of universal gravitation

The force of attraction between any two particles of matter in the universe is directly proportional to the product of their masses and inversely proportional to the square of the distance between their centres of mass.

Newton's second law of motion

The acceleration of a body is directly proportional to the net force exerted on the body, is inversely proportional to the mass of the body, and has the same direction as the net force; also called the law of acceleration.

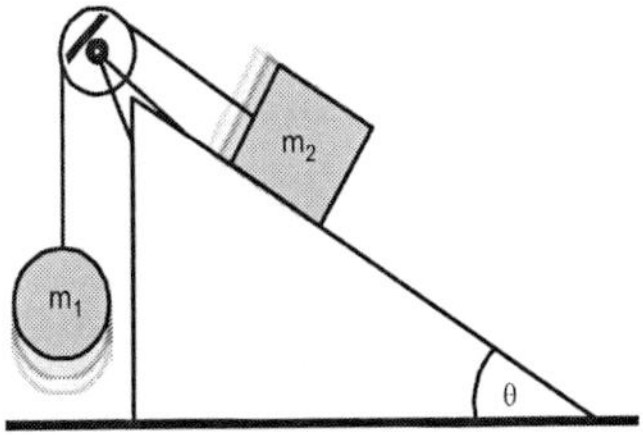

Newton's third law of motion

If one body exerts a force on a second body, then the second body exerts a force equal in magnitude and opposite in direction on the first body; also called the law of interaction.

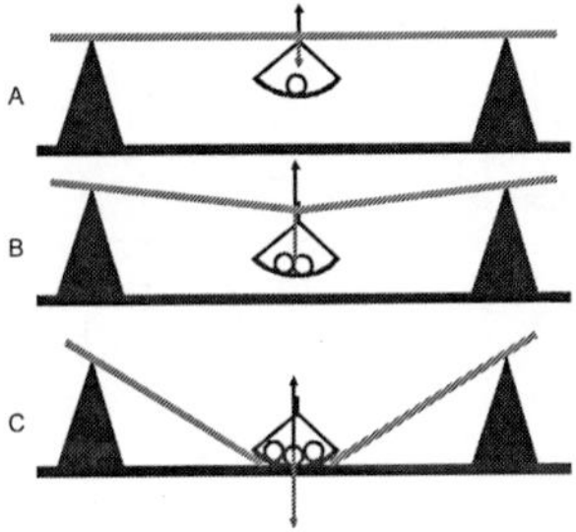

NIM

Nuclear Instrumentation Module. It is standard crate equipment, with a defined protocol, for some devices in the accelerator. "Half-high" NIM crates are used in the MCR and Pre- Acc control room. Other NIM crates are used in the MRRF building. The "half-high" crates in the MCR are only used for power and the modules do not communicate with each other.

Nimbin

A rack mounting receptacle for electronic instrumentation modules standardized according to the NIM (Nuclear Instrumentation Module) system. It uses standardized rear connectors and serves a similar function to a CAMAC crate.

NMR probe

A Nuclear Magnetic Resonance probe used to accurately monitor magnetic fields. Among other places it is found in magnet cage magnets and the LINAC spectrometer magnet.

No q
An error code generated when a GAS-speaking module, such as an 080 or 170 card, fails to "return Q", which is part of the communications protocol. No Q indicated data is not yet available for reading.

No x
An error code generated when a CAMAC module fails to acknowledge its function codes. It can mean that the user is trying to address a nonexistent module or that an incorrect address is being used or the module is busted.

Nodal points
Points on a standing wave that do not move at all due to the destructive interference of the component waves.

Node
A processing point in a network of computers. For example, A VAX 11/785 is the central node of the ACNET system.

Noise
Sound produced by irregular vibrations in matter which is unpleasant to the listener.

Nominal
The desired A/D value of a device, as defined by the user. For alarm purposes there is also a defined tolerance, or min/max value which brackets the nominal value.

Non uniform acceleration
When the velocity of a body increases by unequal amounts in equal intervals of time, it is said to have non-uniform acceleration.

Non uniform speed
When a body travels unequal distances in equal intervals of time then it is said to have non-uniform speed.

Non uniform velocity
When a body covers unequal distances in equal intervals of time in a particular direction, or when it covers equal distances in equal intervals but changes it's direction it is said to have non uniform velocity.

Noninertial frame
An accelerating frame of reference, in which Newton's first law is violated.

Noninertial frame of reference
An accelerating frame of reference in which Newton's first law of motion does not hold true.

Nonthermal particle
A particle that is not part of a thermal gas. These particles cannot be described by a conventional temperature.

Nonthermal radiation
Radiation emitted by nonthermal electrons.

Nonuniform circular motion
Circular motion in which the magnitude of the velocity vector changes.

Normal
A line drawn perpendicular to a line or surface.

Normal force
The force that keeps two objects from occupying the same space.

Normalization
The property of probabilities that the sum of the probabilities of all possible outcomes must equal one.

North pole
One end of a magnet; the end that attracts the south pole.

Northern lights
An older name for the polar aurora.

Notch filter
Notch filters as used in the Stack Tail Dp/p cooling system act to suppress signals at frequencies which correspond to harmonics of the revolution frequency of the p-'s in the core. If the stack tail momentum system is allowed to act on the core, beam heating results (not good). Notch filters also assist in shaping the gain vs. Momentum (frequency) in the stack tail. I think this means that the filters help to provide the correct gain to the

stack tail cooling kicker electrodes as a function of where particles are in the stack radially, which corresponds to the momentum of the particles.

NTF

Neutron Therapy Facility, a medical facility investigating the treatment of malignant tumors with neutrons. Neutrons for the facility are generated by steering 66 mev ions from the linac into a beryllium target. Once called CTF, Cancer Treatment Facility.

NTF beam control module

The module in the NTF control room that actually initiates beam when two switches on the front panel are pressed simultaneously.

NTF interface module

Modules located at RF systems 3 and 4 that sense the time of the RFON pulse. The module at system 4 will send an RF4 INHIBIT to the NTF interlock module if the RFON pulse at system 4 does not shift at the proper time.

NTF interlock module

Also known as the Gannon box. This is the locus of all the NTF interlocks. The logic for producing an NTF enable is contained in this unit, which then sends the enable to the prom module. The interlock module also drives the status modules in the NTF control room and the MCR.

NTF status module

Module that shows the status of the NTF interlocks, generated by the NTF interlock module. The module in the MCR also has keyswitches and toggle switches that are themselves part of the interlock chain. The module in the NTF control room has status only.

NTP

Normal Temperature and Pressure. 70°F and 14.696 psia.

N-type germanium

"Electron-rich" germanium consisting of equal numbers of free electrons and bound positive charges so that the net charge is zero.

Nuclear binding force

The force that acts within the small distances between nucleons.

Nuclear change

A change in the identity of atomic nuclei.

Nuclear energy

Nuclear energy usually means the part of the energy of an atomic nucleus, which can be released by fusion or fission or radioactive decay

Nuclear fission

The splitting a heavy nucleus into more stable, lighter nuclei with an accompanying release of energy.

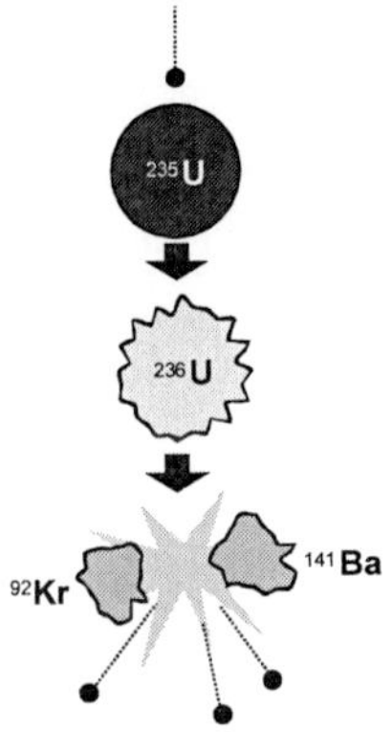

Nuclear force

One of four fundamental forces, a strong force of attraction that operates over very short distances between subatomic particles; this force overcomes the electric repulsion of protons in a nucleus and binds the nucleus together.

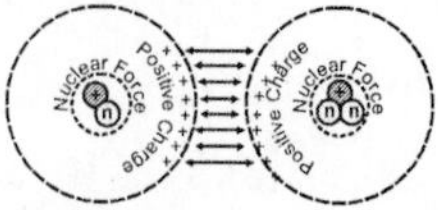

Nuclear fusion

Nuclear reaction of low mass nuclei fusing together to form more stable and more massive nuclei with an accompanying release of energy.

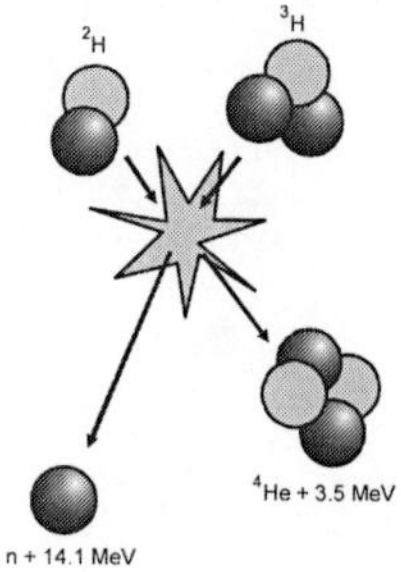

Nuclear magnetic resonance

A spectroscopic technique used by scientists to elucidate chemical structure and molecular dynamics.

Nuclear mass defect

The arithmetic difference between the mass of a nucleus and the larger sum of its uncombined constituent particles.

Nuclear reactor

A nuclear reactor is a device to initiate and control a sustained nuclear chain reaction. Most commonly they are used for generating electricity and for the propulsion of ships. Usually heat from nuclear fission is passed to a working fluid (water or gas), which runs through turbines that power either ship's propellers or generators.

Nucleon

Any particle present in the nucleus of an atom, that is, a proton or neutron.

Nucleus

The positively charged core of an atom, consisting of protons and neutrons (except for hydrogen), around which electrons orbit.

Nuclide

A nuclide (from nucleus) is an atomic species characterized by the specific constitution of its nucleus, i.e., by its number of protons Z, its number of neutrons N, and its nuclear energy state.

O

Object

Optical term referring to one focus of a dipole magnet. Parallel beams entering a dipole will cross at the object.

Oblique

Describes a force that acts at some other angle, one that is not a direct repulsion or attraction. Cf. Attractive, repulsive.

Octave

An octave is the interval between one musical pitch and another with half or double its frequency. The octave relationship is a natural phenomenon that has been referred to as the "basic miracle of music", the use of which is "common in most musical systems".

Octupole

A magnet with eight pole faces used for correcting dipole magnetic field errors. Octupoles also play a role in Tevatron extraction.

Oddmod

Accelerator statistics gathering hardware. Feeds the statistics data to the VAX. If handshaking is interrupted, ie. VAX dies, then ODDMOD continues to collect data. The Datalogger on the other hand is a programme resident in the VAX. When the VAX dies, it dies and no statistics are gathered. ODDMOD was designed as a way to avoid the interruption of data gathering. The module was designed by Todd Johnson and was originally called the Todd Module. A parameter involving TOD MOD was made called T:ODDMOD.

ODH

Oxygen Deficiency Hazard. In areas where the cryogenic system is used a cryogen leak can displace Oxygen creating a hazard to personnel. This necessitates the implementation of special safety procedures and Oxygen monitoring equipment for working in designated ODH areas.

Off tube

One of two Linac thyratrons that control the operation of a 750 keV chopper. After the on tube fires, the off tube fires to ground one side of a series capacitor and draw one of the chopper plates from ground to a negative potential.

Ohm

The ohm is defined as a resistance between two points of a conductor when a constant potential difference of 1 volt, applied to these points, produces in the conductor a current of 1 ampere, the conductor not being the seat of any electromotive force

Ohm's law

The current flowing through a conductor is directly proportional to the potential difference across the ends of the conductor.

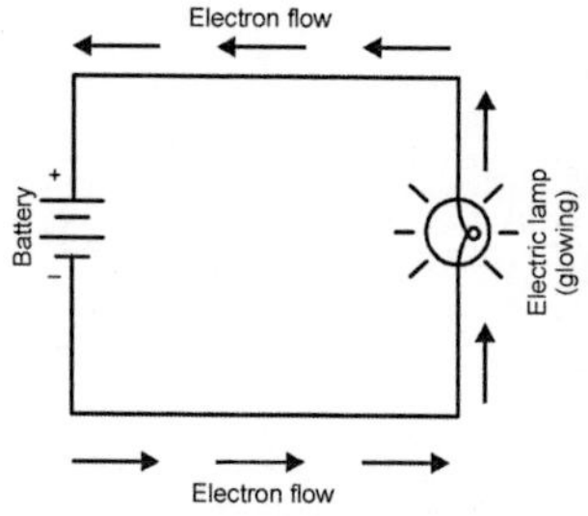

Ohmic
Describes a substance in which the flow of current between two points is proportional to the voltage difference between them.

On tube
One of two Linac thyratrons that controls the operation of a 750 keV chopper. The on tube fires to bring one of the chopper plates from a high potential to ground. The off tube fires at a later time.

Onium/onia
Name for neutral mesons formed from a quark and its own anti-quark.

Opaque
Having the property of not allowing light to pass through.

Open circuit
A circuit that does not function because it has a gap in it.

Open system
A system across whose boundaries both matter and energy can pass.

Operational definition
A definition that states what operations should be carried out to measure the thing being defined.

Operational vax
The VAX 11/785 in the computer room designated for operational use. This computer acts as the central node for the ACNET system. It handles the data base and alarm reporting, and retains the applications programmes to be written onto the console disks when necessary. Either VAX1 or VAX2 may serve as the operational one if the proper connections are made. Currently, VAX3 may not be configured to be the OPER VAX.

Operator (account)
An account on the operational VAX which allows operators to perform certain rebooting tasks and other functions on the ACNET system.

Optical centre
The point in a thin lens through which the secondary axes pass.

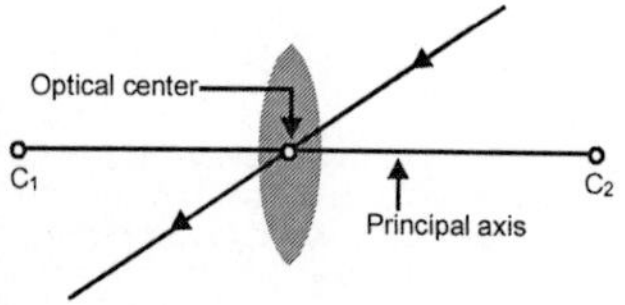

Optical density
A property of a transparent material that is a measure of the speed of light through it.

Optical fibre
A long, thin thread of fused silica, used to transmit light, based on total internal reflection.

Optical isolator
An element in an electrical circuit that converts a signal to a light pulse at one point in the circuit and then back again in another in order to isolate the grounds of each part of the circuit from each other.

Optical radiation
Electromagnetic radiation (light) that is visible to the human eye.

Optical sign conventions

In introductory (freshman) courses in physics a sign convention is used for objects and images in which the lens equation must be written 1/p + 1/q = 1/f. Often the rules for this sign convention are presented in a convoluted manner. We are forced also to declare that the mirror also flips the sign of the surface radius. For reflective surfaces, the radius of curvature is defined to be the directed distance from a surface to its centre of curvature, measured with respect to the axis used for the emergent light. With this qualification the convention for the signs of s' and R is the same for mirrors as for refractive surfaces. In advanced optics courses, a cartesian sign convention is used in which all things to the left of the lens are negative, all those to the right are positive. When this is used, the lens equation must be written 1/p + 1/f = 1/q. (The sign of the 1/p term is opposite that in the other sign convention). This is a particularly meaningful version, for 1/p is the measure of vergence (convergence or divergence) of the rays as they enter the lens, 1/f is the amount the lens changes the vergence, and 1/q is the vergence of the emergent rays.

Opto22

Device which converts a binary signal to a light pulse. Found in the red dot binary I/O boards in the linac secondaries.

Orbit

An applications programme run partially on the operational VAX which "smooths" the Tevatron beam orbit by making adjustments to the correction dipoles. The programme has many other functions all associated with controlling the beam position. Another programme exists, called ORBIT Jr, which performs some of the same functions but runs entirely on the console computer.

Orbital

The probability pattern of position of an electron about the nucleus of an atom.

Orbital period

The amount of time it takes a spacecraft or other object to travel once around it's orbit.

Orbump

A pulsed magnet system in the injection section of the Booster. It moves the injected H- beam from the 200 mev line and the circulating proton beam in Booster so that they overlap and pass through the stripping foil. This allows the Booster to accept and stack up to ten complete turns.

ORC

Operational Readiness Clearence from Research Division

Order of magnitude

A numerical approximation to the nearest power of ten.

Ordinate

The value corresponding to the vertical distance of a point on a graph from the X axis. The Y coordinate.

Origin

The only point on a graph where both the x and y variables have a value of zero at the same time.

O-ring

A vacuum seal of circular cross-section, usually made of Neoprene, which provides a seal between two parallel surfaces. It usually rests in a machined "O-ring groove" in one of the surfaces.

Ortho hydrogen

The product of normal hydrogen liquification. Not in equilibrium at liquid temperatures. Characterized by "ortho" (||) electron spins. Often referred to as "noral" hydrogen.

Oscillatory motion

The to and fro motion of a body about its mean position is called oscillatory motion. Oscillatory motion is also called vibratory motion. Oscillatory motion is periodic in nature.

Oscilloscope

A cathode-ray tube with associated electronic circuits that enable external voltages to deflect the electron beam of the cathode-ray tube simultaneously along both horizontal and vertical axes.

Osha

Occupational Safety and Health Administration

Outgassing

When a beam line or device is under vacuum, any oils or moisture in the device has a lower vapour pressure and evaporates. This is known as outgassing and spoils vacuum making it difficult for the device in question to pump down to operating vacuum levels. For this reason it is necessary to ensure that vacuum devices are exceptionally clean on the inside before they are used.

Overcurrent

In electricity supply, overcurrent or excess current is a situation where a larger than intended electric current exists through a conductor, leading to excessive generation of heat, and the risk of fire or damage to equipment. Possible causes for overcurrent include short circuits, excessive load, and incorrect design. Fuses, circuit breakers, temperature sensors and current limiters are commonly used protection mechanisms to control the risks of overcurrent.

Overcurrent trip

See Fast Trip

Overpass

Section of Main Ring which is used to vertically bypass a colliding beams region. There is presently one at B0 and one at D0.

P

P (Pronounced *pbar*)

The symbol for antiproton is p. p is physicists' shorthand for a proton. A bar atop a symbol denotes that particle's anti-counterpart. p- therefore is representative of an antiproton.

Pa crowbar

Linac RF system trip that occurs when the modulator current is greater than 600 amps during the RF pulse or 125 amps between pulses. A PA crowbar fires the permanent inhibit, shorts the capacitor bank to ground through the ignitron, and resets automatically after 30 seconds.

Page fault

This is a term used to describe the dynamic memory allocation of an executing process on the VAX. In a virtual memory system (see VMS) only part of the information being processed is within physical memory. The remaining information can be assigned to the disk. When the process requires more space than is available in dynamic memory, the memory is broken into pages consisting of 512 contiguous bytes. A "page fault" is the process of exchanging pages between the disk and dynamic memory.

Pagoda

The Pagoda was the main control and tuning area in the Proton Area built in a shape inspired by an oriental pagoda. Control and tuning is now done by the SOD Operations Centre control room. The Pagoda is no longer used. The basement area underneath still has a few power supplies and control diagnostic racks.

Paint can

An inexpensive radiation detector consisting of a simple (non multiplier) phototube mounted through the top of a one pint paint can full of liquid scintillator which produces light in response to ionizing radiation. Because of their low sensitivity these detectors are suitable for primary beam areas like the Main Ring tunnel.

Pair production

The conversion of a photon into an electron and positron when the photon traverses a strong electric field such as that surrounding a nucleus or an electron. Pair production is one of three distinct processes by which a photon can effect the emission of an electron from matter, the other two processes being the photoelectric effect and the Compton effect.

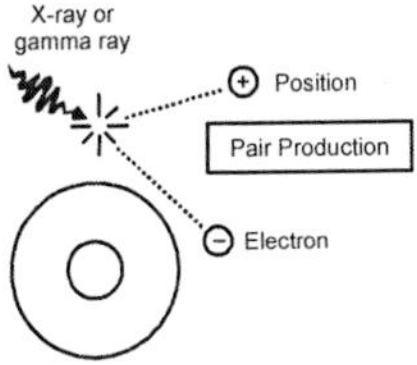

Pair Production and Annihilation

Whenever sufficient energy is available to provide the mass-energy, a particle and its matching antiparticle can be produced. When a particle collides with its matching antiparticle they may annihilate which means they both disappear and their energy appears as some other particles with balanced number of particles and antiparticles for each type. All conservation laws are obeyed in these processes.

Para hydrogen

The equilibrium condition at liquid hydrogen temperatures. Not in equilibrium at ambient temperatures. Characterized by "para" (|~) electron spins.

Parabola

The mathematical curve whose graph has y proportional to x^2.

Parallel

Two lines or surfaces that never intersect. Also, for circuit elements, elements that are connected so that they have the same electrostatic potential difference across them.

Parallel circuit

An electric circuit in which two or more components connected across two common points in the circuit so as to provide separate conducting paths for the current.

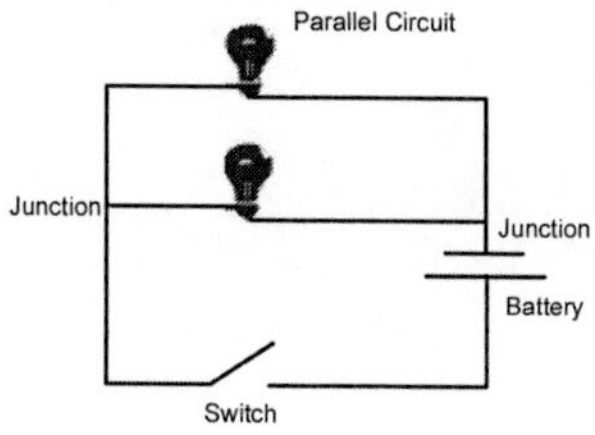

Parallel data

In terms of data transmission it means that all bits of a character or byte are transmitted simultaneously. This requires a multiconductor cable or bus with each conductor carrying a single bit. A 16 bit word requires 16 conductor cable for transmission.

Parallelogram method

The graphic method of finding the resultant of two vectors that do not act along a straight line.

Paramagnetism

The property of a substance by which it is feebly attracted by a strong magnet.

Parasitic

Any activity being carried out which is not the top priority at that time. Parasitic activities are supposed to be carried out with minimal interference to the top priority activity.

Parent

A radionuclide that decays to another nuclide which may be either radioactive or stable.

Particle

A small piece of matter. An elementary particle is a fundamental constituent of matter. Quarks and leptons now appear to be the only elementary particles but the term is often used in referring to any of the subnuclear particles.

Parton

Obsolete term for hypothetical point like constituents of nucleons (protons and neutrons). Partons have since proved to be quark particles.

Pascal

A unit of pressure, equal to the pressure resulting from a force of 1 Newton acting uniformly over an area of $1m^2$.

Pascal's principle of hydrostatics

Pascal actually has three separate principles of hydrostatics. When a textbook refers to Pascal's Principle it should specify which is meant.

Pascal's law

The pressure exerted on a liquid is transmitted equally in all directions.

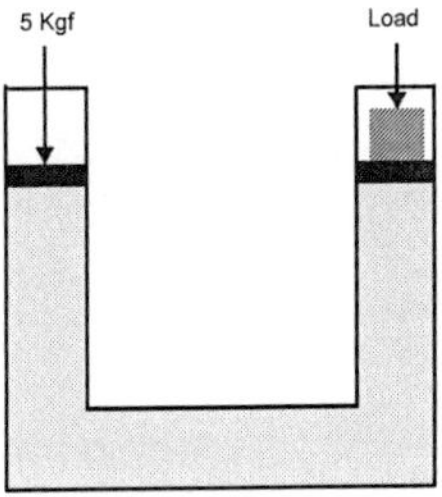

Pascal's Law (Hydraulic Lift)

Paschen series

A group of lines in the infrared region in the spectrum of hydrogen.

Pauli exclusion principle

No two electrons in an atom can have the same four quantum numbers; thus, a maximum of two electrons can occupy a given orbital.

Pbar shot

The injection of antiprotons from the Accumulator into the Main Ring and on into the Tevatron in preparation for colliding beams operation.

PDC

Programmed Data Channel. The MAC-16 includes a set of data, address, and command lines that provide parallel communication (by 16 bit words) between the cpu and external devices. This I/O is controlled by programme instructions (as compared with MDC I/O). I/O rates via the PDC depend on the amount of additional processing necessary in the programme. The maximum data rate is about 60 Kwords/sec. A PDC transfer may be performed to one of up to 255 external device addresses.

PDC crate

An I/O interconnection scheme intended to allow simple interfacing of external devices to a MAC-16's PDC I/O lines. The hardware looks like a CAMAC crate but the internal line designations are definitely not CAMAC. They have been defined to make the crate a buffered fan-in/fan-out for the MAC's PDC bus. The MAC communicates with and controls the crate through two crate modules (the PDC BOX COMMAND BUFFER and the PDC BOX DATA BUFFER). All of the interface modules have been designed and built by Fermilab personnel.

PDP 11

A computer manufactured by Digital Equipment Corporation with 20K of memory. As of 1991 most of the control room consoles are driven by PDP 11 computers. There are plans in the near future to replace these consoles with MicroVAX workstations. PDP stands for Programable Data Processor.

PDP-11/34

Low end minicomputer made by DEC. These 16-bit computers are currently used as the console processors, and one serves as the Linac front-end. These are UNIBUS based machines. Each is equipped with 124 Kwords of MOS memory, a floating point processor, cache memory, and an RL02 disk system.

PDP-11/44

A UNIBUS-based minicomputer built by DEC which contains a separate memory bus capable of holding up to four Megabytes. PDP 11-44's are used for many of the front-end processors.

PDP-11/55

A medium-performance 16-bit minicomputer formerly built by DEC which uses bipolar memory to speed processing. There are three 11/55's (DEC B, DEC C, and DEC D) in the MAC room. The first two are used for Main Ring power supply control and regulation and the third for development and as a spare.

PDP-11/84

The newest and fastest of the PDP-11 series. They are UNIBUS-based. The processor is on a single J11 chip. The 84's are used for the fastest front-end processors.

Peaking strip

An instrument used for magnetic field measurements. It measures the voltage pulse induced in a coil surrounding a sample of magnetic material when the direction of the magnetization is reversed.

Pearlite

A finely divided powder used to insulate when vacuum failure is a serious consideration or the super insulation costs cannot be justified.

Peltier effect

The evolution or absorption of heat at the junction of two dissimilar metals carrying current.

Pendulum

A body suspended so that it can swing back and forth about an axis.

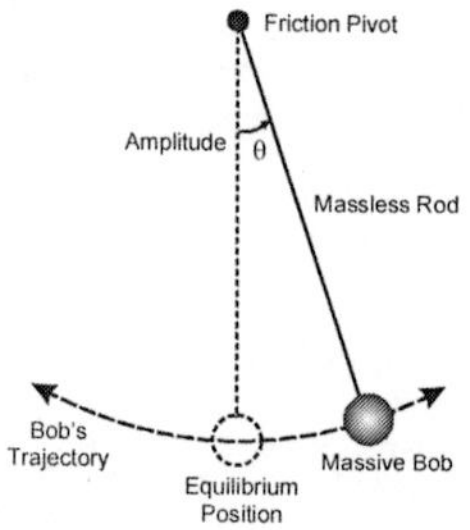

Penetrations key

Key that opens the lock on penetrations that lead into tunnel where beam travels. Most often implies the Key to the LINAC penetrations.

Penumbra

The partially illuminated part of a shadow.

Per unit

In my opinion this expression is a barbarism best avoided. When a student is told that electric field is force per unit charge and in the MKS system one unit of charge is a coulomb (a huge amount) must we obtain that much charge to measure the field? Certainly not. In fact, one must take the limit of F/q as q goes to zero. Simply say: "Force divided by charge" or "F over q" or even "force per charge". Unfortunately there is no graceful way to say these things, other than simply writing the equation.

Period

(1) The time for one complete cycle, vibration, revolution, or oscillation.

(2) The time required for a single wavelength to pass a given point.

Period of oscillation

The time required for one complete oscillation.

Periodic interrupt

This is a software term used to describe an aspect of programme execution timing. For example, all of the console computer processors have a 15 Hz interrupt which signals the APM, and hence the applications programme, to execute some section of code at this rate.

Periodic motion

Periodic motion occurs when an object or system traverses the same path over and over again, always taking the same time (the period) to make a round trip. If the motion is back and forth over the same path it is an oscillation. However, the motion may also be in a circle or other closed loop. If you think your old Uncle Fred, who repeats stories over and over, is boring, take a look at Mother Nature and all her periodic motion. Be glad she doesn't show up at your family reunions.

Periodic wave

A wave in which the particles of the medium oscillate continuously about their mean positions regularly at fixed intervals of time is called a periodic wave.

Permanent inhibit

Linac RF system trip caused by four successive mod blocks in a row. A permanent inhibit shuts off the modulator pulse and shuts down the high-voltage power supply for the capacitor bank.

Permeability

The property of a material by which it changes the flux density in a magnetic field from its value in air.

PET Scan

Positron Emission Tomography scanning uses an array of stationary detectors around the patient and using the spatial 180 degree opposing properties of the 0.511-MeV annihilation radiation from positron-emitting radiopharmaceuticals deposited in the organ or region of interest.

PEX box

Essentially an extension of a PDP-11 console computer or front-end which consists of UNIBUS cards. All PEX boxes have a standard set of cards, including a Universal Clock Decoder and PIOX/PIOR interfaces. The PEX boxes for the front-ends include additional cards for interfacing to the outside world.

Phase

(1) A condition of matter.
(2) In any periodic phenomenon, a number that describes a specific stage within each oscillation.
(3) The angular relationship between current and voltage in an a-c circuit.
(4) The number of separate voltage waves in a commercial a-c supply.

Phase advance

A measure of the stage of the betatron oscillation at some point around the accelerator; usually denoted by the greek letter psi.

Phase angle

Imagine a circular race track with a couple of cars moving around it in the same direction. You could describe the position of each of the cars by how far it was from the starting line. Alternatively, you could describe the angles the cars made from the starting line to their current positions along the circular track as measured from the centre of the track. This would be a kind of phase angle. The difference in their angular positions would be the difference in the phase angles between the cars. If one car were at a position of 100° and the other, trailing behind, at 88° around the track, their phase angles would differ by 12°. If you use the lead car as the reference, this would be a -12° phase angle, since you have to go backwards (negative direction) to locate the trailing car.

Phase change

The action of a substance changing from one state of matter to another; a phase change always absorbs or releases internal potential energy that is not associated with a temperature change.

Phase comparator mixer

An element of the low-level RF systems that looks at the relative phases of two RF signals and produces a signal proportional to the difference in phase.

Phase diagram

Phase diagrams indicate the boundaries between the solid liquid and or gas phases of a material for a given pressure or temperature.

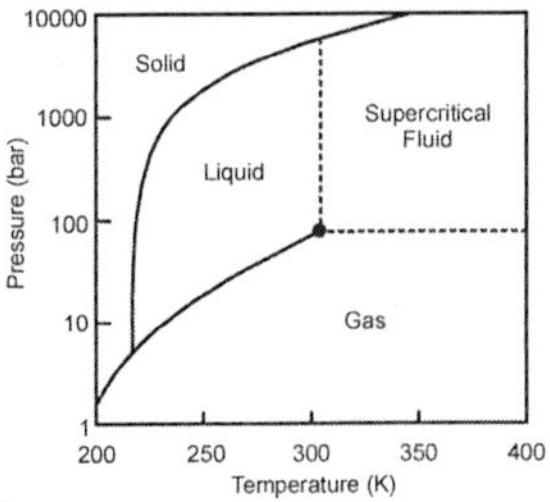

Phase lock input

Output of a Linac phase comparator mixer that looks at the desired RF phase and the cavity RF phase. This signal is raised by 5 volts to produce phase lock output.

Phase lock output

Signal proportional to the difference between the desired RF phase and the cavity RF phase, used to drive a phase shifter that compensates for shifts in cavity RF phase due to beam loading.

Phase reversal

A method of encoding data on a clock where the shifting from one level to the other is shifted in phase for a number of cycles. The number of cycles for which this reversed phase exists constitutes the data being transmitted.

Phase space

Phase space is an abstract space having a dimensionality equal to six times the number of particles in a system. The state of a system is represented by a system point whose components are vectors of the particles. The acceptance of an accelerator is simply the volume in phase space comprising the coordinates and momenta of all particles that will not be lost in the course of subsequent acceleration.

Phase stability

Phase stability enables particles to be accelerated to their final energy. The voltage waveform for the accelerating electric field is sinusoidal. Particles in an accelerator do not advance side by side but are spread out into a column. Therefore if the front end of such a column reaches the accelerating gap when the voltage is at its maximum all later particles experience less voltage and thus less acceleration. Consequently the column lengthens and ultimately many of the particles are decelerated because they arrive at the gap when the electric field is directed in the opposite way. If the phase f of a synchronous particle (frequency of RF = frequency of revolution) is within certain limits then the accelerating voltage can accelerate particles that enter the gap with f Df thus giving a stability. However, if f is outside these limits the RF gets "out of step" with the particles preventing acceleration to the desired full energy.

Phase stability

The principle which gives the range of momenta which can be accelerated in a synchronous accelerator.

Phasor

A representation of the concepts of magnitude and direction in a reference plane; a rotating vector.

Phosphor

A substance that emits light when excited by radiation.

Photoelectric effect

The emission of electrons by a substance when illuminated by electromagnetic radiation of sufficiently short wavelength.

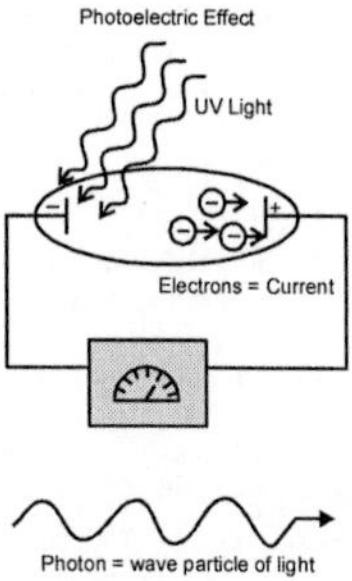

Photoelectrons

Electrons emitted from a light-sensitive material when it is illuminated with light of sufficiently short wavelength.

Photometer
An instrument comparing the intensity source with that of a standard source.

Photometry
The quantitative measurement of visible radiation from light sources.

Photomultiplier
An electronic tube which generates an electrical current roughly proportional to the light intensity impinging on the tube. Photomultiplier tubes are typically used to measure small light signals from a scintillator or Cerenkov counter through which charged particles have passed.

Photon
The carrier particle of the electromagnetic interaction. Depending on its frequency (and therefore its energy) photons can have different names such as visible light, x rays and gamma rays. We describe light in several ways. When we talk about "photons" we generally think of uncharged particles with out mass that carry energy (but be careful, there are other particles like this!). Photons of light are known by other names too, such as gamma rays and x-rays. Low-energy forms are called ultraviolet rays, infrared rays, even radio waves! A photon is one of the fundamental particle in nature and it plays an important role involving electron interactions. Photons are the most familiar particles in everyday existence. The light we see, the radiant heat we feel, microwaves we cook with, make use of photons of different energies. An x-ray is simply a name given to the most energetic of these particles.

Photosphere
The visible surface of the Sun. It consists of a zone in which the gaseous layers change from being completely opaque to radiation to being transparent. It is the layer from which the light we actually see (with the human eye) is emitted.

Photovoltaic effect
The generation of a potential difference across a P-N junction as a consequence of the absorption of incident light of appropriate frequency.

Physical change
A change in which the composition and identifying properties of a substance remain unchanged. physical quantity. A measurable aspect of the universe, such as length.

Physics
The grandest and most exalted science of all. Those who practice it are the best and most important scientists, nay, human beings, in the world today. Besides this, it is the study of space, time, matter, and energy. If you are thinking of going into physics because "space, time, matter, and energy" sound cool, be warned that the profession of physics is filled with huge numbers of really intelligent people competing for a few low-paying jobs.

Pickup loop
In Linac a small (1/8" square) loop at the end of a coaxial cable that is driven by the RF cavity magnetic field to produce a signal proportional to the electric field in the cavity.

Piezoelectric crystal
A symmetric crystal that bends when an electric potential is applied to it. Used in the Pre-Acc ion sources to regulate the gas flow into the source. A piezoelectric crystal is also the heart of a crystal oscillator, such as the master oscillator.

Piezoelectric effect
The property of certain natural and synthetic crystals to develop a potential difference between opposite surfaces when subjected to a mechanical stress, and conversely.

Pig gauge
Means a penning gauge, Phillips gauge, or cold cathode gauge, all of which work on the same principle. Electrons are produced by a cold cathode and accelerated toward a high voltage anode, ionizing gas molecules. The ionization current is measured and converted to a pressure readout.

Pinged beam

A small time slice separated from the slow spill (by a pinger) to give a spill of <100 msec for use with a bubble chamber, for example.

Pinhole magnet

A special pulsed magnet in the extraction line at Fermilab designed to prevent pinged beam from reaching the Proton and Meson experimental areas.

Pion

Pi-Meson. A strongly interacting elementary particle of spin 0 having a rest mass roughly 270 times that of the electron. It exists in neutral, positive, and negative charged states.

PIOR

Programmed Input/Output Retrieval. PIOR is standard hardware for receiving data from links around the accelerator, including PDP-11 to console communication, Tevatron links, and QXR.

PIOX

Programmed Input/Output Transmission. PIOX is standard hardware for transmitting data to many of the links in the accelerator.

Pit

A large temperature and humidity controlled room containing the Haefely high-voltage transformers, voltage multiplier, preaccelerator dome, column, and motor-generator for the preaccelerator.

Pitch

The identification of a certain sound with a definite tone; depends on the frequency which the ear receives.

Pivot point

The point from which the lengths of all torque arms are measured.

Pixel

The term pixel is used to refer to a single scalar element of a multi-component representation (more precisely called a photosite in the camera sensor context, although the neologism sensel is sometimes used to describe the elements of a digital camera's sensor), while in others the term may refer to the entire set of such component intensities for a spatial position.

Planck constant

The proportionality constant (h) which provides the relation between the energy (E) of a photon and the frequency (v) of its associated electromagnetic wave in the so-called Planck Relation E = hv. It is essentially used to describe the sizes of individual quanta in quantum mechanics. Its value depends on the units used for energy and frequency, but it is a very small number.

Planck energy

The super-high energy (approximately 1.22×10^{19} GeV) at which gravity becomes comparable in strength to the other fundamental forces, and at which the quantum effects of gravity become important.

Planck length

The fantastically tiny length scale (approximately 1.6×10^{-35} metres) at which gravity becomes comparable in strength to the other fundamental forces. It is the scale at which classical ideas about gravity and space-time cease to be valid, and quantum effects dominate.

Planck temperature

The temperature of the universe at 1 Planck Time after the Big Bang, approximately equal to 1.4×10^{32}°C.

Planck time

The time it would take a photon travelling at the speed of light to cross a distance equal to the Planck Length. This is the "quantum of time", the smallest measurement of time that has any meaning, and is approximately equal to 10^{-43} seconds.

Planck units

"Natural units" of measurement (i.e. designed so that certain fundamental physical constants are normalized to 1), named after the German physicist Max Planck who first proposed them in 1899. They were an attempt to eliminate all arbitrariness from the system of units, and to help simplify many complex equations in modern physics. Among the most important are the Planck Energy, the Planck Length, the Planck Time and the Planck Temperature.

Planck's constant

Proportionality constant in the relationship between the energy of light waves and their frequency; a value of 6.63 x 10^{-34} joule/sec.

Planetary magnetospheres

The magnetospheres of planets, especially of Jupiter, Saturn, Uranus and Neptune, all of which have dipole-like magnetic fields stronger than the Earths. Mercury has a weak magnetic field, Mars and the Moon are magnetized in patches (probably on their surfaces) and Venus, although non-magntic, has its own interaction with the solar wind, through its thick ionosphere.

Plasma

Plasma consists of a gas heated to sufficiently high temperatures that the atoms ionize. The properties of the gas are controlled by electromagnetic forces among constituent ions and electrons, which results in a different type of behaviour. Plasma is often considered the fourth state of matter (besides solid, liquid, and gas). Most of the matter in the Universe is in the plasma state.

Plasmasphere

A region of relatively dense but cool plasma, surrounding Earth, extending to distances of about 5 Earth radii (RE). The plasmasphere is the upward extension of the Earth's ionosphere, getting less and less dense with increasing distance, and it shares the Earth's rotation.

Plasticity

The property of a solid whereby it undergoes a permanent change in shape or size when subjected to a stress.

Plate

The anode of an electronic tube.

PLD

Programme LoaDer. A managing programme on the console comp- uters which works in conjunction with CPLD (Central Programme Loader) to download applications progra- mmes from the VAX. It also monitors the cache of the 50 most used appli- cations programmes on that console and verifies that the most recent version of each programme is being used.

Plessey box

Plessey is the name of the company which makes the Unibus extender box, or more explicitly the Plessey Peripheral Systems PM-1150/5 extender unit. Same as the PEX box.

P-N junction

The boundary between P and N-type materials in a semiconductor crystal.

Polar orbit

a satellite orbit passing over both poles of the Earth. During a 12-hour day, a satellite in such an orbit can observe all points on Earth.

Polarity check

Procedure used to insure a magnet will have the desired polarity when powered. Checking the polarity of magnets by measuring the magnetic field with a Hall Probe is one way to accomplish this. In the Tevatron it can mean to check which of the superconducting leads on the end of a magnet are upper or lower bus.

Polarization

The preferential alignment of the spin of a particle along a particular axis in space defined e.g. by the electric or magnetic field direction, or the momentum vector of the particle itself.

Polarized light

Light radiations in which the vibrations of all light waves present are confined to planes parallel to each other.

Polarizing angle

A particular angle of incidence at which polarization of reflected light is complete.

Polaroid or polarizer

A device that produces polarized light.

Poloidal radius

The radius of the actual loop structure. For a doughnut, it is measured from the centre to the edge of the pastry (*not* from the centre of the hole).

Polychromatic light

Light composed of several colours.

Port selector

A communications multiplexor for connecting terminals to various computer systems such as the AD VAXcluster and FNAL VAX Cluster.

Position

Position is the location of a point in a coordinate system, for example its x, y, and z coordinates in a 3-D cartesian coordinate system. Position is in reference to the origin of the coordinate system, so called because the coordinate axes emanate from that point.

Position vector

A position can be what a politician says he, or she, believes in. A vector can be a pathogen. Therefore, in a perfect world, a position vector would be a disease contracted by politicians who adopt positions merely to get elected. Unfortunately, due to the existence of mathematics, the world is far from perfect, and we have to settle for the following state of affairs. A position, in the mathematical sense, is a point in a coordinate system, and a position vector is an "arrow" that extends from the origin of the coordinate system to the point in question. The magnitude of the position vector is its length, and the direction is given by angles.

Positive electric charge

One of the two types of electric charge; repels other positive charges and attracts negative charges.

Positive ion

Atom or particle that has a net positive charge due to an electron or electrons being torn away.

Positive rays

Rays coming through holes in a cathode on the side opposite the anode in a discharge tube. Positively charged ions.

Positron

The antiparticle of the electron. It has the same mass as the electron but opposite (positive) electrical charge.

Post coupler

A copper stem with a tab on the end that is used to control the relative field levels in two adjacent cells in a linac RF cavity.

Potential difference

The work done per unit charge as a charge is moved between two points in an electric field.

Potential energy

The energy of position. As in the case of kinetic energy, this energy is relative. But instead of being relative to an arbitrary velocity, as in the case of kinetic energy, it is relative to an arbitrary position. The details depend on what type of potential energy is involved. Each type of potential energy is associated with a force, a conservative force, that depends only on the relative positions of the bodies interacting with each other via that force. It is called "potential" energy, because it can be transformed into the energy of motion, kinetic energy.

Power

Power is defined in physics as the time rate of expenditure of energy. There are numerous kinds of power - mechanical power, electrical power, atomic power, political power, black power, flower power, etc. - because there are numerous kinds of energy. The SI unit of power is the watt and the British unit of power is the horsepower.

Power glitch

A power glitch is an interruption of electrical power lasting only a fraction of a second.

Power on access

Entry into an enclosure in which devices are energized. Because of the lack of electrical insulation in some of these areas electrical hazards may exist.

Power supply programme
A series of computerized commands which tell a power supply what waveform to produce throughout a given cycle.

PPE
Personal Protective Equipment

Preaccelerator
Generally refers to all the hardware associated with the production of 750 keV ions, including the source itself and the Haefely power supply. The general layout is of the Cockcroft-Walton type.

Precess
A rotational motion of a vector about the axis of a coordinate system where the polar angle is fixed and the azmuthal angle changes steadily.

Precession
The motion that results from the application of a torque that tends to displace the axis of rotation of a rotating object.

Precise
Sharply or clearly defined. Having small experimental uncertainty. A precise measurement may still be inaccurate, if there were an unrecognized determinate error in the measurement (for example, a miscalibrated instrument).

Precision
Precision is not the same as accuracy. Precision has to do with reproducing a measurement close to the same value every time the measurement is taken. This does not guarantee the measurement is accurate. For example, you might weigh yourself on the bathroom scale a number of times with the result close to 150 pounds each time. However, if you are supporting yourself with one hand on the vanity, you would have a systematic bias (not to mention a dishonest bias) in your measurement.

Predet timer board
A hardware box which delays a timing event by a predetermined amount. Predets are set manually by switches on the front of the box. They can be thought of as hardwired alternatives to the CAMAC 177 modules. They are used in the Pre- Acc for triggering devices in the domes and in the Linac, as well as in the MCR as delays for scope triggers.

Prepulse
Event on the booster clock that commands the 200 MeV, booster, and 8 GeV pulsed devices to fire in preparation for a beam pulse. Linac beam is not allowed on prepulses.

Prescision
It tells us how consistent repeated measurements are. A precise set of measurements are relatively closer together. An imprecise set of measurements are spread apart.

Pressure
This term usually refers to the type of stress known as "hydrostatic" pressure (due to the common experience of feeling squeezed when under water) or "confining" pressure. Pressure is simply defined as the force exerted per unit area.

Primary
A transformer winding that carries current and normally induces a current in one or more secondary windings.

Primary applications (pa)
Applications programmes which allow interaction with a console user. All of the console resources: screens, touch panels, etc. are allocated to the PA while it is in use.

Primary cell
An electrochemical cell in which the reacting materials must be replaced after a given amount of energy has been supplied to the external circuit.

Primary coil
Part of a transformer; a coil of wire that is connected to a source of alternating current.

Primary collimator
The first collimator after the beryllium target used to produce neutrons for NTF. The primary collimator is made of steel and is of fixed geometry.

Primary colours

Colours in terms of which all other colours may be described or from which all other colours may be evolved by mixtures.

Primary critical device

The principle device that determines whether or not beam will enter a certain enclosure. Critical devices are controlled by the safety system, as well as through the control system. The primary critical device for the linac is the beam stop in the 750 keV line. The secondary critical device for the linac is the pulse shifter.

Primary microprocessor

Choke point of the linac control system that controls messages on the serial data link, and interfaces with the host computers via the Ethernet link.

Primary pigments

The complements of the primary colours.

Principal axis

(1) A line drawn through the centre of curvature and the vertex of a curved mirror.

(2) A line drawn through the centre of curvature and the optical centre of a lens.

Principal focus

A point at which rays parallel to the principal axis converge or from which they diverge after reflection or refraction.

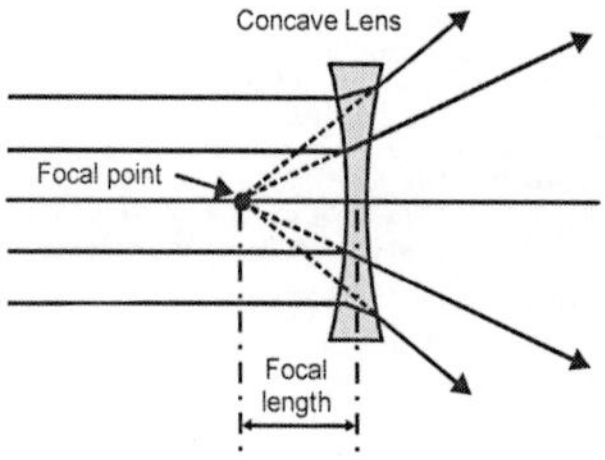

Principia

Actual title: Naturalis Philosophiae Principia Mathematica, which is Latin for, "Up Yours, Robert Hooke". This was Isaac Newton's ground-breaking work on physics, which Edmund Halley finally persuaded him to write. It is so important to the history of physics that I blush to admit I had not read any of it - until, that is, I read where a noted feminist philosopher had referred to it as "Newton's Rape Manual". Now that got my attention. Sexandviolence! I eagerly got a copy and began reading it from cover to cover. Sadly, however, there was nothing from one cover to the other but physics, physics, and more physics. As much as I hate to say it, although it may be a great work of physics, as a rape manual it is pretty much a total loss.

Principle of parity

For every process in nature there is a mirror-image process which is indistinguishable from the original process.

Principle of superpostion

When the paths of two waves of the same type coincide, move through each other or cross, the resultant displacement is the sum of the two individual wave displacements at the point.

Principle quantum number

A quantum number that describes the main energy level of an electron in terms of its most probable distance from the nucleus.

Printed circuit board

An insulating surface containing a circuit made by depositing conductive materials in continuous paths from terminal to terminal. Complex electronic circuits are made by soldering components to these terminals.

Printronix

One of the printers in the computer room accessible through the Development VAX. Also known as the LXY22, it is a dot-matrix line printer that operates between 320 and 600 lines per minute depending on the complexity of the printout (i.e., all upper-case, mixed upper-lower case, or double-height characters). We also have the optional PLXY graphics software package. The DI-3000 graphics package can drive the Printronix in graphics mode.

Probability
The likelihood that something will happen, expressed as a number between zero and one.

Production angle
The angle between a targeted primary beam and a secondary beam is called the production angle.

Progressive travelling wave
Transfers energy with no net motion of the medium through which the wave travels.

Progressive wave
A wave which transfers energy from one part of a medium to another.

Projectile
This is an object that is launched ("projected") with a force of short duration and thereafter travels without propulsion or significant aerodynamic support (such as a glider has), like a spit wad or a water balloon. In other words, the most significant force acting on the object, until it hits the teacher, is gravity. Its path is a parabola in the absence of air and a distorted parabola in the presence of air resistance. The greater the air resistance the greater the distortion.

Prom module
Logic module in the preacc control room that looks at the various beam enable inputs and decides which, if any, will produce a beam pulse. The prom module also selects the chop width to be sent to the choppers.

Proof
A term from logic and mathematics describing an argument from premise to conclusion using strictly logical principles. In mathematics, theorems or propositions are established by logical arguments from a set of axioms, the process of establishing a theorem being called a proof.

Propagate
To travel through a material or space.

Propagation
The act of propagating. The action of traveling through a material or space.

Property
A measurable aspect of matter, e.g., mass and inertia.

Property index (PI)
A secondary address pointer in the VAX database which associates the device index of a parameter with a property. Properties include such things as names, text, alarm limits, basic control, etc.

Proportional wire chamber (PWC)
A PWC is made up of fine parallel wires. The wires serving as anodes are located parallel to a cathode of foil or wires. The voltage and pressure of the gas in the chamber can be adjusted so that ions, liberated by passage of a charged particle, are accelerated to sufficient velocity to produce fresh ionization by collision, a phenomena known as gas multiplication.

Proportionality constant
A constant used to convert one set of units to another.

Proton
An elementary particle that is the positive unit charged constituent of ordinary matter. Its mass is 938 mev and has a spin of 1/2. Protons are one of the particles constituting all nuclei. It is currently believed that protons do not decay although experiments are going on to prove that they do have a half life of approximately 1030 years. It is believed that most of the matter in the universe is in the form of protons. At Fermilab protons and antiprotons are the particles accelerated.

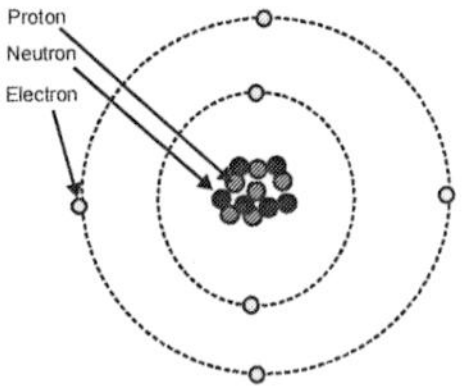

P-type germanium
"Hole-rich" germanium consisting of equal numbers of free positive holes and bound negative charges so that the net charge is zero.

Pull down window
A boxed set of options available upon interrupting. Used especially for copy options on a parameter page.

Pulsar
A neutron star (burnt-out star) that emits radio waves which pulse on and off.

Pulse
A wave of short duration confined to a small portion of the medium at any given time is called a pulse. A pulse is also called a wave pulse.

Pulse interlock module
Linac component in the modulator pulse- forming circuitry that will inhibit the modulator pulse if conditions warrant.

Pulse repeater
Module immediately after the pulse shifter in the preacc control room that sends the pulse to the chopper predets, the H- and I- clock generators, two of the A/D units for secondary G, and secondary G itself.

Pulse sequence
A series of RF pulses and/or magnetic field gradients applied to a spin system to produce a signal whose behavior gives information about some property of the spin system.

Pulse shifter
Module in the preacc control room that will delay the reset pulse to the sources by 1 msec if no beam is desired in the linac. Controlled by the prom module, safety system status, and vacuum valve status.

Pulse shifter status module
Module in the MCR that shows the Linac pulse shifter status and can reset a pulse over count if one occurs.

Pulse skip detector
Module in the preacc control room that senses when one or more of the 1-gap phase reversals from the clock module is missing (should occur at 15 Hz) and sends a message to secondary G so that it can post an alarm.

Pulse train
A stream of electrical pulses representing a single quantity. In the Laboratory it usually represents analogue information from a device such as a SEM or loss monitor which is converted into a stream of pulses which are counted by scalers. This information is generated on the CAMAC controls system by an 040 or 049 CAMAC module and is available via a CAMAC crate.

Pulsed devices
A pulsed device as it relates to accelerator beam line components is one that is triggered to come on at a preset time or event. The pulsed device is powered from a large power reservoir such as a capacitor bank. When the trigger is received the power reservoir dumps its energy into the device. The energy in the device then decays off naturally. The advantage of a pulsed device is that a high level of power can be put through a small device in a short period of time. Some typical pulsed devices are kickers, magnetic septa, and electrostatic deflectors. The pulsed trims in Switchyard for steering fast beam around the electrostatic splitting septa are also pulsed devices.

PV
Pneumatically operated Valve.

PV
Pulsed Vertical trim. A small vertical trim magnet which is pulsed to steer fast spill around splitting septa.

PVT
PVT stands for Pressure, Volume, and Temperature, the fundamental variables of the state of a pure fluid at equilibrium. Any two of the three variables may be specified. The third is then a unique value for a given fluid except where two or more phases coexist in which case the pressure is a unique function of the temperature but the volumes of the phases differ.

Q

Q unit
A unit of energy, used in measuring the heat energy of fuel reserves, equal to 10^{18} British thermal units, or approximately 1.055×10^{21} joules.

QBS
Quench Bypass Switch. System which bypasses the ring current around a quenched magnet cell. It is controlled by the QPM.

QPM
Quench Protection Monitor. The microprocessor system which monitors superconducting magnets for a quench condition or refrigerator problems that could induce a quench. In the event of a quench it takes action to protect the magnet system by firing the HFUs, pulling the Dump and Bypass loops, dropping the TECAR ramp, etc. It is sometimes called Quench Protection Mess.

QPM link
A 50 ohm RG-8U coaxial cable located in the Main Ring tunnel which carries information essential to the quench protection system. TECAR, the Tevatron power supply controller, refreshes the information every 720 Hz. The link carries information about the current in the Tevatron bus which the QPM's decode locally in order to evaluate conditions inside the magnets.

QPM link
A 50 ohm RG-8U coaxial cable located in the Main Ring tunnel which carries information essential to the quench protection system. TECAR, the Tevatron power supply controller, refreshes the information every 720 Hz. The link carries information about the current in the Tevatron bus which the QPM's decode locally in order to evaluate conditions inside the magnets.

Quad enclosures
Three underground enclosures in the Proton-West beam line containing a system of magnets and collimators designed to reduce the halo which accompanies the primary proton beam.

Quadrature detection
Detection of Mx and My simultaneously as a function of time.

Quadrupole
A magnet having four poles which serves to focus the proton beam in one plane. A focussing quadrupole serves to focus in the horizontal plane while a defocussing one focuses in the vertical plane.

Quadrupole steering
The bending of a particle beam by a quadrupole caused by the beam passing through it off-axis.

Quadrupole triplet
A series of three quadrupoles of alternating polarity that produce a net focusing of the beam in both planes. Typically the two outer elements of a triplet are wired in series.

Quality
The property of sound waves that depends on the number of harmonics and their prominence.

Quality factor
The number of oscillations required for a system's energy to fall off by a factor of 535 due to damping.

Quanta
Fixed amounts; usually referring to fixed amounts of energy absorbed or emitted by matter.

Quantized
Describes quantity such as money or electrical charge, that can only exist in certain amounts.

Quantum
When used as a noun (plural quanta): a discrete quantity of energy, momentum or angular momentum, given in units involving Planck's constant *h*. For example electromagnetic radiation of a given frequency *f* is composed of quanta (also called photons) with energy *hf*.

Quantum limit
The shortest wavelength, present in a continuous x-ray spectrum.

Quantum mechanics
Theory describing how things work at small distance scales from atoms on down to quarks. Quantum mechanics describes a duality where particles can be viewed as having a wave function but also letting light (energy) have a particle or localized aspect. It introduces uncertainty into measurement of a physical system such as not being able to measure exactly and simultaneously the position and momentum of an electron. It is also responsible for the quantizing of energy levels of the atom.

Quantum number
Numbers that describe energy states of an electron; in the Bohr model of the atom, the orbit quantum numbers could be any whole number 1, 2, 3, and so on out from the nucleus; in the quantum mechanics model of the atom, four quantum numbers are used to describe the energy state of an electron wave.

Quantum theory
A unifying theory based on the concept of the subdivision of radiant energy into discrete quanta (photons) and applied to the studies of structure at the atomic and molecular levels.

Quark
"Three quarks for Muster Mark" - a quote from James Joyce was the origin of the name for the now-familiar subatomic particle. One of 6 flavours of fundamental particles of which all baryons such as the proton or pi meson are constructed. For each quark, there is a corresponding anti-quark. Quarks interact with each other primarily through the strong force via gluons.

Quasar
A faint blue, star-like object commonly considered to be extremely distant, probably an unusual nucleus of a galaxy. It has a tendency to flare.

Quench
The change of state in a material from super conducting to non superconducting ('normal'). In the Tevatron this process is potentially damaging to the magnets. When the superconductor material quenches the material passes from the super conducting state to a normal resistive state. The Niobium alloy superconductor in the Tevatron that is now a normal resistive conductor heats up very quickly due to the extremely high currents passing through the magnets (4400 amps). Typically only one small piece of the superconductor is the first to quench and the heating of this one spot causes it to expand in volume quickly in relation to the surrounding colder material. Thermal stress induced by this sudden expansion can cause the magnet to break. For this reason very elaborate Quench Protection Monitor (QPM) systems electronically monitor the super conducting state of the Tev magnets. If a quench is detected beam is aborted and Heater Firing Units (HFU) are discharged to heat the entire magnet up evenly. The magnet must then be cooled down to super conducting temperatures again before current can be passed through.

Quiescent

A steady-state condition. The operating condition of an electronic circuit when no input signal is applied.

QXR

Quadrupole eXtraction Regulator. The system which controls the rate of extraction from the Tevatron. It is composed of a microprocessor system which controls special air core quadrupoles in the Tevatron.

QXR link

The link which transmits the programmed waveform to the Quad Extraction Regulator crates. It originates at the QXR microprocessor in the MAC room.

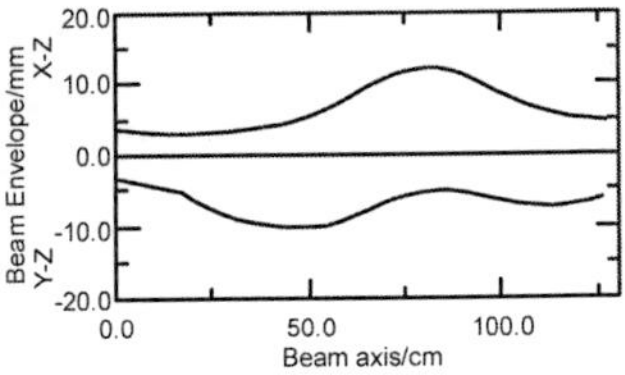

R

R crb stars

Hydrogen-deficient C-type stars.

R galaxy

In the Yerkes9 1974 system, a system showing rotational symmetry, without clearly marked spiral or elliptical structure.

R star

Stars of spectral type R are stars with spectral characteristics similar to those of K stars except that molecular bands of C_2, CN, and CH are present instead of TiO bands.

R zones

Regions in the solar corona in which short-lived radiofrequency variations are observed.

Rabi

It plays a central role in atom-field interactions, showing up in emitted light spectra and in time dependence.

Rabi frequency

This is the frequency at which atomic population is coherently transferred from one state to another by a resonant radiation field; it is named after its discoverer I.

Rad

Radiation Absorbed Dose. The basic unit of an absorbed dose of ionizing radiation. One rad is equal to the absorption of 100 ergs of radiation energy per gram of matter.

Radial

Parallel to the radius of a circle; the in-out direction.

Radial position

Position of a particle or particles in the horizontal plane relative to the centre of the beam pipe.

Radial pulsation

The periodic expansion and contraction of a star that may be merely an optical effect of recession.

Radial velocity

(a) Velocity along the line of sight toward (-) or away from (+) the observer.

(b) The speed at which an object moves toward or away from us. It can be measured from a star's spectrum: a star moving toward us has a blueshifted spectrum, and a star moving away from us has a redshifted spectrum. The larger the blueshift or redshift, the larger the radial velocity. The present radial-velocity champion is a star in the constellation Lacerta named Giclas 233-27, which moves toward us a t 583 kilometers per second.

Radian

The radian is used to measure angles, just like degrees, except that the radian is a natural unit of angular measurement. Practically speaking, this means you don't have to supply a conversion factor in numerous equations where angles appear if your angular measurement is in radians. Imagine a circle of radius r. It could be a pie. In fact, since I'm writing this with Thanksgiving coming up in a few days, it could be a pumpkin pie. With whipped cream on top! Yum! Imagine you slice yourself a piece of this pie. The arc length of the crust, s, divided by the radius of the pie, r, is the angle of your piece of pie in radians.

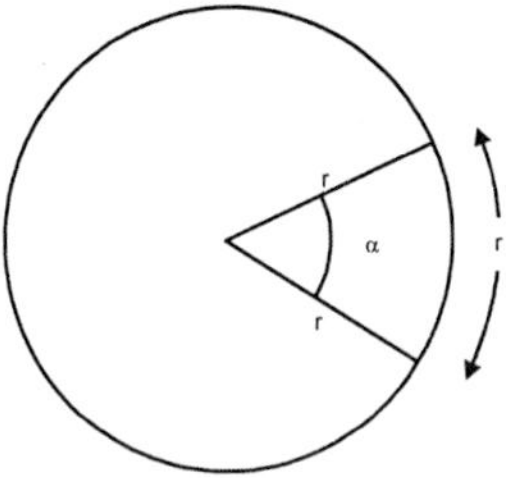

α = 1 radian

Radiant

(a) The point in the sky from which a meteor shower appears to emanate.

(b) The convergent point toward which the stars in a moving cluster appear to travel, or from which the meteors in a shower seem to radiate.

Radiant energy

The form of energy that can travel through space; for example, visible light and other parts of the electromagnetic spectrum.

Radiation

Radiation is energy in transit in the form of high speed particles and electromagnetic waves. Radiation is further defined into ionizing and non-ionizing radiation:

(1) Ionizing radiation is radiation with enough energy so that during an interaction with an atom, it can remove tightly bound electrons from their orbits, causing the atom to become charged or ionized. Examples are X-rays and electrons.

(2) Non-ionizing radiation is radiation without enough energy to remove tightly bound electrons from their orbits around atoms. Examples are microwaves and visible light.

Radiation baffles

An inactive set of shields designed to reduce the effects of cryogenic radiation.

Radiation belt

A ring-shaped region around a planet in which electrically charged particles (usually electrons and protons) are trapped. The particles follow spiral trajectories around the direction of the magnetic field of the planet. The radiation belts surrounding Earth are known as the Van Allen belts.

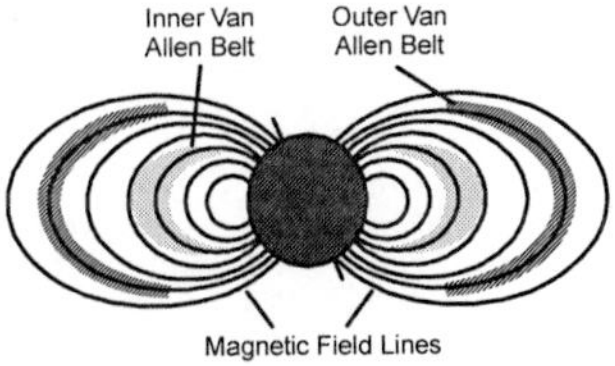

Radiation damping

A decrease in the amplitude of an oscillation due to the emission of energy by radiation.

Radiation era

The era from about 10 sec to about 10^{12} sec after the Big Bang, when the temperature had dropped to 10^9K and the rate of electron-positron pair annihilation exceeded the rate of their production, leaving radiation the dominant constituent of the universe. At t = 200 sec, nucleosynthesis began rather abruptly and virtually all Deuterium was synthesized to Helium. The radiation era was followed by the matter era.

Radiation length

The mean path length required to reduce the energy of relativistic charged particles by the factor 1/e, or 0.368, as they pass through matter. Also known as cascade unit; radiation unit.

Radiation oncology

Treatment of tumours with ionization radiation.

Radiation pressure

The transfer of momentum by electromagnetic radiation incident on a surface. $p_{rad} = (4/3)s T^4 / c$.

Radiation shield

An active (cooled) shield designed to intercept cryogenic radiation. Often cooled by LN2.

Radiation sickness

The syndrome associated with intense acute exposure to ionizing radiation.

Radiation temperature

The temperature that a blackbody of similar dimensions would have that radiated the same intensity at the same frequency.

Radiation transport

The field of nuclear science dealing with the prediction and measurement of the movement of electromagnetic radiation or particles through matter.

Radiative braking

The slowing down of rotation of a star due to radiation.

Radiative capture

The capture of a free electron by an ion with the subsequent emission of an X-ray (or gamma-ray) photon.

Radiative equilibrium

In a star, represents an even process by which energy (heat) is transferred from the core to the outer surface without affecting the overall stability of the star.

Radiative transfer

The process by which radiation travels through a medium.

Radiative viscosity

The friction produced by the collisions between matter and radiation.

Radio

Electromagnetic radiation with the lowest energy and longest wavelength. Unlike visible light, radio waves penetrate dust and can be detected from throughout the Galaxy.

Radio astronomy

the astronomy associated with radio observations of celestial objects. The waveband extends from low radio frequencies (10 MHz,l: 30 m) to centimeter and millimeter wavelengths. At the low frequency end of the range, the limit is imposed by the Earth's ionosphere and at the upper end by water vapor absorption in the atmosphere. Within this waveband, many sophisticated radio telescope systems have been constructed, either using single dishes or combining them in arrays using the principles of aperture synthesis and interferometry to obtain high angular resolution.

Radio frequency

In comparison with other electro- magnetic waves or oscillations, radio frequencies are low frequencies ranging between 3KHz to 300GHz. The frequency of the accelerating electric field falls in the range of radio frequencies and RF in an accelerator refers to this accelerating field.

Radio galaxy

A galaxy that is extremely luminous at radio wavelengths. A radio galaxy is usually a giant elliptical - the largest galaxy in a cluster - and is a strong emitter of synchrotron radiation. M87 and M82 are examples.

Radio interferometer

Type of radio telescope that relies on the use of two or more aerials at a distance from each other to provide a combination of signals from one source which can be analyzed by computer. Such an analysis results in a resolution that is considerably better than that of a parabolic dish aerial by itself because of the greater effective diameter.

Radio lobes

The extended regions of diffuse radio emission, often dumbbell shaped, that surround a radio galaxy.

Radio map of the sky

Celestial chart depicting sources and intensities of radio emission.

Radio scintillation

The scintillation in received radio emission; the equivalent of "twinkling" in visible light from the stars.

Radio source

A source of extraterrestrial radio radiation. The strongest known is Cas A, followed by Cyg A and the Crab Nebula (Tau A) (the capital letters following the name of a constellation refer to the radio sources of the constellation, A being the strongest source). Radio sources are divided into two main categories: Class I, those associated with our Galaxy (which is a weak radio source), and Class II, extragalactic sources. Most radio sources are galaxies, supernova remnants, or H II regions.

Radio source counts

The integral number of radio sources per unit solid angle whose measured flux density at the operating frequency of a radio telescope exceeds a certain given value; plot of log N (number of sources) versus log S (where S is in flux units).

Radio stars

Stars with detectable emission at radio wavelengths. They include pulsars, flare stars, some infrared stars, and some X-ray stars.

Radio telescope

Non-optical telescope (of various types) which, instead of focusing light received from a distant object, focuses radio signals onto a receiver-amplifier.

Radio waves

Electromagnetic waves of relatively low frequency.

Radio window

The wavelength range between a few millimeters and about 20 meters within which Earth's atmosphere is transparent to radiation.

Radioactive

A word distinguishing radioactive materials from those which aren't. Usage: 'U-235 is radioactive; He-4 is not.'

Radioactive dating

A technique for estimating the age of an object by measuring the amounts of various radioisotopes in it.

Radioactive decay

The natural spontaneous disinte-gration or decomposition of a nucleus.

Radioactive decay constant

A specific constant for a particular isotope that is the ratio of the rate of nuclear disintegration per unit of time to the total number of radioactive nuclei.

Radioactive decay law

The rate of disintegration of a radioactive substance is directly proportional to the number of undecayed nuclei.

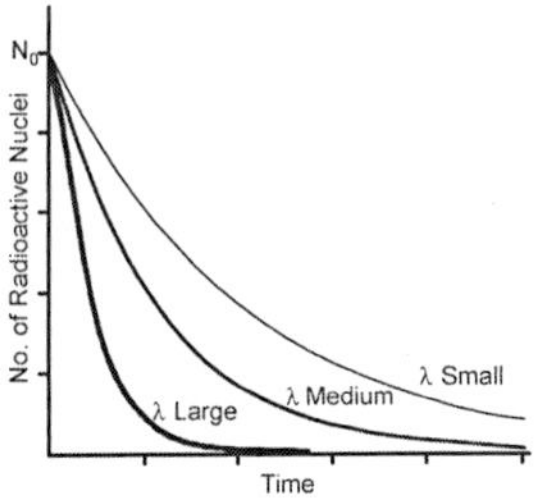

Radioactive decay series
Series of decay reactions that begins with one radioactive nucleus that decays to a second nucleus that decays to a third nucleus and so on until a stable nucleus is reached.

Radioactive material
A material whose nuclei spontaneously give off nuclear radiation. Naturally radioactive materials (found in the earth's crust) give off alpha, beta, or gamma particles. Alpha particles are Helium nuclei, beta particles are electrons, and gamma particles are high energy photons.

Radioactive waste
Materials which are radioactive and for which there is no further use.

Radioactivity
(a) Emission of particles by unstable elements as they decay.

(b) The spontaneous disintegration of unstable atomic nuclei. All natural radioactive elements heavier than lead are daughter products of either ^{232}Th (half-life 1.39×10^{10} yr), ^{235}U (half-life 7.13×10^{8} yr), or ^{238}U (half-life 4.51×10^{9} yr). The radioactive output of the Earth averages 1.7 ergs g^{-1} yr^{-1}.

Radiocarbon dating
Determination of the age of a substance containing radioactive carbon by means of its radioactive half-life.

Radiography
The making of shadow images on a photographic emulsion by the action of ionization radiation. The image is the result of the differential attenuation of the radiation in its passage through the object being radiographed.

Radioimmunotherapy
This type of radiotherapy is the application of monoclonal antibodies that have been tagged with high activities of suitable radionuclides. These tumor-specific antibodies are derived from the patient's own cancer and, hence, they selectively target this tumor when injected into the patient. Also known as monoclonoal antibody therapy.

Radio isotope
A radioactive isotope. A common term for a radionuclide.

Radiology
The branch of medicine that deals with the diagnostic and therapeutic applications of radiation.

Radiometer
A device that detects radio waves from space and measures their direction.

Radiometric dating
Determination of the age of objects - e.g., earth and moon rocks - by means of the half-life of the unstable elements they contain.

Radionuclide
Radionuclides are materials that produce ionization radiation, such as X-rays, gamma rays, alpha particles, and beta particles.

Radiosonde
A sounding balloon used to transmit information on Earth's upper atmosphere.

Radiotelescopes
Sensitive radio antennae employed to detect the radio energy emitted by nebulae, galaxies, pulsars, etc.

Radius
In astronomy, an old instrument for measuring the angular distance between two celestial objects.

Radius vector
In astronomy, an imaginary line connecting the centre of an orbiting body with the centre of the body (or point) that it is orbiting.

Raleigh criterion
For images of two wave sources to be just resolved the maximum of one diffraction pattern is coincident with the first minimum of the other.

Ram

Random access memory. A silicon micro-chip capable of temporary storage of information in the form of binary digits, either 0 or 1, and enabling rapid access to any part of its storage area.

Ram pressure

The motion of a blunt body at supersonic velocity through an ambient gaseous medium causes a strong drag or ram pressure to be exerted on the body. In the case of a galaxy moving through the intergalactic gas, the ram pressure is capable of stripping the galaxy of much of its interstellar gas.

Raman effect

(a) In spectroscopy, the change in the wavelength of light scattered by molecules.

(b) The change of wavelength on scattering. It arises from radiation exciting (or de-exciting) atoms or molecules from their initial states.

Ramp

Varying the output current/voltage of a device as a function of time.

Ramp enable

A permit sent to the NTF 58 deg magnet power supply telling it that it may ramp. The ramp enable comes from the NTF interlock module.

Ramsauer effect

An anomalously large mean free path for low-energy electrons.

Random error

These are errors that tend to fall with equal probability on either side of the actual value. Therefore the more measurements you have, the more the negative errors will tend to cancel the positive ones. The total error resulting from random errors can be lessened by increasing the number of measurements. Just think of what this means. If only our government could make lots of errors on both sides of a policy, eventually they might get it right.

Random walk

If a point experiences successive displacements such that each displacement is in a random direction and of a length also governed by a frequency distribution, then the point is said to experience a random walk. It is a law of statistical behavior closely allied to Brownian motion and the diffusion of molecules. It can be proved that the root mean square displacement experienced in *N* mean free paths is related to the diffusion coefficient by $D_{rms} = \sqrt{N}$.

Range

This term is used to describe how far a projectile goes when it is launched on a horizontal surface. Therefore, the distance traveled by the projectile when it reaches the same level it had when it was launched (strikes the ground) is the range. It is a little known fact that, during the Texas Revolution, artillerymen had limited training facilities. To sharpen their skills against a mobile enemy, they would conduct target practice by trying to hit cattle roaming on the prairie. This is where the term "range cattle" comes from.

Ranger spaceprobes

The series of 9 US spaceprobes only the final 3 of which were successful. All were meant to photograph the surface of the Moon before crashing onto it. Some good results were obtained.

Rankine scale

A temperature scale with the same division as the Fahrenheit scale and the zero point at 0° absolute. 0° R = - 470° F.

Rare gases

The inert gases He, Ne, Ar, etc.

Rarefaction

A part of a longitudinal wave in which the density of the particles of the medium is less than the normal density is called a rarefaction.

Raster

The area of an oscilloscope upon which the image is produced.

Rate

A quantity of one thing compared to a quantity of another. In physics the comparison is generally made by taking a quotient. Thus speed is defined to be the dx/dt, the 'time rate of change of position'.

Rate meter

An electronic instrument that indicates, on a meter, the number of radiation induced pulses per minute from radiation detectors such as a Geiger-Muller tube.

Ratio

The quotient of two similar quantities. In physics, the two quantities must have the same units to be 'similar'. Therefore we may properly speak of the ratio of two lengths. But to say "the ratio of charge to mass of the electron" is improper. The latter is properly called "the specific charge of the electron."

Raw data

The Mx and My data as a function of time and/or other parameters in an NMR pulse sequence. This is also called k-space data.

Ray

A straight line representation of the path of a light wave.

Ray diagram

A drawing of light rays used to analyze a set of optical devices, such as a lens or mirror.

Ray tracing

The computer simulation of light ray paths through an optical system.

Rayleigh

(a) Unit of flux. 1 rayleigh = 10^6 photons emitted in all directions per cm^2 vertical column per second. It is used in measuring the luminous intensity of the aurora.

(b) The luminous intensity of the aurora and the night sky may be measured in rayleighs, where one rayleigh is equivalent to 10^6 quanta per square centimetre. The unit, proposed in 1956, is named after the fourth Lord Rayleigh (1875-1947), who included in his numerous scientific achievements a thorough investigation of glow discharges in gases. The luminous intensity of the night sky is about 250 R, whereas that from an auroral display lies between 1 and 1000 kR.

Rayleigh limit

The minimum resolvable angle between the wavelengths of two spectral lines.

Rayleigh scattering

Selective scattering (i.e., preferential scattering of shorter wavelengths) of light by very small particles suspended in the Earth's atmosphere, or by molecules of the air itself. The scattering is inversely proportional to the fourth power of the wavelength.

Rayleigh-jeans law

An approximation of Planck's blackbody formula valid at long wavelengths ($hv << kT$). It is often used in radio astronomy; it gives the brightness temperature of a radio telescope.

Rayleigh-jeans limit

An approximation valid at sufficiently long wavelengths (longward of the peak intensity) to the energy distribution of a blackbody.

Rayleigh-jeans spectrum

The low-frequency portion of a blackbody spectrum.

Rayleigh-taylor instability

A type of hydrodynamic instability for static fluids in which the density increases outward.

Razin effect

The strong suppression of low-frequency (synchrotron) radiation by electrons moving in a cool, collisionless plasma. It is a theoretical calculation of the Tsytovitch effect specifically directed toward radio astronomy. (also called Razin-Tsytovitch Effect)

R-branch

A set of lines in the spectra of molecules corresponding to unit decreases in rotational energy.

RC circuit
A circuit that contains a resistor and a capacitor in series with one another.

RCRA
Resource Conservation and Recovery Act.

Reactance
The nonresistive opposition to current in an a-c circuit.

Reaction
Reaction forces are those equal and opposite forces of Newton's Third Law. Though they are sometimes called an action and reaction pair, one never sees a single force referred to as an action force.

Reaction motor
A heat engine whose acceleration is produced by the thrust of exhaust gases.

Reaction rate
The rate at which a chemical or nuclear reaction proceeds. Particles interacting via the strong nuclear force react together in roughly 10^{-23} seconds, while particles interacting via the weak nuclear force, such as the disintegration of a neutron, might take seconds.

Real
The component of a signal perpendicular to the imaginary signal.

Real image
A place where an object appears to be, because the rays diffusely reflected from any given point on the object have been bent so that they come back together and then spread out again from the new point. Cf. Virtual image.

Real object
The point(s) from which light rays diverge as they enter a lens or mirror.

Reboot
To restart a computer by using the "bootstrap loader" to retrieve the correct program from a peripheral device, e.g., disk.

Receiver
General term for a radio detection system.

Reciprocal
The inverse of a number; for example, the reciprocal of 3 is 1/3, the reciprocal of 1/2 is 2.

Reciprocal linear dispersion
The inverse of the linear dispersion of a spectrometer which is the rate of change of position along the spectrum (in millimeters) with wavelength (in angstroms). The reciprocal gives the number of angstroms per millimeter.

Reciprocity failure
The non-linear behavior of a photographic emulsion in which an increase in exposure time does not correspond to an increase in sensitivity by the same factor.

Recombination
(a) The capture of an electron by a positive ion. It is the inverse process to ionization.

(b) At about 300,000 years after the Big Bang, the plasma of free electrons and nuclei condensed to form a neutral gas, in a process called recombination. The prefix "re-" is not meaninful here however since according to the Big Bang theory the electrons and protons were combining for the first time ever.

(c) That point in time during the expansion of the Universe at which almost all of the electrons recombine with protons to form hydrogen atoms. Batter and radiation consequently decouple from one another because no further scattering of the radiation occurs.

Reconnection
The rejoining of magnetic lines of force severed by the annihilation of the field across the neutral region.

Rectifier
A device for changing alternating current to direct current.

Rectilinear motion
The motion of a body in a straight line.

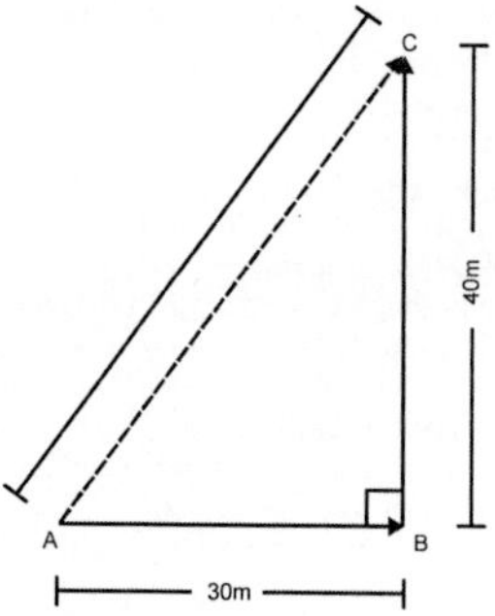

Rectilinear propagation

Traveling in a straight line.

Recycler ring

A proposed ring of permanent magnets which would be installed in the Main Injector tunnel to store antiprotons in order to help the accumulator stack more. This will increase the available intensity of the antiproton beam used for collisions.

Red dwarf

A main-sequence star with spectral type M. Red dwarfs are much fainter, cooler, and smaller than the Sun but are the most common type of star in the Galaxy, accounting for 70 percent of all stars. The nearest red dwarf, Proxima Centauri, lies just 4.25 light-years away, but neither it nor any other is visible to the naked eye.

Red giant

(a) Large, highly luminous but relatively cool star that has reached a late stage in its "life". It is running out of nuclear "fuel" and has accordingly expanded greatly and become less dense. Many also become variable stars of long periodicity. Its next evolutionary stage is to become a white dwarf, in developing into which the star has to cross the main sequence on the Hertzsprung-Russell diagram.

(b) A giant star with spectral type M. Such stars are in a more advanced state of evolution than the Sun, for they do not burn hydrogen into helium at their cores. Instead, they may fuse hydrogen into helium in a layer surrounding their cores, or they may fuse helium into carbon and oxygen, or they may do both. Often, astronomers use "red giant" loosely, to include not only M giants but G and K giants, too.

(c) A late-type (K or M) high-luminosity (brighter than $M_v = 0$) star that occupies the upper right portion of the H-R diagram. Red giants are post-main-sequence stars that have exhausted the nuclear fuel in their cores. The red-giant phase corresponds to the establishment of a deep convective envelope. Red giants in a globular cluster are about 3 times more luminous than RR Lyrae stars in the same cluster.

Red giant tip

The upper tip of the red-giant branch in the H-R diagram. The red-giant tip represents the "flash" point (e.g., helium flash, carbon flash) where the density and temperature of the core have become high enough that the "ash" in the core is ignited and serves as the fuel for a new series of nuclear reactions.

Red spot

An elliptical spot about 40,000 × 15,000 km on the southern hemisphere of Jupiter. Its color and intensity vary with time. It has been observed for at least a century, and an examination of earlier records shows that Cassini had sketched it in the seventeenth century.

Red supergiant

A supergiant with spectral type M. Red supergiants are the largest stars in the universe: if put in place of the Sun, some would touch Saturn. The two brightest red supergiants in Earth's sky are Betelgeuse and Antares.

Reddening

The process by which light from an astronomical object grows red as the light travels through interstellar dust. Dust scatters blue light more than red, thus leaving predominantly red light transmitted.

Red-dot board

One type of binary I/O board found in a linac secondary connected to OPTO22 devices to provide optical input and output to the secondary.

Redshift

(a) The shift of spectral lines toward longer wavelengths in the spectrum of a receding source of radiation.

(b) If a star or galaxy is moving away from us, the radiation from the star or galaxy appears shifted towards longer wavelengths, or towards the red end of the spectrum.

(c) The shift to the red of a star's spectrum caused by the star's movement away from us. This movement stretches the star's light waves and increases their wavelength. Since red has a longer wavelength than blue, this shift is called a redshift. The larger a star's redshift, the faster the star is moving away from us. Most galaxies also show redshifts, not because of the galaxy's movement away from us (although the galaxy is moving away from us) but because of the expansion of the universe. As a galaxy emits a light wave toward us, the light wave travels through the fabric of space; en route to Earth, it is stretched by the expansion of space and exhibits a redshift. The farther the galaxy, the larger the redshift. To distinguish this type of redshift from one caused by movement, astronomers call it the "cosmological redshift".

(d) The shift of spectral lines toward longer wavelengths, either because of a Doppler effect or because of the Einstein effect (gravitational redshift). The redshift $z = \delta\lambda/\lambda$ where is the laboratory wavelength of the spectral line and is the difference between the laboratory and the observed wavelengths. The redshift of distant galaxies was first noted by Slipher in 1926.

Redshift survey

The methodical tabulation of the redshifts of a large number of galaxies in a particular region of the sky. Redshifts directly measure the recessional speeds of galaxies. If Hubble's law is assumed, this speed can be translated to distance. Under such an assumption, a redshift survey provides the third dimension, depth, for the galaxies in a survey. The other two dimensions for each galaxy are provided by its position on the sky. The redshift of a galaxy is obtained by measuring its spectrum of light; in this way it is possible to see how much its colors are shifted.

Redshift-distance relation

The correlation between redshift in the spectra of galaxies and their distances.

Redshift-magnitude test

A cosmological test involving the plotting of redshifts and apparent magnitudes of distant galaxies. Deviations from the relation expected in Euclidean space can help determine whether the universe is open or closed. The redshift-magnitude test is very sensitive to evolutionary effects (whether galaxies were brighter or dimmer in the past).

Reduced proper motion

The observed proper motion of a star (in seconds of arc per year) reduced to absolute proper motion (in kilometers per second).

Reference source

Part of the monitor/control module in the PreAcc Haefely control system that produces a command voltage for the power supply in response to computer commands or local input.

Reflectance

The ratio of the light reflected from a surface to the

light falling on it, expressed in percentage.

Reflected ray

A line representing direction of motion of light reflected from a boundary.

Reflecting telescope

Telescope that uses mirrors to magnify and focus an image onto an eyepiece.

Reflection

What happens when light hits matter and bounces off, retaining at least some of its energy.

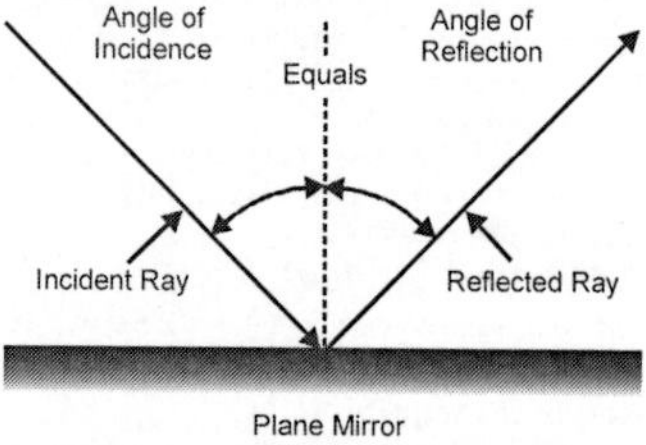

Reflection nebula

A cloud of interstellar gas and dust whose spectrum contains absorption lines characteristic of the spectrum of nearby illuminating stars. The emission component of its spectrum is due to gas; the reflection component, to dust.

Refracting telescope

Telescope that uses lenses to magnify and focus an image onto an eyepiece. (refractor).

Refraction

Motorists traveling rural Texas highways aren't the only ones who have to put up with annoying speed zone changes. Waves have to also, because as they propagate along, minding their own business, the medium through which they propagate may change its propagation characteristics, causing the waves to either speed up or slow down. This phenomenon is called refraction. If a wavefront runs into a situation where the wave speed in the medium varies from faster to slower across the wavefront, it bends toward the slower side, causing a change in the direction of propagation of the wave. If the left side of a wavefront is slower than the right side, for example, the direction of propagation of the wave will slant toward the left.

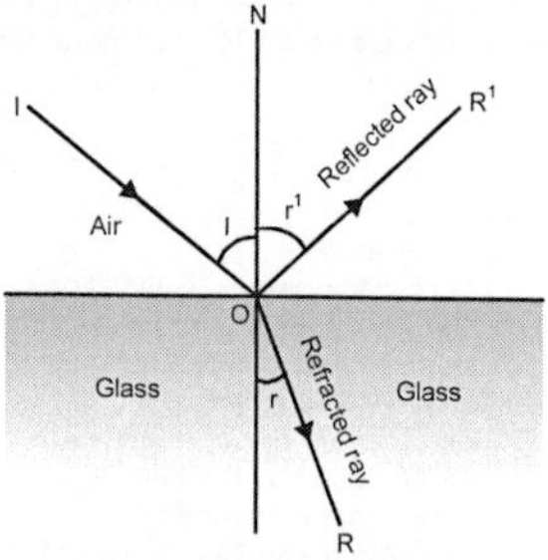

Refraction and Reflection of Light

Refraction, astronomical

The change in direction of travel (bending) of a light ray as it passes obliquely through the atmosphere. As a result of refraction, the observed altitude of a celestial object is greater than its geometric altitude. The amount of refraction depends on the altitude of the object and on atmospheric conditions.

Refraction, refractive index

(a) Deflection (or "bending") of light - or any ray as it passes from one medium into another of greater or lesser density, representing a change in overall speed of the ray. Refracting telescopes rely on the refraction of light through lenses. The refractive index of a medium (e.g., glass) is a measure of the medium's "bending" power.

(b) A number which characterizes the properties of a material when light is transmitted through it. A vacuum has a refractive index of 1.0; air is fairly close to this also. As the refractive index rises, light waves travel more slowly in the material, more light is reflected and the bending or refraction of light is greater. Some materials have a different refractive index depending on the plane of vibration of the electromagnetic wave, they are called birefringent.

Refractive index

The ratio of speed of light in vacuum to that in the medium.

Refractor

A telescope in which the light is focused by a lens at the viewing side of the telescope. By contrast, a reflecting telescope is one in which light is focused by a mirror.

Refrigeration

The extraction of heat at lower than ambient temperature.

Regelation

The melting of a substance under pressure and the refreezing after the pressure is released.

Regge trajectory

Derived from S-matrix theory, the Regge Trajectories were theoretical plots that attempted to account for the position of elementary particle resonances. One of the triumphs of early string theory was to describe the general shape of these Regge Trajectories.

Regolith

The layer of fragmentary debris produced by meteoritic impact on the surface of the Moon or a planet.

Regression of the Nodes

The slow ($19^{\circ}.35$ per year, 360° in 18.6 years), westward motion of the nodes of the Moon's orbit due to perturbations of the Earth and Sun.

Regular reflection

Reflection from a polished surface in which scattering effects are negligible.

Regulator (a0)

Transistor power supply used to provide a smoother output to the Main Ring quadrupole bus at injection than is possible with standard SCR power supplies.

Regulator/oscillator module

Module in the Pre acc Haefely control system that receives the digitized command and monitor voltages from the monitor/control module and uses them to generate a drive signal for the power amplifier. The regulator/oscillator also receives an input that represents the high-voltage transformer output and uses it for regulation.

Regulus (αleo)

A triple star situated in the body of constitution leo at a distance of 77.5 light years from the sun.

Relation

A rule of correspondence between the set of values of one quantity to the values of another quantity, often (but not always) expressible as an equation.

Relative

Colloquially 'compared to'. In the theory of relativity observations of moving observers are quantitatively compared. These observers obtain different values when measuring the same quantities, and these quantities are said to be relative. The theory, however, shows us how the differing measured values are precisely related to the relative velocity of the two observers. Some quantities are found to be the same for all observers, and are called invariant. One postulate of relativity theory is that the speed of light is an invariant quantity. When the theory is expressed in four dimensional form, with the appropriate choice of quantities, new invariant quantities emerge: the world-displacement ($x + y + z + ict$), the energy-momentum four-vector, and the electric and magnetic potentials may be combined into an invariant four-vector. Thus relativity theory might properly be called invariance theory.

Relative density

The ratio of density of a substance to the density of water at 4°C.

Relative deviation

Percentage average deviation of a set of measurements.

Relative error

Percentage absolute error of a set of measurements.

Relative humidity

The percentage of the amount of water vapor actually present in a certain volume of the air to the amount of water vapor needed to saturate it.

Relative uncertainty

The uncertainty in a quantity compared to the quantity itself, expressed as a ratio of the absolute uncertainty to the size of the quantity. It may also be expressed as a percent uncertainty. The relative uncertainty is dimensionless and unit less.

Relativistic

Particles moving at these speeds demonstrate effects predicted by the special theory of relativityincreased mass, slowing of time, etc. - that must be taken into account by combining relativity with quantum theory if accurate predictions are to be made.

Relativistic beaming

Theory devised by Francis Smith regarding the generation of polarized radiation in neutron stars (pulsars).

Relativistic mass

The mass of an object in motion with respect to the observer.

Relativistic particles

Particles whose velocities approach the speed of light.

Relativistic plasma

A plasma consisting of particles which have relativistic energies, i.e. for typical particles, their kinetic energies exceed their rest-mass-energies mc^2. Relativistic plasmas are found in such astronomical objects as supernova remnants, radio galaxies, the interstellar medium and the nuclei of galaxies. In many of these cases, the relativistic plasma provides most of the pressure of the medium. The spectrum of the particle energies is generally of power-law rather than Maxwellian form so that many of the particles are ultrarelativistic, i.e. $E >> mc^2$.

Relativistic quantum field theory

The quantum-mechanical theory of fields, such as the electromagnetic field, that incorporates special relativity.

Relativistic zone

For a pulsar, the region in which *M*[grams] / R[cm] is not negligible compared with unity.

Relativity

(a) The theory of how motion and gravity affect the properties of time and space. The special theory of relativity establishes, among other things, the nonabsolute nature of time. The amount of time elapsed between two events will not be the same for two observers or clocks in relative motion to each other. The general theory of relativity describes how gravity affects the geometry of space and the rate at which time passes.

(b) The special theory concerns time and distance measurements by two observers in uniform relative motion, and clarifies the notion of simultaneity relative to such observers. The general theory of relativity is concerned with the generalization of Newton's law of gravitation when masses moving under their mutual influence acquire velocities comparable to that of light; its basic postulate, derived from the equality of the inertial and the gravitational mass, is that all accelerations are metrical in origin.

Relaxation

The process of gravitational interaction (in the case of a cluster of stars or galaxies) whereby a random distribution of motions is eventually established. The system is said to relax to a state of thermal equilibrium.

Relaxation time

Period required for the reestablish- ment of thermal equilibrium; in particular (in the astronomical context) the period required for the reestablishment of a random distribution of motion in a cluster of stars.

Relief valve

There are two uses. (1) Pressure, set to MWP + 10% and (2) Thermal, set to relieve at a pressure conveniently above the system working pressure but below MWP to provide for cryogen expansion. The Frig building relief valves on the roof tops are an example of the first usage. The Kautzky valves are an example of the second.

Rem

Roentgen Equivalent for Man. A measurement of radiation dosage. It is the amount of radiation required to deposit 1 Joule of energy per kilogram (i.e., 100 ergs/gm) of body tissue. REM = (Quality Factor)x(RAD) Q.F. depends upon substance.

Remnant field

(Also spelled remanent). The field remaining in the magnet after its excitation current has been removed. It is particularly important in ring magnets at injection, where the total magnetic field is made of the powered field plus the remnant field; this causes field errors which must be compensated for during the injection process.

Renormalisation

Strictly, the rescaling of some parameter in a field theory. In practice, nearly all renormalizations involve an infinite rescaling, so the term has come to be identified with a mathematical procedure for circumventing otherwise nonsensical infinite terms in quantum field theory by absorbing them into observable constants in the theory, such as mass, charge, etc.

Renormalisation group

The way in which coupling constants enter into field theory often involves certain simple scaling relations that are described by a group (in the mathematical sense), In statistical mechanics, the renormalization group method systematically implements some form of coarse-graining operation to expose the character of the large-scale phenomena, in physical systems where many scales are important.

Renormalization

(a) The mathematical process which ensures that the basic quantities in quantum field theory (e.g. in QED: the photon, electron and electric charge) are well-defined and not infinite.

(b) A mathematical procedure in quantum mechanics that allows one to make a correspondence between the formal quantities of the theory and the actual quantities observed in the lab. Some of the formal quantities, such as the mass of an electron, have infinite values before renormalization.

(c) When a theory such as quantum electrodynamics is approximated by a perturbation expansion, the first approximation is found to give answers that agree well with experiment. The second approximation, however, is found to produce mathematical expressions that are infinite, and hence meaningless. Renormalization is a technique for reformulating the theory so that the infinities are avoided, developed independently by Feynman, Tomonaga, and Schwinger in the 1940s.

Repeater

A module which receives information from a link and retransmitts it to points further downstream.

Repetition time

The time between repetitions of the basic sequence in a pulse sequence.

Reproducing universes

The process in some inflationary universe models whereby the universe is constantly spawning new universes, causally disconnected from each other and from the parent universe.

Repulsive

Describes a force that tends to push the two participating objects apart. Cf. Attractive, oblique.

Reseau

A grid that is photographed by a separate exposure on the same plate with star (or galaxy) images.

Reset noise

The unwanted and uncertain electrical signal transmitted to the output pin of a CCD during the process of recharging, via the reset transistor, the output storage capacitor to its preset value in readiness for the next pixel charge.

Residual intensity

Ratio of correlated flux in the line to correlated flux in the continuum.

Residual interaction

Interaction between objects that do not carry a charge but that contain constituents that do have a charge. Although some chemical substances involve electrically-charged ions, much of chemistry is due to residual electromagnetic interactions between electrically neutral atoms. The residual strong interaction between protons and neutrons, due to the strong charges of their quark constituents, is responsible for the binding of the nucleus.

Residual magnetism

Magnetism retained in a magnet after the magnetizing field has been removed.

Resistance

The ratio of the voltage difference to the current in an object made of an ohmic substance.

Resistive wall effect

As beam intensity is increased in a synchrotron, image currents flowing in the walls are increased, attracting the beam at high betatron oscillation points thus enhancing the betatron oscillations toward an unstable state.

Resistivity

A proportionality constant that relates the length and cross-sectional area of a given electric conductor to its resistance, at a given temperature.

Resistor

A circuit element that impedes the flow of current.

Resolution

The ability of an optical system, including detector, to separate two adjacent objects - this is called "spatial resolution" or two adjacent wavelengths in a spectrometer - this is called "spectral resolution".

Resolution of forces

The resolving of a single force into component forces acting in given directions on the same point.

Resolving power

(a) The ratio of the mean wavelength of two lines to the minimum resolvable angle. The resolving power of the human eye is about 1 minute of arc (its integration time is about 1/15 second).

(b) The ratio of the wavelength of radiation to the smallest interval of wavelength that the instrument can measure.

Resonance

(a) One of the natural states of oscillation of a physical system.

(b) The selective response of any oscillating system to an external stimulus of the same frequency as the natural frequency of the system. Under such conditions the nodes of the two wave trains coincide, and the waves of the initial system increase in amplitude. The natural mode of oscillation of a star varies inversely as the square root of its mean density; if the Sun were to start resonating at its natural frequency, it would have a period of about an hour.

(c) Resonances are sometimes found when elementary particles collide and interact together. They represent tiny regions of space in which energy is temporarily bound.

Resonance capture

Capture by an atomic nucleus of a particle whose energy is equal to one of the energy levels of the nucleus. Under such circumstances the particle's chances of being captured are greatly increased.

Resonance line

The longest-wavelength line arising from the ground state.

Resonance particles

(a) Hadronic particles which exist for only a very brief time (10^{-23} seconds) before decaying into hadrons. (also called resonances)

(b) Strongly interacting particles which are born and decay within the short time span of the strong interaction (10^{-23} seconds). The existence of a resonance cannot be observed directly; it can only be inferred from studying the longer-lived products of its decay. An asterisk is commonly used to designate a resonance, e.g., λ^*.

Resonant reaction

A nuclear reaction that has an energetically favorable probability of occurring (see resonance capture).

Rest mass

The mass of an object not in motion.

Rest-mass energy

The energy which a particle has even when it is at rest. According to the famous relation $E = mc^2$ of special relativity, this rest energy is equal to the rest mass of the particle-the mass it has when a rest-times the square of the speed of light. If the mass is in grams and the speed of light in centimeters per second ($c = 2.998 \times 10^{10}$ centimeters per second), then the energy is given in ergs.

Restoration

A process used by radio astronomers to eliminate the smoothing effect observed in radio maps that is caused by the finite width of the telescope beam.

Restoring force

The force which tends to bring an oscillating body towards its mean position whenever it is displaced from the mean position is called the restoring force.

Resultant

A vector representing the sum of several vector components. resultant force. The single force that has the same effect as two or more forces applied simultaneously at the same point.

Resultant force

A single force, which acts on a body to produce the same effect in it as, done by all other forces collectively, is called the resultant force.

Retarder

A device for introducing a phase delay, such as half-wave or quarter-wave, between two orthogonally polarized components of an electromagnetic wave.

Retdat

RETurns DATa. A program present on all front-ends which receives request lists for data from consoles and organizes those lists to be sent out to the appropriate CAMAC crates in the field.

Reticle

A system of cross-hairs in the eyepiece of a telescope.

Retraction spring

A small piece of wire used to keep broken septum wires from shorting the cathode to ground.

Retrograde

(a) In a backwards direction; in astronomy this means in a direction corresponding to east-to-west.

(b) Apparent motion of a planet in a direction opposite to its normal progress across the sky produced by the orbital motion of the earth.

Reverberation

The prolongation of sound at a given point after direct reception from the source has ceased, it is due to reflections from the boundary surfaces.

Reverse bias

Voltage applied to a semiconductor P-N junction that reduces the electron current across the junction.

Reverse power

The RF power from an amplifier that is reflected back by the load. The power not reflected back is the forward power. The sum of the two represent the total power of the amplifier. In RF station tuning, the reverse power between stages is always tuned for a minimum.

Reversing layer

Lower chromosphere of the Sun, a comparatively cool region in which radiation at certain wavelengths is absorbed from the continuous spectrum emitted from the Sun's photosphere.

RF

Radio Frequency. It is the type of electromagnetic energy used in acceleration systems.

RF bucket

That area in RF phase where particles oscillate about the synchronous phase angle. Particles in an RF bucket will normally remain in the bucket. Particles outside the bucket will not be accelerated.

Rf cavity

An electrically-resonant standing-wave cavity designed to impart energy to particles as they pass through a gap or number of gaps in the cavity by virtue of the electric field gradient across the gap(s).

RF coil

An inductor-capacitor resonant circuit used to set up B_1 magnetic fields in the sample and to detect the signal from the sample.

RF defocussing

Phenomenon caused by the curved fields in the gap between drift tubes and the changing electric field strength that results in radial defocussing of the beam as it is accelerated between drift tubes.

RF east mac

A MAC-16 minicomputer which handles digital control of Booster stations 1-8 in the East Gallery. Digital control means such things as turning stations or anode supplies on and off, etc.

RF phase adjust module

Linac module in the low-level RF system that adjusts the phase of the input RF from the master oscillator under the direction of the local secondary microcomputer. This adjustment controls the intertank phase.

RF power

Radio-Frequency power. Electromagnetic fields alternating at the frequencies of radio waves (up to 10^{10} Hz), which can be used to accelerate charged particles in accelerators.

RF pulse

A short burst of RF energy which has a specific shape.

RF west mac

A MAC-16 minicomputer which handles digital control of Booster stations 9-18 in the West Gallery. Digital control means such things as turning stations or anode supplies on and off, etc.

RFGE

RF Gap Envelope. RF abbreviation. This is the RF voltage that is present on the gaps of the cavity beam tube that accelerate the beam. There are two gap monitors on each cavity and are referred to as upstream and downstream. They both read the same gap voltage and should present readings that are within 2% accuracy.

RHEA

Sixth satellite of Saturn, discovered by Cassini in 1672. Diameter about 1500 km; rotation period $4^{d}12^{h}25^{m}$. Albedo 0.57.

Rheostat

A variable resistance.

Richardson-lucy method

An image reconstruction algorithm.

Riemannian geometry

A large class of non-Euclidean geometries. The mathematics of general relativity uses Riemannian geometry.

Riemannian geometry

Mathematical framework for describing curved shapes of any dimension. Plays a central role in Einstein's description of spacetime in general relativity.

Rigging

The heavy material or instrumentation of an experiment must be moved into or rigged into a certain location. This usually requires a crane and a special crew referred to as riggers.

Right ascension

The angular distance on the celestial sphere measured eastward along the celestial equator from the equinox to the hour circle passing through the celestial object. Right ascension is usually given in combination with declination.

Right bends

A set of bending magnets that initially direct the beam toward the Proton Area. Also known as the MH-300's.

Right-hand rule

One version of this is the fact that everything is made for right-handed people. Left-handed people are "sinister" (from the Latin word for "left") and not be trusted or given an appropriate table setting. For example, in baseball you have right-handed pitchers and "crafty" left handers. You never hear right handers being described as "crafty". Instead, you may hear announcers use the phrase, "He's a hard-throwing right hander." Honest. Dependable. A paragon of decency, not like those crafty lefties.

Rigid body

A rigid body in physics is one where every atom is always in the same position with respect to every other atom in the body, even when outside forces are applied to the body. In other words the body cannot be deformed - its shape is always exactly the same. Of course, no real body, with the possible exception of Al Gore, is perfectly rigid, but it makes a good approximation in physics, since many objects are only minutely deformed by ordinary external forces.

Ring current

A very spread-out electric current circling around the Earth, carried by trapped ions and electrons.

Ring galaxy

A galaxy with a ring-like appearance. The ring contains luminous blue stars, but relatively little luminous matter is present in the central regions. It is believed that such a system was an ordinary galaxy that recently suffered a head-on collision with another galaxy.

Ring nebula

A famous planetary nebula (M57, NGC 6720) in the constellation Lyra.

Ripple

An a.c. component or a periodic fluctuation of a direct current or voltage. Ripple is generally the result of inadequate filtering of the voltage produced by an a.c. source.

Ritz combination principle

A principle discovered empirically before the advent of quantum mechanics which states that every spectral line of a given atom corresponds to the difference of some pair of energy levels.

RL circuit

A circuit that contains a resistor and an inductor in series with one another.

RL02 disk drive

The disk drive common to all PDP-11 computers. The console computers have two disks, one of which carries the cache memory while the other one carries the management programs. The front-ends have only one disk.

RLC circuit

A circuit that contains a resistor, a capacitor, and an inductor in series with one another.

RM80 disk drive

A fixed media 124 Mb (formatted) disk drive used on the Development VAX.

Robertson-walker metric

(a) An equation which describes the spacetime continuum in a Universe which adheres to the cosmological principle.

(b) A metric which is appropriate for a spacetime which is homogeneous and isotropic. It was derived by Robertson and Walker with a minimum of assumptions; but the metric had been used earlier by Friedmann to derive the cosmological models (without a cosmological constant) that are currently in use.

(c) A mathematical description of the geometrical properties of a homogeneous and isotropic universe. Friedmann cosmologies all use the Robertson-Walker metric.

Roche limit

The minimum distance at which a satellite under the influence of its own gravitation and that of a central mass about which it is describing a circular Keplerian orbit can be in equilibrium. For a satellite of negligible mass, zero tensile strength, and the same mean density as its primary, in a circular orbit around its primary, this critical distance is 2.44 times the radius of the primary.

Roche lobe

The first equipotential surface for two massive bodies describing circular orbits around one another which forms a figure eight enclosing the two objects. The Roche lobes are the two lenticular volumes enclosing the two bodies.

Rods

The more sensitive cells of the retina of the eye. They are of most importance in vision in poor light, but cannot provide color information. Their action is not known in detail. It appears to be based on the photochemical breakdown of a reddish dye called rhodopsin.

Roentgen

Measurement of radiation dosage caused by X-rays and gamma radiation. It is the amount of radiation required to deposit 97 ergs of energy per gram of air.

Root mean square (rms)

The square root of the average of the squares of a group of numbers or values. For example, the RMS value of {2, 4, 3, 2.5} is $[2^2 + 4^2 + 3^2 + 2.52)/4]^{1/2}$ = 5.937. For continuous quantities, such as alternating electric current, the root-mean-square value is used to measure the average effect. The root-mean-square value of an alternating current (also called the effective value) is the value of the direct current that would produce the same energy transfer per second in a given resistor. For a sine wave, this is $I_m/2^{1/2}$, where I_m is the peak value.

Root-mean-square (rms) current

The effective value of an alternating current; the square root of the mean of the instantaneous values squared.

Rosette nebula

Is a large circular H11 region (M16, NGC 2237-2244) in Monoceros, on the milky way galaxy more than 1.6 kpc distant. It has a fairly high degree of symmetry about a centrally located cluster of about six hot, young O-type stars.

Rossby number

This gives the ratio of the inertial to the Coriolis forces in a moving fluid. It is named after the Swedish meteorologist C. A. Rossby (1899-1959).

Rossby waves

Cyclonic convection waves in a rotating fluid. Such waves occur in the atmosphere, in the oceans, and in the fluid core of the Earth.

Rosseland mean absorption coefficient

A coefficient of opacity which is a weighted inverse

mean of the opacity over all frequencies. It is applied when the optical depth is very large.

Rossiter effect
A rotational distortion of the velocity curves of eclipsing binaries.

Rotary motion
Motion of a body about an internal axis.

Rotation
Of a single body in space: spinning on an axis. Of a planetary system, rotation is generally planar in relation to the parent star. Galactic rotation, however, is usually differential.

Rotation curve
A quantitative description of how fast each part of a galaxy is rotating about the centre. A rotation velocity is the velocity of a rotating galaxy at a certain distance from the centre of the galaxy. A "flat" rotation curve is one in which the rotational velocity of the galaxy remains constant with distance away from the centre of the galaxy. This indicates that the mass of the galaxy increases linearly with distance from its centre.

Rotation matrix
A matrix used to describe the rotation of a vector.

Rotational equilibrium
The state of a body in which the sum of all the clockwise torques in a given plane equals the sum of all the counterclockwise torques about a pivot point.

Rotational inertia
The intrinsic property of an object that causes it to resist changes in rotational motion. Also called moment of inertia.

Rotational invariance
The property of being unchanged by a rotation. A sphere is rotationally invariant, but a rectangle is not. As far as we know the fundamental laws of physics are rotationally invariant.

Rotational transition
A slight change in the energy level of a molecule due to the rotation of its constituent atoms about their centre of mass.

Roughing
The first stage of vacuum pumping. It generally ranges from atmospheric pressure down to a few microns (one micron is 0.001 mm).

Roughing pump
A rotating-vane pump used in the initial stage of vacuum pump down, good down to about 1×10^{-3} torr.

R-Process
The capture of neutrons on a very rapid time scale (i.e., one in which a nucleus can absorb neutrons in rapid succession, so that regions of great nuclear instability are bridged), a theory advanced to account for the existence of all elements heavier than bismuth (up to *A* 298) as well as the neutron-rich isotopes heavier than iron. The essential feature of the *r*-process is the release of great numbers of neutrons in a very short time (less than 100 seconds). The presumed source for such a large flux of neutrons is a supernova, at the boundary between the collapsing neutron star and the ejected material. However, other proposed sources have included such things as supernova shocks and black-hole-neutron-star collisions. The heavier *r*-process elements are synthesized at a temperature of about 10^9 K and an assumed neutron density of 10^{20}-10^{30} per cm^3. The r-process is terminated by neutron-induced fission. The existence of ^{244}Pu (half-life 82 million years) in the early solar system shows that at least one *r*-process event had occurred in the Galaxy just before the formation of the solar system.

RR LYR
(a) Periodic variables with periods less than one day, and of spectral types A to early F.

(b) Type of short-period variable stars. Spectrally classified as A to F giants. They were once called cluster-cepheids.

(c) An old metal-poor white or yellow-white giant star that pulsates like a Cepheid and therefore varies in brightness. Most RR Lyrae stars have periods of under one day, which is shorter than periods for Cepheids. RR Lyrae stars are also fainter than Cepheids, with absolute magnitudes around +0.7, corresponding to a luminosity about 45 times the Sun's. RR Lyrae stars are excellent distance indicators because they all have nearly the same intrinsic brightness. They take their name from the star RR Lyrae, in the constellation Lyra.

RSS

Radiation Safety System. Logic system for a particular enclosure that controls the primary and secondary critical devices for that area. Inputs to the RSS include the status of the gates leading to the enclosure, the emergency switches in the enclosure, and whether or not the enclosure has been secured.

Rubidium

A soft silvery highly reactive element. Naturally occurring rubidium comprises two isotopes, one of which, ^{87}Rb, is radioactive (half-life 5×10^{10} years). The element is used in vacuum tubes, photocells, and in making special glass. Symbol: Rb; m.p. 39.05°C; b.p. 688°C; r.d. 1.532 (20°C); p.n. 37; r.a.m. 85.4678.

Runaway stars

(a) Early type stars (O and B) outside the Galactic plane, which reached large distances (from the Galactic plane) because of their high velocities.

(b) Stars of spectral type O or B with unusually high space velocities. The three best known are AE Aur, 53 Ari, and μ Col, all of which diverge from a comparatively small area in Orion. Runaway stars are thought to be produced when there is a supernova explosion in a close binary system.

Runge-kutta method

A step-by-step method of numerical integration.

Ruthenium

A transition metal that occurs naturally with platinum. It forms alloys with platinum that are used in electrical contacts. Ruthenium is also used in jewelry alloyed with palladium. Symbol: Ru; m.p. 2310°C; b.p. 3900°C; r.d. 12.37; p.n. 44; r.a.m. 101.07.

Rutherfordium

A radioactive metal not found naturally on earth. It is the first transactinide metal. Atoms of rutherfordium are produced by bombarding ^{249}Cf with ^{12}C or by bombarding ^{248}Cm with ^{18}O. Symbol: Rf; m.p. 2100°C (est.); b.p. 5200°C (est.); r.d. 23 (est.); most stable isotope ^{261}Rf (half-life 65s).

Rv tau variables

Periodic variables with periods 60-100 days, and of spectral types G and K.

Rydberg

A unit of energy ($R = {}^3c / me^4$) equal to 13.5978 eV (the ionization potential of hydrogen).

Rydberg atom

extremely highly excited atoms are called Rydberg atoms (Rydberg was an early systematizer of atomic spectra). These atoms are huge (the size of viruses for the largest) and fragile but interact very strongly with radiation. Quantum opticians use them to test basic ideas about atom-photon interactions.

Rydberg constant (r)

A constant found in the description of the line spectra of gases.

S

S band

A radiofrequency band at a wavelength of 11.1 cm.

S stars

Red-giant stars of spectral type S are similar to M stars except that the dominant oxides are those of the metals of the fifth period (Zr, Y, etc.). They also have strong CN bands and contain spectral lines of lithium and technetium. Pure S stars are those in which ZrO bands are very strong and TiO bands are either absent or only barely detectable. Almost all S stars are LPVs. (S1,0. The number following the comma is an abundance parameter.)

S1, S2

Pulsed magnetic septums located at the start and end of the 200 MeV line.

SA0040

The secondary applications program which operates the AEOLUS alarm screen.

Sachs-wolfe effect

A supergiant whose spectral type has changed from B4 Ia in 1955 to A5 Ia in 1967 to F6 Ia in 1972. It ejected a planetary nebula some 6000 years ago. It showed s-process elements in its surface layer in 1972 that did not exist in 1965 - an indication of deep mixing.

Saddle coil

A coil geometry which has two loops of a conductor wrapped around opposite sides of a cylinder.

Saddle Coil

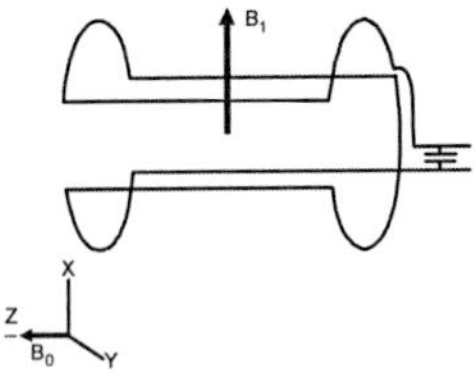

Safety lead

Connection from the Tevatron main magnet bus to the QBS's. They are found at each spool piece downstream of a defocussing quadrupole.

Sagittarius A

The very centre of the Milky Way, Sagittarius A is a strong source of radio waves and probably a massive black hole.

Sagittarius arm

One of the spiral arms of the Milky Way, lying between us and the centre of the Galaxy in the direction of Sagittarius. It includes the Scutum arm, the 3-kpc arm, and the Norma arm. It is about 1.5 kpc from the Sun and about 8.7 kpc from the galactic centre. Density of H I and H II in Sagittarius arm is about 1.2 atoms cm^{-3}.

Sagittarius B2

A massive (3×10^6 *M*), dense (up to 10^8 particles per cm^3) H II region and molecular cloud complex - the richest molecular source in the Galaxy. It is in the galactic plane about 10 kpc distant, near the galactic centre.

Saha equation

An equation that determines the number of atoms of a given species in various stages of ionization that exist in a gas in thermal equilibrium at some specified temperature and total density.

Salpeter function

A simple functional interpolation for the distribution by mass of newly formed stars. Also referred to as the initial mass function of stars, the Salpeter function (the number of stars formed per unit mass range) is proportional to $m^{-2.35}$, where m is the mass of a star.

Samarium

A silvery element of the lanthanoid series of metals. It occurs in association with other lanthanoids. Samarium is used in the metallurgical, glass, and nuclear industries. Symbol: Sm; m.p. 1077°C; b.p. 1791°C; r.d. 7.52 (20°C); p.n. 62; r.a.m. 150.36.

Sample and hold

This is a circuit, used throughout the accelerator, which upon command records the value (analog or digital) of a device in a buffer and holds this value until it receives a command to reset its buffer.

Sample probe

That portion of the NMR spectrometer containing the RF coils and into which the sample is placed.

Sample time

The time, unique to each accelerator subsystem, when data is loaded into buffers for use by the MCR or sampled by the front-end computers.

Saros

(a) A particular cycle of similar eclipses (lunar or solar) known to the Babylonians, that recur at intervals of 6585 days (about 18 tropical years). The interval contains 223 synodic months (6585.32 days) and 19 ecliptic years (6585.78 days). (It also contains 242 nodical months.) The difference of a fraction of a day causes each eclipse to fall about 120° west of the previous eclipse.

(b) A Babylonian lunar cycle of 6585.32 days, or 18 years 11.33 days, or 223 lunations, at the end of which the centres of the Sun and Moon return so nearly to the relative positions of the beginning that all the eclipses of the period recur approximately as before, but in longitudes.

Satellite

The term has also been applied to man-made (artificial) satellites; many astronomers make the distinction by calling natural satellites moons (and the Earth's natural satellite the Moon).

Satellite galaxy

A galaxy that orbits a larger one. The Milky Way has at least ten satellite galaxies: the Large Magellanic Cloud, the Small Magellanic Cloud, Ursa Minor, Draco, Sculptor, Sextans, Carina, Fornax, Leo II, and Leo I.

Satellite lines

Of an OH source: The lines arising from transitions at 1612 and 1730 MHz. (a) Sixth major planet out from the Sun. The most spectacular of the Solar System, it is circled by a series of concentric rings. (b) Sixth planet from the Sun. Mean distance from Sun 9.540 AU; e = 0.056, i = 2°29'33". Sidereal period 29.458 years; synodic period 378 days. Equatorial diameter 116,340 km. Oblateness 0.1. Mass 5.7×10^{29} g = 95.2 M_E; mean density 0.7 g cm^{-3}; surface gravity 11 m s^{-2}; V_{esc} 33.1 km s^{-1}. Rotation period at equator 10^h14^m; at poles 10^h38^m. Obliquity 26°44'. T_{eff} about 160 K. V_{orb} 9.65 km s^{-1}. Albedo 0.50. Atmosphere hydrogen and helium. Ten satellites, all of which are locked in synchronous rotation.

Saturated air

Air in which equilibrium exists between evaporation and condens- ation; the relative humidity is 100 percent.

Saturated solution

The apparent limit to dissolving a given solid in a specified amount of water at a given temperature; a state of equilibrium that exists between dissolving solute and solute coming out of solution.

Saturation (loss monitor)

A loss monitor read back which has exceeded its maximum of 10.23 volts. At this point further losses do not result in a larger read back.

Saturation (of a magnet or of iron)

A magnet is said to be showing saturation when its field no longer rises linearly with the excitation current. The term properly applies to the steel of the magnetic core in which the permeability falls from a large value at low excitation to a value approaching that of vacuum at high excitation when all the magnetic domains are aligned with the field.

Saturn nebula

A double-ring planetary about 700 pc distant.

Save file

This term generally refers to a filesharing file containing some type of data or information related to accelerator operation. These files are generally temporary.

Sawtooth wave

A waveform generated electronically (such as the variation of voltage with time), having a uniform increase that regularly and rapidly drops to the initial value. A sawtooth wave is used as the time base for scanning circuits in a cathode-ray tube.

SC stars

Stars which appear to be intermediate in type between S stars and carbon stars (C/O ratio near unity).

Scalar

Any quantity that has only magnitude as opposed to both magnitude and direction. For example mass is scalar quantity. By convention in physics the word speed is a scalar quantity, having only magnitude, while the word velocity is used to denote both the speed and the direction of the motion and is thus a *vector* quantity.

Scalar field

A field of energy generated by scalar particles. These hypothesized particles have no intrinsic spin. All known elementary particles have some intrinsic spin; thus scalar particles and scalar fields are theoretical to date.

Scalar quantity

A physical quantity, which is described completely by its magnitude, is called a scalar quantity.

Scalar-tensor theory

A class of theories of gravity more complex than Einstein's theory, general relativity. The best known scalar-tensor theory is the Brans-Dicke theory. In some scalar-tensor theories, the gravitational constant is not constant, as it is in general relativity.

Scale factor

A measure of changing distances in cosmology. The distance between any two galaxies, for example, is proportional to the scale factor, which is always increasing in an expanding Universe. If the scale factor doubles in size, then the distance between any two galaxies doubles.

Scale height

The mean distance of a group of stars from the Galactic plane. In general, old stars have larger scale heights than young ones. The height at which a given parameter changes by a factor e. For example, an atmospheric scale height of 100 km means that the value at 100 km is $1/e$ the value at the surface.

Scale invariance

S physical system is said to exhibit scale-invariance if its appearance remains unchanged (in a statistical sense, and to within simple readjustments of the units of measurements) when its scales of length energy or other variables are multiplied by a common factor.

Scale length

A measure of the size of a physical system or region of space.

Scale-invariant

The most inflationary models predict that the spectrum of density perturbations is nearly scale-invariant, meaning essentially that each wavelength has the same strength. This spectrum is also called the Harrison-Zeldovich spectrum, named for two astrophysicists who proposed the spectrum a decade before inflation was invented.

Scale-limited

A measuring instrument is said to be scale-limited if the experimental uncertainty in that instrument is smaller than the smallest division readable on its scale. Therefore the experimental uncertainty is taken to be half the smallest readable increment on the scale.

Scaler

An electronic instrument for counting radiation induced pulses from radiation detectors such as a Geiger-Muller tube.

Scaling

The phenomenon observed in deep inelastic scattering, and predicted by James Bjorken, whereby the structure functions which describe the shape of the nucleon depend not on the energy or momentum involved in the reaction, but on some dimensionless ratio of the two. The structure functions are hence independent of any dimensional scale. In scattering experiments, the property whereby the likelihood of a reaction depends not so much on the amount of energy transferred to the target as on the ratio between energy transferred and momentum transferred.

Scandium

A lightweight silvery element. It is found in minute amounts in over 800 minerals, often associated with lanthanoids. Scandium is used in high-intensity lights and in electronic devices.

Scattering

The 'spreading out' of a beam of radiation as it passes through matter, reducing the energy moving in the original direction. Depending on the circumstances, scattering can follow any combination of three processes as the radiation interacts with matter particles - reflection (elastic scattering), absorption followed by re-radiation (inelastic or Compton scattering), and diffraction. Thus sunlight is scattered (or diffused) as it passes through cloud and dust in the atmosphere. However, even perfectly clear air scatters sunlight, making the sky color blue - high frequencies are scattered more than low frequencies. The process whereby light is absorbed and reemitted in all directions, with essentially no change in frequency. Scattering by free electrons was the dominant source of opacity in the early Universe.

Scattering matrix

The S-matrix relates the incoming and out-going states of elementary particles during interactions and scattering experiments. The mathematical structure and properties of the S-matrix has received considerable attention.

Schmidt camera

Telescopic camera incorporating an internal corrective lens or plate that compensates for optical defects and chromatic faults in the main mirror. The system was invented by Bernhard Schmidt.

Schmidt plates

Photographic plates obtained with a Schmidt telescope, which is a type of telescope with a particularly large field of view.

Schmidt telescope

(a) A telescope with a spherical primary mirror and a thin refractive corrector plate with a complex, non-spherical shape. Very wide-field performance for surveys.

(b) A type of reflecting telescope (more accurately, a large camera) in which the coma produced by a spherical concave mirror is compensated for by a thin correcting lens placed at the opening of the telescope tube. The Schmidt has a usable field of 0°.6.

Scholastics

Adherents to the philosophy and cosmology of Aristotle. Their dominance in the universities, which had been founded largely to study Aristotle, constituted an obstacle to acceptance of the Copernican system advocated by Kepler and Galileo.

Schottky (pickup, signal, bands)

Schottky pickups are beam detectors, like BPM's, which are tuned to be sensitive to the revolution frequency of the circulating beam as well as the revolution frequency harmonics. If the signal from a Schottky pickup is looked at via a spectrum analyzer, the momentum spread and tunes can be measured by looking at the width of the Schottky bands and by looking at the amplitude of the revolution harmonic sidebands.

Schottky barrier

A metal to semiconductor interface without any insulation layer produces an energy barrier in the semiconductor which can be used like a diode.

Schrödinger equation

Equation governing the evolution of probability waves in quantum mechanics.

(a) A quantum-mechanical wave equation describing the nonrelativistic motion of a particle or system of particles under the influence of forces. The solutions to Schrödinger's equation yield the wave function describing the system (particle, atom, molecule). This is the fundamental equation in nonrelativistic quantum mechanics.

(b) The equation that describes the propagation of the waves associated with subatomic particles. In a more general context it describes the time evolution of the state of a quantum system. (c) The equation from quantum theory that tells how to calculate the effects of the forces on the particles, It is the quantum theory equivalent of Newton's second law.

Schuster mechanism

A scattering mechanism in the continuum, which under certain conditions can yield emission lines in the spectrum even under the assumption of LTE. It is the modifica- tion of the emergent radiation, for a given temperature distribution. by variations in the ratio of pure absorption to scattering opacity.

Schwarzschild black hole

A nonrotating, spherically symmetric black hole derived from Karl Schwarzchild's 1916 exact solution to Einstein's vacuum field equations.

Schwarzschild filling factor

Ratio of the actual density to the limiting value for a system.

Schwarzschild radius

(a) The critical radius, according to the general theory of relativity, at which a massive body becomes a black hole, i.e., at which light is unable to escape to infinity. $R_s = 2GM / c^2$; R_s for Sun, 2.5 km; R_s for Earth, 0.9 cm.

(b) The event horizon of a spherical black hole; the critical radius from which light is unable to escape to infinity. The Schwarzschild radius of a star of solar mass is 2.5 km.

(c) The "surface" of a black hole, within which the strength of gravity is so strong that light cannot escape. The Schwarzschild radius is proportional to the mass of the black hole and would be about 2 miles for a black hole of the mass of our sun. Black holes were first "theoretically" discovered by Karl Schwarzschild in 1917.

(d) The effective radius of a spherically symmetric black hole, r_g: $(2GM/c^2)^{1/2}$: 3(M/M) km. The gravitational redshift of radiation emitted at this radius is infinite to an external observer. Photons cannot escape from a black hole to the outside world from within this radius. The Schwarzschild radius is therefore the smallest physical size which an astronomical object of mass M can have. Matter falling within the radius r_g inevitably collapses into the singularity.

Schwarzschild singularity

The centre of a black hole. According to Einstein's theory of general relativity, the entire mass of a black hole is concentrated at a point at its centre, the "singularity". It is believed that quantum mechanical effects, not included in the theory, would cause the mass to spread out over a tiny but nonzero region, thus preventing an infinite density of matter and doing away with the singularity.

Schwarzschild solution

Solution to the equations of general relativity for a spherical distribution of matter; one implication of this solution is the possible existence of black holes.

Science

(a) Systematic study of Nature, based upon the presumption that the Universe is based upon rationally intelligible principles and that its behavior can therefore be predicted by subjecting observational data to logical analysis.

(b) Science can be defined as a self-correcting way to get knowledge about the natural universe, plus the body of knowledge obtained that way. It is both a method and the resulting understanding and knowledge. The method requires making models to explain phenomena, testing them experimentally, and revising them until they work. The goal of science is understanding. Once part of the natural world is understood, it may be possible to develop applications of the new knowledge. The process of developing such applications is properly called technology, not science.

Scientific law

A relationship between quantities, usually described by an equation in the physical sciences; is more important and describes a wider range of phenomena than a scientific principle.

Scientific notation

A positive number expressed in the form of $M \times 10^n$ in which M is a number between 1 and 10 and n is an integral power of 10.

Scientific principle

A relationship between quantities concerned with a specific, or narrow range of observations and behavior.

Scintillation

(a) In radio astronomy, a rapid oscillation in the detected intensity of radiation emitted by stellar radio sources, caused by disturbances in ionized gas at some point between the source and the Earth's surface (usually in the Earth's own upper atmosphere).

(b) Variations in the brightness of starlight (i.e., "twinkling") caused by turbulent strata very high in Earth's atmosphere. Scintillation increases with distance from the turbulent zone.

Scintillation counter

An instrument that detects and measures gamma radiation by counting the light flashes (scintillations) induced by the radiation.

Scintillator

A detector for high-energy photons such as gamma-rays. The impact of a gamma-ray causes a burst of light which can be observed with a PMT.

Sco-cen association

An association of very young stars about 200 pc distant in the Gould Belt. The most luminous member is a B star of $M_v = -4.9$.

Scorpius OB1

An extremely young association of OB stars in Scorpius about 2 kpc distant.

Scorpius X-1

A compact eclipsing X-ray source about 9000 light years distant in the constitution scorpios. It is the brightest X-ray source in the sky (besides the Sun) and was discovered in 1962. It has day-to-day variations (period about 0.78 days) of as much as 1 mag; it also has optical and radio counterparts but no correlation has been found among the flares observed at the three different wavelengths. It is a thermal X-ray source, probably associated with a rotating collapsed star surrounded by an extensive envelope. Tentative optical identification with the 13th mag blue variable V818 Sco. The spectrum of Sco X-1 is similar to that of an old nova. (3U 1617-15)

Scott effect

A selection effect in the study of the magnitude-redshift relation in cosmology. It was pointed out by Elizabeth Scott in 1957 that at great distances only the most luminous clusters of galaxies would be visible, and this fact would introduce a bias into the data.

SCR

Silicon Controlled Rectifier. Also called a thyristor. A semiconductor rectifier whose forward anode-cathode current is controlled by a signal applied to a third electrode. The SCR will latch into a forward bias. Widely used in power supplies throughout the laboratory.

SCR (save/compare/restore)

A program which reads the current value of D/A settings, A/D readbacks, nominal values and alarm states and loads this information into a semipermanent buffer residing in the VAX. The program, currently found on page D1, can also read the saved values and display them on the console TV, load them back into the devices, or compare differences between two save files.

Screen image editor (SIE)

A primary applications program, currently found on D10, which allows editing of the TV screen and touch panel on behalf of another applications program.

Sculptor

A faint constellation in the southern sky. 2. A dwarf galaxy that orbits the Milky Way in the constellation Sculptor. It is 255,000 light-years from the Galactic centre.

Sculptor group

The nearest group of galaxies to the Local Group, 4 to 10 million light-years away. Its brightest member is the beautiful edge-on spiral NGC 253.

Scuti stars

A group of pulsating variable stars of spectral class A-F with regular periods of 1-3 hours and with small variations in amplitude. They lie in the lower part of the Cepheid instability strip.

SDA

Sequenced Data Acquisition. Used to gather data about a shot from start of shot set up to end of low beta squeeze. Runs on the VAX and saves information to a file to be reviewed later.

SDB

Subdwarf B-type stars with very broad and shallow Balmer lines; fewer lines of the Balmer series are visible than for normal dwarfs.

SDLC

Synchronous Data Link Control. A data link communication protocol developed by IBM and used to control a serial data link (or SDLC link).

SDLC fiber optic link

Serial Data Link Controller. The Linac secondaries and Tevatron QPMs use an IBM serial link protocol which transmits and receives data along an external fiber-optic link.

SDO

Subdwarf O stars showing few very broad and shallow Balmer lines and a very strong He II 4686 line.

Search and secure

The method of searching an accelerator enclosure in a logical fashion and resetting safety system interlocks to ensure that no personnel are in the enclosure before turning on power supplies and sending beam through that enclosure.

Second

A unit of time defined as the duration of 9,192,631,770 periods of the radiation corresponding to the transition between the two hyperfine levels of the ground state of the cesium-133 atom. In 1967 the General Conference of Weights and Measures (CGPM) adopted this as the tentative definition of the second in SI units, replacing the ephemeris second, which remains in the IAU system of astronomical constants.

Second law of motion

Since Galileo came up with the first law of motion, this is not really Newton's second law. Also, since it is apparently the definition of force, it is presumably not a law in the sense of what is usually meant by a law of nature. So maybe it should be called "Newton's one and only definition of force no pictures or accounts of which can be reproduced without express written permission of the NFL.

Second law of photoelectric emission

The kinetic energy of photoelectrons is independent of the intensity of the incident light.

Second law of thermodynamics

It is not possible for an engine to transfer heat from one body to another at a higher temperature unless work is done on the engine.

(a) A physical law formulated in the nineteenth century and stating that any isolated system becomes more disordered in time.

(b) Law stating that total entropy always increases.

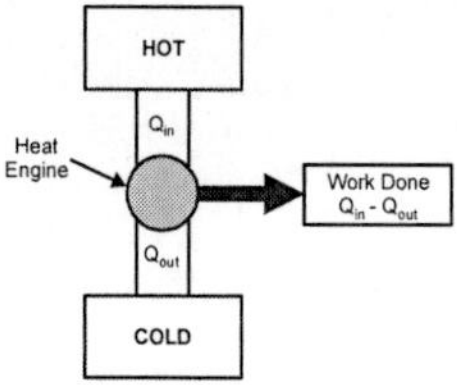

Second parameter

The color of a globular cluster's horizontal branch is determined largely by its metallicity: all other things being equal, the more metal-poor a cluster, the bluer its horizontal branch. However, all other things are not always equal, because globulars with similar metallicities sometimes have different horizontal-branch colors, so a second parameter must be responsible. Searle and Zinn speculated that the second parameter was age and said that all globulars had not formed at the same time.

Second quantization

This goes beyond the quantum theory of Heisenberg and Schrödinger by applying the act of quantization a second time. In this way, matter and energy fields can themselves become quantized. The quantum excitations of these fields are the elementary particles.

Second superstring revolution

Period in the development of string theory beginning around 1995 in which some nonperturbative aspects of the theory began to be understood.

Second's pendulum

A simple pendulum whose time period on the surface of earth is 2 seconds is called the second's pendulum.

Secondary

A transformer output winding in which the current is due to inductive coupling with another winding called the primary.

Secondary applications (SA)

An operating program for which console control has been relinquished. Typically an SA continues to update a Lexidata or storage scope with fresh data, although the console is also being used for other purposes.

Secondary axis

Any line other than the principal axis drawn through the centre of curvature of a mirror or the optical centre of a lens.

Secondary coil

Part of a transformer, a coil of wire in which the voltage of the original alternating current in the primary coil is stepped up or down by way of electromagnetic induction.

Secondary cosmic rays

Atomic fragments mainly muons produced by collisions between primary cosmic rays and the molecules in Earth's atmosphere.

Secondary emission

Emission of electrons as a result of the bombardment of an electrode by high-velocity electrons.

Secondary mirror

The second reflecting surface encountered by the light in a telescope. The secondary is usually suspended in the beam and therefore obstructs part of the primary.

Secondary particles

Those particles that are produced by hitting a target with the primary proton beam from the accelerator.

Secondary station

Same as a Linac secondary. It provides local control and monitoring for a given Linac station.

Second's pendulum

A simple pendulum whose time period on the surface of earth is 2 seconds.

Secular

In astronomy, gradual, taking aeons to accomplish.

Secular acceleration

Apparent acceleration of the Moon and Sun across the sky, caused by extremely gradual reduction in speed of the Earth's rotation (one 50-millionth of a second per day).

Secular change

A continuous, nonperiodic change in one of the attributes of the states of a system. Often, a change in an orbit due to dissipation of energy.

Secular equilibrium

A state of parent-daughter equilibrium which is achieved when the half-life of the parent is much longer than the half-life of the daughter. In this case, if the two are not separated, the daughter will eventually be decaying at the same rate at which it is being produced. At this point, both parent and daughter will decay at the same rate until the parent is essentially exhausted.

Secular instability

Instability caused by the dissipation of energy.

Secular stability

The condition in which the equilibrium configuration of a system is stable over long periods of time.

Seed nuclei

Nuclei from which other nuclei are synthesized.

Seeing

It describes the blurring of a stellar (point-like) image due to turbulence in the Earth's atmosphere, both at high altitudes and within the telescope dome. Seeing estimates are often given in terms of the full-width in arcseconds of the image at the points where the intensity has fallen to half its peak value. The typical value at a good site is a little better than 1 arcsecond.

Segmented mirrors

A large mirror construction technique in which many smaller elements are built and then actively controlled to conform to the shape of the required large mirror.

Segmented wire ion chamber (SWIC)

A SWIC resembles a wire spark chamber consisting of three parallel wire planes. A plane of horizontal signal wires, a high voltage plane, and a plane of vertical signal wires. The wires are connected to an integrating and scanning circuit capable of holding, scanning, and dumping the ionization current collected by the wire when the proton beam passes through the device. Its purpose is to give a profile of the beam.

Selected areas

262 small (75' square) regions of the sky in which magnitudes, spectral types, and luminosity classes of stars have been accurately measured and which have served as standards for magnitude systems.

Selective absorption

The reddening of starlight in passing through fine particles of interstellar dust.

Selectivity

The property of a tuned circuit that discriminates between signal voltages of different frequencies.

S-Electron

An orbital electron whose *l* quantum number is zero.

Selenium

A metalloid element existing in several allotropic forms. The common gray metallic allotrope is very light-sensitive and is used in photocells, solar cells, some glasses, and in xerography. The red allotrope is unstable and reverts to the gray form under normal conditions.

Selenocentric

With reference to, or pertaining to, the centre of the Moon.

Self-absorption

Reduction in relative intensity in the central portion of spectral lines resulting from selective absorption by a cooler shell surrounding the hot source.

Self-consistent field approach

An approach in which the density distribution and state of motion in a system are determined so as to be self-consistent with the force field (e.g., gravitational or electromagnetic) arising from the system itself.

Self-inductance

The ratio of the induced emf across a coil to the rate of change of current in the coil.

Self-organisation

Spontaneous emergence of order, arising when certain parameters built in a system reach critical values.

SEM (grid)

The diagnostic devices used to measure beam position in the Antiproton source transport lines. SEM's are close relatives of multiwires as found in the 750 keV, 200 MeV, and 8 GeV lines as well as Switchyard SWIC's. The grids crossed x,y 10 micron titanium strips with either 1.5 or 3.0 mm grid spacing. The electronics includes modified up-based SWIC scanners as used in the fixed target experimental areas.

Semi-conductor

A material like silicon or germanium in which the valence band and the conduction band are separated by a small (forbidden) energy gap. Such materials have some of the properties of a good electrical conductor - in which the energy gap is zero - and some of the properties of an insulator - in which the gap is very large.

Semi-convection

The partial convective mixing that takes place in a convectively unstable region where stability can be attained by the results of the mixing before the region is completely mixed.

Semi-diameter

The angle at the observer subtended by the equatorial radius of the Sun, Moon, or a planet.

Semi-forbidden lines

Spectral lines from "semiforbidden" transitions, i.e., those whose transition probabilities are perhaps 1 in 10^6 instead of about 1 in 10^9 for forbidden transitions. One bracket - e.g., [C III] - is used to indicate semiforbidden lines.

Semi-major axis

Half the length of the major axis of an ellipse; a standard element used to describe an elliptical orbit.

Semi-minor axis

Half the length of the minor axis of an ellipse; a standard element used to describe an elliptical orbit.

Semi-regular variable

A class of giant and supergiant pulsating stars of spectral class M, K, N, R, or S with a periodic (or semiperiodic) light curve of varying amplitude. Betelgeuse is one.

SEND button

A button at the lower left-hand corner of the keypad at a console terminal. It provides interrupt capability for the AEOLUS screen. Nowadays this button is blue and is labeled RESET.

Sense

One of two opposite directions describable by the motion of a point, line, or surface.

Sense switch

This is an external device (generally a set of switches) which is capable of modifying program flow or control by the orientation of the switches. For ACNET consoles the sense switches are areas defined on the touch panel screen which when activated modify the program function or display in some way. A typical use of the switches at a console terminal might be to modify the format (A/D, D/A, etc.) Of the data displayed on the TV screen, or modify the characteristics of the keypad interrupts.

Separatrix

In a phase space diagram, the boundary which divides the stable beam region from the unstable beam region.

Septum

A magnetic or electrostatic device used to deflect charged particles along one of two paths. Typically, a solid metal sheet or plane of wires separates a region with and electric or magnetic field from a region of no field. Beam entering the first region is deflected while beam entering the second region is not.

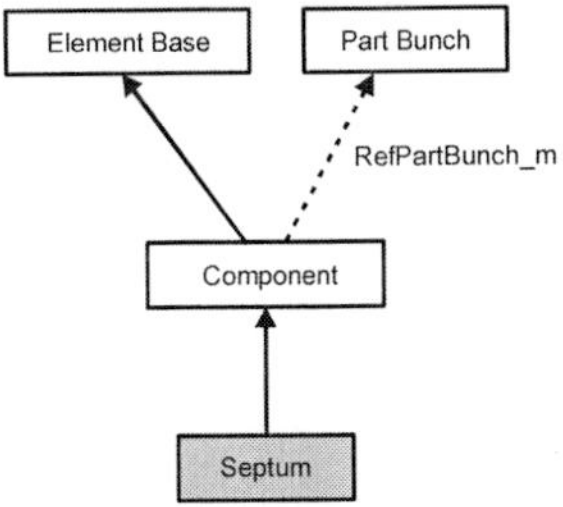

Septum, electrostatic

A device which splits the proton beam into two beams. It consists of a chamber bisected by a row of fine wires. On one or both sides of the wires there exists an electrostatic field(s) which serves to separate the two beams.

Sequencer

That part of an electronic system responsible for the accurate phasing of time-critical events such as CCD clocking and readout.

Serial

Data transmitted one bit at a time. Many of the links at Fermilab are serial links. Normally this data must be reconstructed into a parallel format before it can be used by a computer.

Serial data link

Also SDLC link. A fiber-optic data link that connects the primary and secondary microcomputers in the linac control system. Data is transmitted on a 1 mhz Manchester-encoded clock under SDLC protocol.

Serial register

The final (horizontal) row of a CCD in which the controlling electrodes are arranged at right angles to those on the rest of the CCD. This enables charges coupled onto this row to be transferred in single-file through the CCD output amplifier.

Series

For circuit elements, elements that are connected so that they have the same electrical current conducted through them.

Series circuit

An electric circuit in which the components are arranged to provide a single conducting path for current.

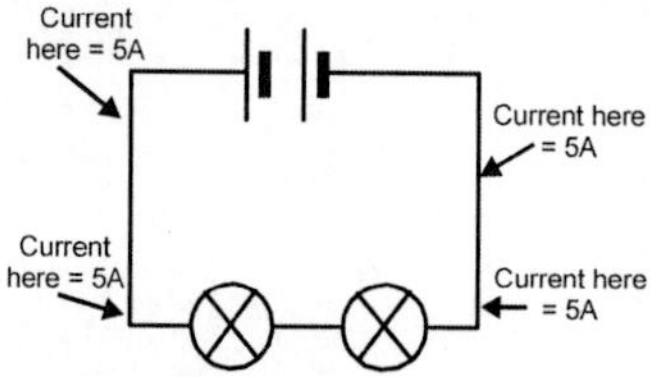

Series resonance

A condition in which the impedance of a series circuit containing resistance, inductance, and capacitance is equal to the resistance of the circuit and the voltage across the circuit is in phase with the current.

Series SCR

The SCR which bypasses Tevatron current around the dump resistor except under ramp dump conditions.

Serpentis

A G0 V star almost identical to the Sun in its energy distribution.

Set point

In the context of feedback systems it is the nominal value toward which the system strives. In a controls context it is the D/A value of any parameter when an applications program is entered.

Setdat

A program present on all of the front-ends which organizes lists of D/A setting values before they are sent to the hardware.

Seti

The Search for Extraterrestrial Intelligence, by using radiotelescopes to listen for signals transmitted by intelligent alien beings.

Sextans dwarf

A dwarf companion to the Milky Way. Discovered by computer in 1990, Sextans lies about 300 kpc from the Galactic centre.

Sextant

Instrument employed to measure the elevation of astronomical objects above the horizon. Based upon an arc equal to a sixth of a circle, sextants are more compact and easier to use than are the quadrants that preceded them.

Sextupole

A magnet with six pole faces, used for correcting magnetic field errors.

Seyfert galaxy

(a) A type of spiral galaxy first discovered by Karl Seyfert in the 1940s. The central region of a Seyfert galaxy is distinguished by powerful radiation, much of it focused into narrow frequencies.

(b) One of a small class of galaxies (many of which are spirals) of very high luminosity and very blue continuum radiation with small, intensely bright nuclei whose spectra show strong, broad, high-excitation emission lines probably caused by discrete clouds moving at velocities that are higher than the escape velocity. Seyferts possess many of the properties of QSOs, such as the ultraviolet excess of the continuum, the wide emission lines, and the strong infrared luminosity.

Seyfert's sextet

A compact group of galaxies surrounding NGC 6027. It has both spiral and irregular members.

S-factor
A nuclear cross-section factor measured in keV-barns.

Shadow matter
Theoretical classes of particles, their existence intimated by supersymmetry, theory, that participate in few if any of the four known fundamental forces. Planets, stars, and galaxies made of shadow matter could conceivably exist in the same space and time we occupy without our sensing their presence.

Shane-wirtanen catalogue
A catalogue of all galaxies brighter than seventeenth magnitude (a measure of brightness). There are about a million galaxies in the Shane-Wirtanen catalogue.

Shapley-ames catalogue
A catalogue of galaxies brighter than thirteenth magnitude, completed in 1932. There are about 1200 galaxies in this catalogue.

Shear
A stress applied to a body in the plane of one of its faces.

Shear modulus
The ratio of shear stress to shear strain (scalar; n/m^2).

Shear strain
The ratio of the amount of deformation of the side of a body to the length of the side.

Shear strain (scalar)
The ratio of the horizontal distance a sheared face moves to the height of the object.

Shear stress
The restoring force developed per unit area when deforming force acts tangentially to the surface of body producing change in the shape of the body without any change in volume.

Sheath
The boundary layer of charged particles between a plasma and its surrounding material.

Shell star
A hot main-sequence star, usually of spectral class B-F, whose spectrum shows bright emission lines presumed to be due to a gaseous ring or shell surrounding the star.

Shield
A mass of attenuating material used to prevent or reduce the passage of radiation or particles.

Shielding
A protective barrier, usually a dense material, which reduces the passage of radiation from radioactive materials to the surroundings.

Shift plot
A plot done at the end of each shift and posted in the crew chiefs log. The plot is an indication of overall productivity of the accelerator. For fixed target mode Tev accelerated intensity is plotted over the duration of the shift. For collider mode luminosity and the pbar stack are plotted. Any downtime is also indicated on the shift plot.

Shift save
A methodical saving of pertinent accelerator parameters, rf curves and ramped devices. The save is done according to a checklist once every 24 hours during accelerator operation. In the event of a failure of the accelerator, the last running conditions can be recalled from the shift save to restore the accelerator to running condition.

Shock
A sudden transition at the front of fast flow of plasma or gas, when the flow moves too fast for the undisturbed gas to flow out of the way. Also occurs when a steady fast flow hits an obstacle.

Shock wave
A sharp change in the pressure, temperature, and density of a fluid which develops when the velocity of the fluid begins to exceed the velocity of sound.

Shooting star
The streak of light in the sky produced by the firey entry of a meteoroid into the Earth's atmosphere;

also the glowing meteoroid itself. The term "fireball" is sometimes used for a meteor approaching the brightness of Venus; the term "bolide" for one approaching the brightness of the full Moon.

Short circuit

A circuit that does not function because charge is given a low-resistance "shortcut" path that it can follow, instead of the path that makes it do something useful.

Short sample limit

This is the figure of merit for a superconducting magnet. It is the highest field possible just before the critical magnetic field of the superconducting wire is exceeded.

Short scale

The cosmological distance scale which uses a Hubble constant of approximately 100 km/s/Mpc.

Shot noise

Noise, or fluctuations in the current of a detector, due to the fact that the current is carried not by a smooth fluid, but by a large number of individual electrons (cf. wave noise; correlator).

Shower (also called Electro- magnetic Cascade Shower)

Shower can create photons by interacting with a medium. In a similar way, photons can create electrons and their antiparticles, positrons, by interacting with a medium. So, imagine a very high-energy electron, of the sort used at SLAC, impinging on some material. The electron can set photons into motion and these photons can, in turn, set electrons and positrons into motion, and this process can continue to repeat. One high-energy electron can set thousands of particles into motion. Albert Einstein's famous relation governing the equivalence of matter and energy ($E = mc^2$) governs this process — namely, matter (electrons and positrons) can be creased from pure energy and vice versa. The particle creation process only stops when the energy runs out.

Shunt impedance

Technically, an impedance in parallel with an electrical circuit. In this application, the ratio of the square of the electric field strength on the axis of an RF cavity to the power dissipated per meter of length.

Shunt SCR

The SCR which bypasses a Tevatron power supply from the circuit in the event of a ramp dump or fast bypass.

Shuttered kicker

Kicker magnets are used to put the injected antiprotons from the Debuncher onto the Accumulator injection orbit and to kick out bunches of p-'s from the Accumulator towards the Main Ring. Since there is almost always circulating beam in the Accumulator during stacking or unstacking operations, a magnetic shield, or shutter, is placed between the circulating beam and the beam to be kicked, thereby shielding the circulating particles from the effects of the kickers. These shutters are physically moved out of the beam once the kicker pulse is completed. The use of these kickers would be impossible were it not for the the use of high dispersion regions, which permit radial separation of the circulating beam as a function of momentum. Both the injection and extraction kickers are located in straight section 20.

SI

Stands for "Systeme International", the international system of units, which forms the basis for other recognized units, such as those of the BS. The SI is a metric system, whose fundamental units for mechancis are the meter, the kilogram, and the second. Derived units include the radian, newton, the joule, the watt, the hertz, and the pascal.

Sibling

A device which is logically or sequentially related to other devices; for example, two consecutive horizontal correction dipoles.

Side lobe
In radio astronomy, a component of the reception pattern of an antenna away from the main beam, representing a direction in which the antenna is sensitive when it should be insensitive.

Sideband
A range of frequencies contained in a modulated carrier wave, either above or below the unmodulated frequency (hence upper and lower sidebands). The existence of sidebands is a consequence of the modulation process. For instance, in an amplitude modulated wave, if the carrier frequency is f_c and the modulating signal frequency is f_s, then the modulated wave has three components of frequency $f_c - f_s$, f_c, and $f_c + f_s$.

Sidereal
In astronomy, relating to the period of time based on the apparent rotation of the stars, and therefore equivalent to the rotation of the body from which the observation is made. Thus on Earth a sidereal year is 365.256 times the sidereal day of 23 hours, 56 minutes and 4 seconds.

Sidereal day
The length of time ($23^h56^m4^s.091$) between two successive meridian transits of the vernal equinox (cf. mean solar day). Because of precession the sidereal day is about 0.0084 second shorter than the period of rotation of Earth relative to a fixed direction ($23^h56^m4^s.099$).

Sidereal hour angle
Angular distance on the celestial sphere measured westward along the celestial equator from the catalog equinox to the hour circle passing through the celestial object. It is equal to 360° minus right ascension in degrees.

Sidereal period
The time it takes for a planet or satellite to make one complete circuit of its orbit (360°) relative to the stars. Earth's sidereal period (or sidereal year) is equal to 365.2564 mean solar days.

Sidereal time
The measure of time defined by the apparent diurnal motion of the catalog equinox; hence a measure of the rotation of the Earth with respect to the stars rather than the Sun.

Siderite
An iron (or iron and nickel) meteorite. Siderites comprise about 6 percent of known falls.

Siderolite
A stony iron meteorite. Siderolites comprise less than 2 percent of known falls. (lit.: "sky stone")

Sido
Generally used as a friendly derision for any person that is extremly knowledgable about computers and computer systems. Sidos consider it a point of honor to be known by such a title. Such knowledge extends way beyond that gained from everyday work usage or study. There are many computer professionals that work with computers every day that do not qualify for SIDO status. The level of computer edification needed to qualify someone as a SIDO can only be had by those who posses a passionate interest that borders on the fanatical in anything to do with computers. Sidos appear as true wizards able to do things that others thought difficult or impossible to accomplish. Sidos willingly and often spend all hours of the night exploring new systems and devices, communicating among themselves in a language totally foreign to anyone who is not a SIDO.

Siemens
The derived S.I. unit of electrical conductance, equal to the conductance of an element that has a resistance of 1 ohm, also written as ohm-1.

Sigma
In astronomy, a quantitative measure of the random speeds of stars in a collection of stars. If the stars were molecules of gas, darting this way and that, then sigma would be directly related to the temperature of the system. A high sigma is analogous to a high temperature. Sigma is also called the velocity dispersion.

Signal band

The wavelength interval within which a feature (e.g., the 21-cm line) is measured (cf. comparison band).

Signal-to-noise ratio

The ratio of the amount of intelligible meaning in a signal to the amount of background noise.

Signature

A new particle will have some characteristic behavior in a detector that allows it to be recognized. Particles that decay into others do so in a unique way that is different for every kind of particle. Knowing the properties of the particle allows us to calculate how it will decay. The features that allow a new particle to be identified in a detector are called its signature.

Significant figures

The only digits in a number that are meaningful. The rightmost significant figure is called the "least significant figure" and represents the best estimate of the precision. There is disagreement about the meaning of the most significant figure.

Silicon

(a) Element with atomic number fourteen and the sixth most common metal in the Universe. It is produced by high-mass stars that explode.

(b) A hard brittle gray metalloid element. It has the electronic configuration of neon with four additional outer electrons; i.e., $[Ne]3s^2 3p^2$. Silicon accounts for 27.7% of the mass of the Earth's crust and occurs in a wide variety of silicates with other metals, clays, micas, and sand, which is largely SiO_2. It is used widely in semiconductor applications.

Silicon burning

The end of the line for a high-mass star, silicon burning creates iron and other elements of similar mass and presages a supernova.

Silicon controlled rectifier

A rectifier having the ability to begin conducting at an arbitrary phase of an AC current cycle. A normal rectifier conducts for 180° of phase (Zener diodes excepted). An SCR conducts only after it has received a firing pulse, then continues to conduct until the polarity changes, so one can selectively chose to conduct on any phase F, such that 0<F.

Silicon vertex detector

This is a silicon based detector similar to that in a digital camera. It provides precision particle tracking by connecting the dots due to a particle passing through its multiple layers. This allows one to reconstruct any vertex from which two or more tracks emerge. Such a vertex, if outside the beam collision region, indicates the position of a particle decay.

Silver

(a) Element with atomic number 47. It is produced by both the r-process and the s-process, but more by the former.

(b) A transition metal that occurs native and as the sulfide and chloride. It is extracted as a by-product in refining copper and lead ores. Silver darkens in air due to the formation of silver sulphide. It is used in coinage alloys, tableware, and jewelry. Silver compounds are used in photography.

Simple harmonic motion

Take a rock, tie it to a string, and twirl it in a horizontal circle at a constant rate. Do this at sunrise or sunset next to a wall such that the stone's shadow is projected on the wall by the sun shining brightly from a clear horizon. The shadow the rock makes on the wall will go back and forth in simple harmonic motion.

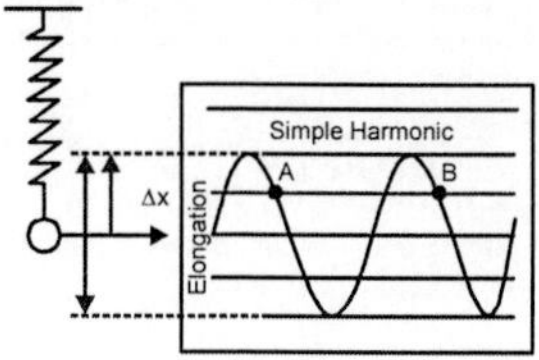

Simple harmonic oscillator

An oscillator that oscillates in simple harmonic motion is a simple harmonic oscillator. A simple harmonic oscillator has the property that the magnitude of its restoring force is proportional to the displacement of the system from equilibrium. (When this is the case, the force is said to be elastic.) The restoring force is therefore greatest when the system is farthest from equilibrium. This also means, from Newton's second law of motion, the acceleration towards equilibrium is greatest when the system is farthest from equilibrium. The farthest distance from equilibrium is called the amplitude of the motion.

Simple pendulum

A heavy point mass (actually a small metallic ball), suspended by a light inextensible string from a frictionless rigid support is called a simple pendulum. A simple pendulum is a simple machine based on the effect of gravity.

Simulations

In science, simulations of physical systems with a computer.

Sinc pulse

An RF pulse shaped like Sin(x)/x.

Singularity

(a) Anomaly in space-time at which a state not in accord with the classical laws of physics obtains. An example is a black hole; another is the moment of the big bang.

(b) A point of infinite curvature of space where the equations of general relativity break down. A black hole represents a singularity; so, perhaps, did the Universe at the first moment of time.

(c) A place, either in space or in time at which some quantity, such as density, becomes infinite. The laws of physics cannot describe infinite quantities and, in fact, physicists believe that infinities do not exist in nature. All singularities, such as the Schwarzschild singularity, are therefore probably the artifacts of inadequate theories rather than real properties of nature.

(d) A point in space-time at which the space-time curvature and other physical quantities become infinite and the laws of physics break down.

(e) If the standard big bang theory is extrapolated all the way back to time zero, one reaches an instant of infinite density, infinite pressure, and infinite temperature - an instant that is frequently called the initial singularity. This singularity is sometimes said to mark the beginning of time, but it is more realistic to recognize that an extrapolation to infinite density cannot be trusted.

(f) A region of space-time where physical variables become infinite, such as density, tidal forces, pressure, and world line of observer terminates; a bad place to be.

Singularity theorems

In astronomy and cosmology, mathematical proofs that show the conditions under which a mass will gravitationally collapse to form a singularity. The singularity theorems of cosmology, proved in the 1960s, indicate that the current behavior of the Universe, together with the laws of general relativity without quantum mechanical corrections, require that at some definite time in the past the Universe was compressed to a state of zero size and infinite density, called a singularity. The laws of physics break down at a singularity and cannot be used to predict anything during or before the singularity occurred.

Sink

In general, a region where energy is given up, in contrast to a source, where energy is released.

Sirius (CMA)

(a) The brightest star in the night sky. It is a white, A-type star that lies just 8.6 light-years from Earth in the constellation Canis Major. Orbiting the main star (officially called Sirius

A) is a faint white dwarf, Sirius B. Sirius A is the nearest A-type main-sequence star to Earth; Sirius B is the nearest white dwarf to Earth.

(b) Also called Dog Star. An A1 V star 2.7 pc distant - the (apparently) brightest star in the sky. Its companion (Sirius B) is a white dwarf of about 0.96 *M* but only about 0.03 *R*. Period 49.9 years.

Skew correction element

An n-pole correction element which is rotated by an angle of 180/n degrees. (Note that in this scheme, a vertical dipole is actually a skew horizontal dipole.)

Skew dipole

Dipole magnet rotated from the horizontal plane by some fraction of 90 degrees so that it bends the beam both horizontally and vertically.

Skylight

The faint, diffuse glow of the night sky. It comes from four main sources : airglow, diffuse Galactic light, Zodiacal light, and the light from these sources scattered by the troposphere.

SLAC

The acronym for the Stanford Linear Accelerator Centre at Stanford University in California, USA. It is distinguished by having a 2-mile-long linear accelerator in which electrons and positrons can be accelerated for subsequent injection into storage rings such as PEP, an e^+e^- collider which was commissioned in 1980. However, the most fascinating of SLAC's facilities is the novel SLC (Stanford Linear Collider), consisting of the old linear accelerator together with two new collider arcs.

Slepton

The supersymmetric partner of any of the leptons.

Slew

The relatively rapid motion of a telescope (under computer control) as it moves to point at a new position in the sky. Once at the new position the motion of the telescope returns to that required to cancel the effect of the Earth's rotation relative to the stars the sidereal rate.

Slope

In the world of graphs, slope refers to the rate of climb or descent of the curve on the graph. So, it is just like the slope you are familiar with if you are a skier. There are your bunny slopes and your expert slopes. The measure of slope is "rise over run", that is, vertical change (rise) divided by how far horizontally you went to get that vertical change (run). Now, "rise" does not necessarily refer to an increasing altitude; a negative "rise" is actually a fall. Thus for a positive slope you are either trudging uphill (if you are a cross-country skier) or taking the ski lift (if you are a downhill skier).

Slow nova

A nova whose light curve shows a much more gradual development - i.e., rise time of several days, maximum of several weeks, slower decline, amplitude only about 10 mag.

Slow spill

Ejection of the circulating beam from a circular accelerator over many turns (up to tens of thousands of turns or times of the order of a second). In modern synchrotrons slow spill is achieved by slowly adjusting the focusing field toward a betatron resonance so that the oscillations are stable for a steadily decreasing range of amplitudes until at the end of the spill no oscillation is stable.

Small magellanic cloud

The second largest, and the second nearest, of the galaxies that orbit the Milky Way. It lies in the southern sky, 190,000 light-years away.

Smart module

A relative term used to designate a module which can do some amount of internal data processing or error checking. All of the microprocessors, such as the HOG's, BPM's, QPM's, and Refrigerators, can do this, as well as many smaller units such as 080, 160, and 165 cards, etc.

S-matrix
The S-matrix relates the incoming and out-going states of elementary particles during interactions and scattering experiments. The mathematical structure and properties of the S-matrix has received considerable attention (also called the scattering matrix).

Smatter
The superpartners of the Standard Model particles. This book argues th at the experimental discovery of smatter will provide us with information that will be essential for gaining insights into the ultimate laws of nature, the primary theory.

Smeds module
Module in the MCR built by Jim Smedinghoff (Smeds) that allows computer enabling of 15 Hz beam for use by the linac steering program (L36).

Smooth space
A spatial region in which the fabric of space is flat or gently curved, with no pinches, ruptures, or creases of any kind.

Snapshot
In general terms, this refers to data taken at some specific time over a small time interval. The data obtained may or may not be representative of events over a longer time interval. A specific use is the Beam Position Monitor (BPM) data averaged over a number of turns and stored in a circular buffer. Another important use is for diagnosis of problems; for example, when the ramp trips a snapshot of the voltage-to-ground is taken and may be placed in a circular buffer to be analyzed at a later time.

Snell's law
The ratio of sin i to sin r is a constant and is equal to the refractive index of the second medium with respect to the first.

Snickers
A putative satellite galaxy of the Milky Way, reported in 1975. Its reality is in dispute.

Snowplow model
A sunspot model in which the expanding current sheath scoops up material like a snowplow, but discards all the accumulated matter when the magnetic field reverses.

Sodium
A soft reactive metal. It has the electronic configuration of a neon structure plus an additional outer 3s electron. Electronic excitation in flames or the familiar sodium lamps gives a distinctive yellow color arising from intense emission at the so called 'Sodium-D' line pair. The metal has a body-centreed structure.

Software
The programs, routines, etc. For use in a digital computer, as distinguished from the physical components (hardware) of the computer.

Software Documentation Memo (SDM or SODOM)
A publication distributed by the Controls group which is intended to clarify operational aspects of software usage. This is primarily used for descriptions of major software utilities, control system theory, and not for application program documentation.

Solar apex
A point on the celestial sphere lying in the constellation Hercules toward which the Sun and the solar system are moving with respect to the Local Standard of Rest at a rate of about 19.4 km per second (about 4.09 AU per year).

Solar atmosphere
The atmosphere of the Sun. An atmosphere is generally the outermost gaseous layers of a planet, natural satellite, or star. Only bodies with a strong gravitational pull can retain an atmosphere. Atmosphere is used to describe the outer layer of the Sun because it is relatively transparent at visible wavelengths. Parts of the solar atmosphere include the photosphere, chromosphere, and the corona.

Solar constant

(a) Mean radiation received from the Sun at the top level of Earth's atmosphere: 1.95 cal cm^{-2} min^{-1}.

(b) Energy received per cm^2 per second by a planet at r astronomical units from the Sun (equal to 1.39×10^6 ergs $cm^{-2}s^{-1}/r^2$).

Solar cycle

The 11-year period between maxima (or minima) of solar activity. Every 11 years the magnetic field of the Sun reverses polarity; hence the more basic period may be 22 years.

Solar energy

Is produced by nuclear fusion and comprises almost entirely electromagnetic radiation (particularly in the form of light and heat); particles are also radiated forming the solar wind.

Solar flare

Sudden and dramatic release of a huge burst of solar energy through a break in the Sun's chromosphere in the region of a sunspot. Effects on Earth include aurorae, magnetic storms and radio interference.

Solar limb

The apparent edge of the Sun as it is seen in the sky.

Solar mass

The amount of mass in the Sun, and the unit in which stellar and galactic masses are expressed.

Solar motion

The velocity of the Sun through space, relative to the Local Standard of Rest. The solar motion is U = -9 kilometers per second, V = +12 kilometers per second, and W = +7 kilometers per second.

Solar neutrino unit (snu)

1 SNU = 10^{-36} solar-neutrino captures per second per target atom.

Solar neutrinos

The reactions that fuel the sun lead to the emission of photons, which reach the earth as sunlight, and of neutrinos, which we do not see with our eyes but which can be detected in special neutrino detectors. At present there is great interest in these neutrinos, because the number being detected is fewer than expected, and this may be a signal that neutrinos have mass, in which case we could account for the lesser number detected. If they have mass, the experiments to detect them will allow the value of their mass to be measured.

Solar parallax

(a) The parallax of the Sun, now measured as 8.794".

(b) Angle subtended (8".79) by the equatorial radius of the Earth at a distance of 1 AU.

Solar phase angle

Angular distance at the planet between the Earth and the Sun.

Solar prominence

Mass of hot, hydrogen rising from the Sun's chromosphere, best observed indirectly during a total eclipse. Eruptive prominences are violent in force and may reach heights of 2 million km; quiescent prominences are relatively pacific but may last for months.

Solar rotation

Is differential, the equatorial rotation taking less time than the polar by up to 9.4 Earth-days.

Solar spectrum

The band of colors produced when sunlight is dispersed by a prism.

Solar system

The Sun and all objects gravitationally bound to it. The solar system is roughly a sphere with a radius greater than 100,000 AU, with the Sun at the centre. The Sun is overwhelmingly the dominant object. Planets, satellites, and all interplanetary material together comprise only about 1/750 of the total mass. Geochemical dating methods show that the solar system chemically isolated itself from the rest of the Galaxy $(4.7 \pm 0.1) \times 10^9$ years ago.

Solar velocity

Velocity of the Sun (19.4 km sin the direction l^{II} =

51°, b^{II} = 23°) with respect to the local standard of rest.

Solar wind

(a) Stream of charged particles flowing from the Sun at a speed of about 600 km sec^{-1}. It is the effects of the solar wind that produce aurorae in the Earth's upper atmosphere, that cause the tails of comets to stream back from the Sun, and that distort the symmetry of planetary magnetospheres.

(b) A radial outflow of energetic charged particles from the solar corona, carrying mass and angular momentum away from the Sun. Mean number density of solar wind (1971), 5 per cm^3; mean velocity at Earth 400 km s^{-1}; mean magnetic field 5 × 10^{-5} gauss; mean electron temperature 20,000 K; mean ion temperature 10,000 K. The Sun ejects about $10^{-}13$ *M* per year via the solar wind.

(c) A radial outflow of hot plasma from the solar corona. The sun ejects about 10^{-13} of its mass per year in the solar wind, which carries both mass and angular momentum away from the sun.

Solenoid

A cylindrical coil of wire that becomes electromagnetic when a current runs through it.

Solid angle

(a) A measure of the angular size of an extended object, equal to the area it subtends on the surface of a sphere of unit radius.

(b) Symbol: The three-dimensional analog of angle; it is subtended at a point by a surface (rather than by a line). The unit is the steradian (sr), which is defined analogously to the radian - the solid angle subtending unit area at unit distance. As the area of a sphere is $4r^2$, the solid angle corresponding to the revolution (2 radians) is 4 steradians.

Solid state detector

A device used to detect the passage of charged subatomic particles by their crystal-distorting or ionizing effects on a nonconducting or nonconducting solid.

Solidification

The change of phase from a liquid to a solid.

Solids

A phase of matter with molecules that remain close to fixed equilibrium positions due to strong interactions between the molecules, resulting in the characteristic definite shape and definite volume of a solid.

Solid-state

Usually implies crystalline semiconductor materials used in the electronics industry.

Soliton

A finite-amplitude hydrodynamic disturbance which is propagated through a fluid without any change of shape. MHD solitons are also known.

Solstice

One of the two points on the ecliptic at which the Sun appears to be farthest away from the celestial equator (representing therefore mid-summer or mid-winter).

Sombrero galaxy

A spiral galaxy in the constellation Virgo. It was the first galaxy whose rotation was detected.

Sonde

A rocket or balloon carrying instruments to probe conditions in the upper atmosphere.

Sonic boom

Sound waves that pile up into a shock wave when a source is traveling at or faster than the speed of sound.

Sonometer

A device, consisting of two or more wires or strings stretched over a sounding board, used for testing the frequency of strings and for showing how they vibrate.

Sound
The series of disturbances in matter to which the human ear is sensitive. Also similar disturbances in matter above and below the normal range of human hearing.

Sound intensity
The rate at which sound energy flows through a unit area.

Source
A radioactive material that produces radiation for experimental or industrial use.

Source function
The amount of radiant energy per unit mass per unit solid angle emitted in a specified direction. For the case of LTE, it is equal to the Planck function; for pure, isotropic scattering, it is equal to the mean intensity.

South atlantic anomaly
A disturbance in the geomagnetic field (a region of intense charged-particle fluxes) over the south part of the Atlantic Ocean. It was discovered in early OAO (Orbiting Atronomical Observatory) flights that when the detector passed over that area, the data it collected were not valid.

South galactic pole
A point in the constellation Sculptor toward which our line of sight is perpendicular to and below the Galactic disk.

South pole
One end of a magnet; the end that attracts the north pole.

Space
We can define coordinate systems and locate points in space. We know that there is a property called distance that can be defined between points. We know that we can only define three perpendicular coordinate axes (as far as we can tell), and we say we live in three dimensions. In relativity theory space is an aspect of a larger entity called spacetime, reflecting the intimate connection between the spatial directions and time.

Space charge
A radially defocussing force caused by electrostatic repulsion and magnetic fields generated by the moving protons within an accelerator.

Space charge forces
Divergent forces on a charged particle beam caused by nonzero net charge density, i.e.: mutual repulsion.

Space charge wave
An electrostatic wave brought about by oscillations of the charges.

Space motion
Velocity of a star with respect to the Sun; hypotenuse of the right triangle formed by its radial and tangential velocities (cf. peculiar velocity). Space motion vectors are U (in the direction of the galactic anticentre), V (in the direction of galactic rotation), and W (in the direction of the galactic north pole).

Space tether
an experiment in which a satellite was released from the space shuttle at the end of a long insulated cable. Theplan was for the dynamo processdue to the motion of the tether through the Earth's magnetic field to generate a large current in it.

Space velocity
A star's total velocity with respect to the local

standard of rest. This is the combination of the star's U, V, and W velocities: space velocity = sqrt $(U^2 + V^2 + W^2)$. For example, the Sun (U = -9, V = +12, W = +7) has a space velocity of 17 kilometers per second.

Space weather

The popular name for energy-releasing phenomena in the magnetosphere, associated with magnetic storms, substorms and shocks.

Space-like path

A trajectory along which $U \cdot U > 0$.

Spacetime

(a) Arena in which events are depicted in the theory of relativity. The orbit of a planet for instance, can be described as a "world line" in a four-dimensional space-time continuum.

(b) The three physical dimensions of space are combined with time, treated as a fourth dimension, to constitute the space-time continuum that is used as the fundamental framework of the theory of relativity.

(c) A union of space and time originally emerging from special relativity. Can be viewed as the "fabric" out of which the Universe is fashioned; it constitutes the dynamical arena within which the events of the Universe take place.

(d) In both the special and general theories of relativity it is necessary to treat space and time on an equal footing. The ensuing mathematical space is called 'space-time'.

Spacetime continuum

A four-dimensional framework in which events take place. Einsteinian concept of the Universe in accordance with his theories of relativity; Four-dimensional actuality, in which any anomaly is known as a singularity.

Spacetime foam

Frothy, writhing, tumultuous character of the spacetime fabric on ultra-microscopic scales, according to a conventional point-particle perspective. An essential reason for the incompatibility of quantum mechanics and general relativity prior to string theory.

Spallation

The process in which an incoming beam of particles or energy collides with a substance, reacts with it, and knocks off pieces of it.

Spark chamber

An instrument for detecting and measuring the paths of elementary particles in an experiment. It is analogous to the cloud chamber and bubble chamber. It consists of numerous electrically charged metal plates mounted in a parallel array the spaces between the plates being filled with an inert gas. Any interaction causes sparks to jump between the plates.

Spark gap

Electrodes found on the Haefely voltage multiplier and the accelerating column that will arc in the event of a voltage imbalance and thus prevent an arc from occurring in expensive/inaccessible components.

Spark spectra

The spectra of ions often produced by a spark discharge (cf. arc spectra).

Sparticles

Hypothetical particles which are predicted by some Grand Unified Theories.

SPEAR

Stanford Positron Electron Accelerating Ring.

Special relativity

Theory used to describe objects moving at speeds close to the speed of light. At slow speeds such as autos or aeroplanes, the effect is too small to be observed but for beams of particles in accelerators, the effect must be dealt with cautiously. All massive particles travel at less than the speed of light (c = 186,000 miles per second) no matter how hard you try to accelerate them. Photons though have no mass so they travel at the speed of light (in a vacuum).

Special relativity

(a) Einstein's theory of time and space, formulated in 1905, which shows how measurements of length and time differ for observers in relative motion.

(b) Theory formulated by Albert Einstein comprising two basic yet very original propositions: that a spaceship (or other enclosed vessel) traveling at uniform speed through space contains its own space-time continuum, and that a ray of light passes an observer at the speed of light no matter how (uniformly) fast nor in what direction the observer is travelling. One consequence of this theory was the equation of mass (m) with energy (E), formulated as $E = mc^2$ (where c is the speed of light). Ten years later, Einstein produced his General Theory of Relativity.

(c) A theory of space, time and motion formulated by Einstein in 1905. The theory was generalized in 1915 to include gravity.

(d) The constraints of special relativity are two conditions that Einstein pointed out should be satisfied by any acceptable physical theory. Somewhat oversimplified, these conditions are, first, that light moves at the same speed in vacuum regardless of how it is emitted and, second, that scientists working in different labs moving with different relative speeds should formulate the same natural laws. The constraints imposed by these conditions have surprising implications for the structure of acceptable theories. For example, the Schrodinger equation of quantum theory does not satisfy these conditions.

Specific

In physics and chemistry the word specific in the name of a quantity usually means divided by an extensive measure that is, divided by a quantity representing an amount of material. Specific volume means volume divided by mass, which is the reciprocal of the density. Specific heat capacity is the heat capacity divided by the mass.

Specific gravity

Ratio of the mass of a given volume of a substance to that of an equal volume of water.

Specific heat

Each substance has its own specific heat, which is defined as the amount of energy (or heat) needed to increase the temperature of one gram of a substance by one degree Celsius.

Speckle interferometry

The technique of recovering the diffraction-limited angular resolution of a telescope by analysis of images obtained using a very high speed camera system to "freeze" the blurring due to atmospheric turbulence.

SPECT

Single-Photon Emission Computerized Tomography involves scanning involving the rotation of detectors around a patient and acquires information on the concentration of radionuclides introduced to the patient's body. This is analogous to CT imaging with x-rays.

Spectra

Atoms can exist in a number of discreet energy levels. They emit or absorb photons when they make transitions from one level to another. The energies of the photons emitted or absorbed by one atom are different from those of all other atoms. The photon energies are directly related to their frequencies, which set their colors in the spectrum, so by observing the colors of the photons, it is possible to determine which atoms are being observed.

Spectral bandwidth

The wavelength, or frequency range over which photons are detected at any one time; some detectors can operate in one or more bands placed within a broader range of spectral response.

Spectral classification

The system devised by Annie Cannon combining the perceived colour of a star with its spectral characteristics. Very generally, of the overall sequence O B A F G K M R N S, stars in the group O B A are white or blue and display increasing characteristics of the presence of hydrogen; in F G are yellow and show increasing calcium; in K are orange and strongly metallic; and in M R N S are red and indicate titanium oxide through carbon to zirconium oxide bands. The groups are numerically subdivided, according to other characteristics, and there are further small classes for very unusual categories of star. Different methods of classification exist but are not in such common use.

Spectral index

The power of the frequency to which the intensity at that frequency is proportional. It is positive for thermal radiation, negative for nonthermal radiation.

Spectral line

A line in a spectrum due to the emission or absorption of electromagnetic radiation at a discrete wavelength. Spectral lines result from discrete changes in the energy of an atom or molecule. Different atoms or molecules can be identified by the unique sequence of spectral lines associated with them.

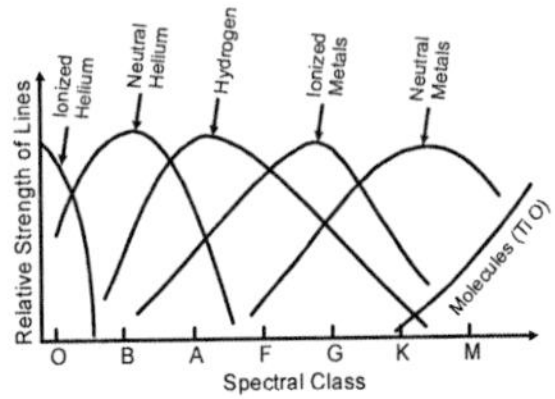

Spectral range

The range of wavelengths of the electromagnetic radiation that can be produced.

Spectral ratio

The ratio of electromagnetic wavelengths from different cosmic epochs. This gives the expansion factor of the Universe.

Spectral series

(a) All spectral lines of a given atom arising from transitions with a common lower energy level.

(b) A group of related lines in the absorption or emission spectrum of a substance. The lines in a spectral series occur when the transitions are all between the same energy level and a set of different levels.

Spectral type

The classification of a star's spectrum, which correlates with the star's temperature and color. There are seven main spectral types. From hot and blue to cool and red, they are O, B, A, F, G, K, and M. For further precision, astronomers divide each spectral type. For example, from warmest to coolest, spectral type G is G0, G1, G2, G3, and so on to G9. The Sun is spectra] type G2.

Spectrograph

(a) A device, usually based on a finely etched grate that performs the function of a prism, for breaking up light into its constituent parts and making a photographic or electronic record of the resulting spectrum. When lacking a means for recording the spectrum, the device is called a spectroscope.

(b) An instrument that records the amount of light in each range of wavelength, that is, in each range of color. In general, each type of astronomical object, such as a star or a galaxy, will emit a characteristic spectrum of light.

Spectrograph

An instrument that spreads light or other electromagnetic radiation into its component wavelengths (spectrum), recording the results photographically or electronically.

Spectroheliograph

Device with which spectra of the various regions of the Sun are obtained and photographed.

Spectrometer

A device for producing a spectrum. The 40R bending magnet in the Linac momentum analysis line comprises a magnetic spectrometer. Particles with different momenta will follow different paths through the magnet and will appear in different positions at the scanning wire.

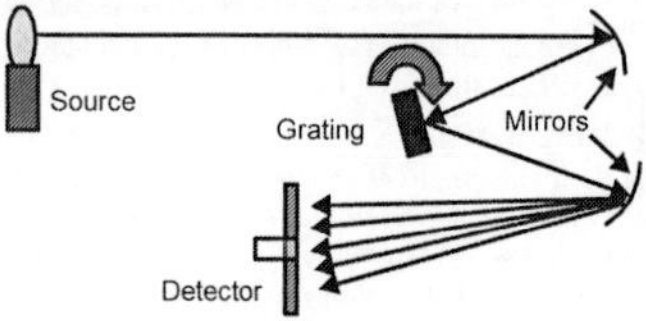

Spectroscope

Optical instrument used for the study of spectra.

Spectroscopic binaries

Stars whose binary nature can be detected from the periodic Doppler shifts of their spectra, owing to their varying velocities in the line of sight. Double-lined spectroscopic binaries have two sets of spectral features, oscillating with opposite phases. Single-lined spectroscopic binaries have only one set of oscillating spectral lines, owing to the dimness of the secondary component. Spectroscopic binaries are typically of spectral type B, with almost circular orbits (whereas long-period M-type binaries have highly eccentric orbits).

Spectroscopic parallax

Parallax for a group of stars based on the magnitudes and spectral types of the member stars. Spectroscopic parallax is by far the most common method of determining stellar distances.

Spectroscopy

1. The production and analysis of spectra. There are many spectroscopic techniques designed for investigating the electromagnetic radiation emitted or absorbed by substances. Spectroscopy, in various forms, is used for analysis of mixtures, for identifying and determining the structures of chemical compounds, and for investigating energy levels in atoms, ions, and molecules. In astronomy it is used for determining the composition of celestial objects and for measuring red shifts.
2. Any of various techniques for analyzing the energy spectra of beams of particles or for determining mass spectra.

Spectroscopy

The science of finding the energy levels of a physical system which obeys the laws of quantum mechanics.

Spectrum

(a) The breakdown of light into a rainbow of colors. A good spectrum reveals a star's spectral type, radial velocity (from the spectrum's Doppler shift), and metallicity.

(b) A record of the distribution of matter or energy (e.g., light) by wavelength. Spectra can be studied to learn the chemical composition and motion of stars and galaxies.

(c) The amount of light in each range of wavelength, that is, in each range of color. The term spectrum can also be applied more generally to the intensity of something at each length scale. An object that emits radiation in a continuous range of colors is said to have a continuous spectrum. An object that emits radiation only at certain wavelengths is said to have emission lines; objects that absorb radiation only at certain wavelengths are said to have absorption lines.

Spectrum variables

Main-sequence Am or Ap stars whose spectra show anomalously strong lines of metals and rare earths which vary in intensity by about 0.1 mag over periods of about 1-25 days. They are characterized by large magnetic fields (10^3-10^4 gauss) at the surface, small variations in light and color, and small projected rotational velocities. These peculiarities are sometimes interpreted in terms of an oblique rotator.

Specular reflection

Reflection from a smooth surface, in which the light ray leaves at the same angle at which it came in.

Speed

The absolute value of or, in more then one dimension, the magnitude of the velocity, i.e. The velocity stripped of any information about its direction Spring constant. The constant of proportionality between force and elongation of a spring or other object under strain.

Speed of Light

(a) c = 299,792 km sec^{-1} (186,180 miles sec^{-1}).

(b) Light and all other massless particles travel in vacuum with a speed, usually labeled c, whose value is about three hundred million meters a second. Special relativity implies that no particle or signal can move faster than the speed of light and that photons always have this speed, regardless of the speed of their source.

Sphere

The outer surface of a ball. The surface of a familiar three-dimensional ball has two dimensions (which can be labeled by two numbers such as "latitude" and "longitude," as on the surface of the earth). The concept of a sphere, though, applies more generally to balls and hence their surfaces, in any number of dimensions. A one-dimensional sphere is a fancy name for a circle; a zero-dimensional sphere is two points (as explained in the text). A three-dimensional sphere is harder to picture; it is the surface of a four-dimensional ball.

Spherical aberration

The failure of parallel rays to meet at a single point on a spherical surface after reflection or refraction.

Spherical collapse

Initial stage in the collapse of a star, followed by gravitational collapse and finally singularity.

Spherical coordinate system

There is no truth to the story that this system was invented by Orson Wells. It was invented by Orson's doctors, who needed a reference system for his body. Anyway, the coordinate system is defined thusly. As usual some point is chosen as the origin. Then what is essentially a polar coordinate system is established in an arbitrary plane centreed on the origin.

Spherical space

A three-dimensional space whose geometry resembles that of the surface of a sphere and is said to have positive curvature.

Spicule

A short-lived (about 5 minutes), narrow jet of gas spouting out of the solar chromosphere. Spicules tend to cluster at the edges of super-granulation cells.

Spike

An undesired intense portion of the spill.

Spill

Beam extracted from the Tevatron. Using resonant extraction, the beam "spills" out of the machine a little at a time.

Spill duty factor

The spill duty factor is a quantitative measure of the quality of the beam being extracted from the accelerator. The spill duty factor is given the range 0% - 100% and measures: (1) The amount of time extracted beam is on divided by the maximum time it could be on and (2) The uniformity of the instantaneous intensities over the length of the flattop.

Spill duty factor

The spill duty factor is a quantitative measure of the quality of the beam being extracted from the accelerator. The spill duty factor is given the range 0% - 100% and measures:

(1) The amount of time extracted beam is on divided by the maximum time it could be on and

(2) The uniformity of the instantaneous intensities over the length of the flattop.

Spill structure

The regularity or lack thereof of spill intensity over time.

Spin

The name given to the angular momentum carried by a particle. For composite particles the spin is made up from the combination of the spins of the constituents plus the angular momentum of their motion around one-another. For fundamental particles spin is an intrinsic and inherently quantum property, it cannot be understood in terms of motions internal to the object.

Spin density

The concentration of spins.

Spin network

A term used by Roger Penrose to denote collections or networks of quantum mechanical spinors. Although they were not created within any background space, Penrose discovered that these spin networks had properties that were similar to those of Euclidian angles in a three-dimensional space. One of Penrose's early goals was to extend the spin network idea by employing twistors and in this way derive the properties of the space-time quantum mechanically.

Spin packet

A group of spins experiencing the same magnetic field.

Spin quantum number

From quantum mechanics model of the atom, one of four descriptions of the energy state of an electron wave; this quantum number describes the spin orientation of an electron relative to an external magnetic field.

Spin-echo

An NMR sequence whose signal is an echo resulting from the refocusing of magnetization after the application of 90° and 180° RF pulses.

Spin-flip collisions

Collisions between particles in which the direction of the spin angular momentum changes. Since the total angular momentum is conserved, the orbital angular momentum must be changed in magnitude or direction or both.

Spin-lattice relaxation

The return of the longitudinal magnitization to its equilibrium value along the +Z axis.

Spin-lattice relaxation

The return of the longitudinal magnitization to its equilibrium value along the +Z axis.

Spin-lattice relaxation time (t_1)

The time to reduce the difference between the longitudinal magnitization and its equilibrium value by a factor of e.

Spinor

A mathematical object that reverses sign after a rotation by 360 degrees and returns to itself only after a rotation by 720 degrees. (More familiar mathematical and physical objects return to themselves after a rotation by 360 degrees.) A physical example showing spinor behavior is the following: Paint each face of a cube a different color and connect each of the eight corners of the cube to the corresponding corners of the room with threads. Now rotate the cube by 360 degrees. The threads are hopelessly tangled up, even though the cube has returned to its original position. Rotation of the cube by *another* 360 degrees, however, allows one to untangle the threads.

Spin-spin relaxation

The return of the transverse magnitization to its equilibrium value (zero).

Spin-spin relaxation time

The time to reduce the transverse magnetization by a factor of e.

Spinthariscope

A device used to detect subatomic particles by the light flashes they produce on a zinc sulfide screen.

Spin-up

A discontinuous increase in the pulse frequency of a pulsar.

Spiral density wave

A wave, due to a local increase in the gravitational field, that produces a series of alternate compressions and rarefactions as it propagates with fixed angular velocity in a rotating galaxy. The compression also acts on interstellar gas in the galaxy, which is triggered to form stars on the leading edges of the spiral arms. The large-scale structure of spiral galaxies can be understood in this way.

Spiral galaxy

A galaxy with a prominent nuclear bulge and luminous spiral arms of gas, dust, and young stars that wind out from the nucleus. Masses span the range from 10^{10} to 10^{12} M.

Spiral nebula

A spiral galaxy - not really a nebula at all (although many do appear nebulous).

Spiritualism

Belief that material interactions alone cannot account for all phenomena, and that some - e.g., thought - are due to the fundamentally insensible actions of intangibles.

Spitzer-oort hypothesis

A hypothesis which explains the mass motion of the interstellar gas in terms of the gas pressure gradients existing between H I and H II regions.

Spitzer-schwarzschild scattering mechanism

The process by which stars in the Milky Way's disk encounter interstellar clouds and are accelerated by them. Over time, this perturbs the stars, so that older disk stars have more elliptical orbits, larger velocity dispersions, and greater scale heights than younger disk stars. This mechanism cannot, however, explain the motions of halo stars.

Split

The split ratio is the amount of beam going to a particular external experimental area divided by the amount of extracted beam, usually given as a percentage. It also refers to the septa, and bump magnets that control this ratio, i.e., a splitting station.

Splitting station

Place where a single incoming proton beam is split into two or more beams. The primary elements of a splitting station are septa and lambertsons.

Spontaneous emission

(a) Radiation emitted by an isolated body.

(b) An excited atom can shed its excitation by radiating a photon in a spontaneous emission. This emission is independent of external radiation and is entirely random and uncontrolled.

Spontaneous symmetry breaking

(a) The breaking of an exact symmetry of the underlying laws of physics by the random formation of some object. For example, the rotational in variance of the laws of physics can be broken by the randomly chosen orientation of an orthorhombic crystal that condenses as the material is cooled. In the standard model of particle physics, the symmetry between electrons and neutrinos is spontaneously broken by the values that are randomly chosen by the Higgs fields. In grand unified theories, the symmetry between electrons, neutrinos, and quarks is spontaneously broken by the values chosen randomly by the Higgs fields.

(b) Any situation in physics in which the ground state (i.e. the state of minimum energy) of a system has less symmetry than the system itself. For example, the state of minimum energy for an iron magnet is that in which the atomic spins are all aligned in the same direction, giving rise to a net macroscopic magnetic field. By selecting a particular direction in space. the magnetic field has broken the rotational symmetry of the system.

However, if the energy of the system is raised, the symmetry may be restored (e.g. the application of heat to an iron magnet destroys the magnetic field and restores rotational symmetry).

(c) In many physical systems the actual state of the system does not reflect the underlying symmetries of the dynamics because the manifestly symmetric state is unstable. The system then trades stability for asymmetry. The symmetry breaking in this case is said to be spontaneous.

(d) Often the equations of a theory may have certain symmetries, though their solutions may not; the symmetries are hidden, or broken. For example, the equations may describe several particles in identical ways, so the equations are unchanged if the particles are interchanged, but the solutions may give the particles different properties. This phenomenon is called spontaneous symmetry breaking.

Spool piece

The device that contains the Tevatron correction element coils.

Spörer's Law of Zones

The equatorward drift of average sunspot latitudes.

Spot size

The transverse size of the proton beam at a given point. It is usually referred to at a target.

Spring constant (scalar; n/m)

The constant of proportionality between the applied force and the resulting change in length of a given spring.

S-process

Slow Neutron Capture: A process in which heavy, stable, neutron-rich nuclei are synthesized from iron-peak elements by successive captures of free neutrons in a weak neutron flux, so there is time for b-decay before another neutron is captured (cf. r-process). This a slow but sure process of nucleosynthesis which is assumed to take place in the intershell regions during the red-giant phase of evolution, at densities up to 10^5 g cm^{-3} and temperatures of about 3×10^8 K (neutron densities assumed are 10^{10} cm^{-3}). The *s*-process slowly builds stable nuclear species up to $A = 208$ (time between captures about 10-100 years).

Sputnik 1

First artificial Earth satellite, launched by the Soviet Union on 4 October 1957.

Squark

The supersymmetric partner of any of the quarks.

SSDN

Sub-System Device Number. Each database entry in a given subsystem (e.g. Linac, Tevatron, etc.) has a unique number assigned to it. This number is used by the front-ends and describes characteristics such as module type, location, etc. The format of these numbers is different between front-ends and different for each property of a device.

S-state/S-level

The state of an atom in which the orbital angular momentum *L* (the vector sum of the orbital angular momenta *l* of the individual electrons) is zero.

Stability

A measure of how hard it is to displace an object or system from equilibrium. Three cases are met in statics (*see* equilibrium). They differ in the effect on the centre of mass of a small displacement. An object's stability is improved by: (a) lowering the centre of mass; or (b) increasing the area of support; or by both.

Stable

Non-radioactive.

Stack

Antiprotons are stored in the pbar Accumulator storage ring. Antiprotons are produced by bombarding the antiproton target with protons, sweeping the antiprotons into the circulating

Accumulator antiproton beam, and stochasticaly cooling them. This process is called stacking. The antiprotons collected in this manner are collectively called the stack.

Stack tail

The least dense region of the p- beam in the Accumulator. Beam is deposited onto the stack tail by ARF1 and the stochastic cooling systems, specifically the Stack tail Dp system, move the p-'s from the tail towards the core. The particle density of the stack increases in an approximately exponential fashion from the stack tail to the core.

Stacking (RF & momentum)

The means by which successive pulses of antiprotons are combined into one beam in the Accumulator. This is accomplished by first moving an injected pulse of p-'s from the injection orbit to the edge of the stack tail by means of RF deceleration (ARF1). The beam is then pushed towards the core by the stack tail momentum cooling system.

Stage

To write (or cache) an applications program onto the console disk from the VAX, where it may be easily retrieved.

Stainless steel

18% NiCr steel with low conductivity, nonmagnetic, and good cryogenic material properties. Typical cryogenic types are 304, 304L, and 316, all low carbon.

Standard big bang model

The Friedmann - Lemaître cosmological models of an isotropic and homogeneous Universe composed of expanding matter and radiation. There are three possible choices for the geometry of space in a standard Big Bang model: space can be positively curved, like the surface of a sphere, in which case the Universe is finite, closed, and will eventually recollapse; or, space can either be Euclidean or have negative curvature (like a saddle-shaped surface), in which case the Universe is infinite, open, and will expand forever. In all three models, space is unbounded.

Standard candle

An object - usually a star or a galaxy of known intrinsic brightness. Measuring the apparent brightness of a standard candle yields its distance.

Standard deviation

The root mean square deviation from the arithmetic mean.

Standard epoch

A date and time that specifies the reference system to which celestial coordinates are referred. Prior to 1984 coordinates of star catalogs were commonly referred to the mean equator and equinox of the beginning of a Besselian year.

Standard Error (S.E.)

The standard deviation of a distribution of means or any other statistical measure computed from samples. It is equal to 1.4826 times the probable error.

Standard model

Physicists' name for the current theory of fundamental particles and their interactions.

Standard Model of Cosmology

Big bang theory together with an understanding of the three nongravitational forces as summarized by the standard model of particle physics.

Standard Model of Particle Physics

(a) A theory of particle interactions, developed in the early 1970's, which successfully describes electromagnetism, the weak interactions, and the strong interactions. The theory consists of two parts, quantum chromodynamics to describe the strong interactions, and the unified electroweak theory to describe the electromagnetic and weak interactions.

(b) The very successful theory of quarks and leptons and their interactions is called the Standard Model by particle physicists. The name arose historically as the theory developed and then was difficult to change because it is widely used. The Standard Model is the most complete mathematical theory of the natural world ever developed and is well tested experimentally.

Standard pressure
A convenient measure of pressure equivalent to 1 atmosphere or 1.01×10^5 pascal.

Standard ruler
Any extended celestial object which is more or less constant diameter. It can be used to gauge distances, because the further away it is, the smaller it will appear.

Standard temperature
Zero degrees Celsius.

Standard volume
The volume of an ideal gas at standard temperature and standard pressure, namely, 22.4 liters.

Standing wave
A traveling wave, like a traveling salesman, gets around. It is created by a disturbance at one point and then propagates away from that point, as if afraid it might be blamed for the disturbance. Now if you get two or more traveling waves to interfere with each other in just the right way, you can create a vibrating pattern, like the one on a plucked cello string, that vibrates in place. In the case of the string you have two waves, traveling in opposite directions due to being reflected at the ends of the string, combining to produce the stationary pattern. Such a superposition of traveling waves is called a standing wave.

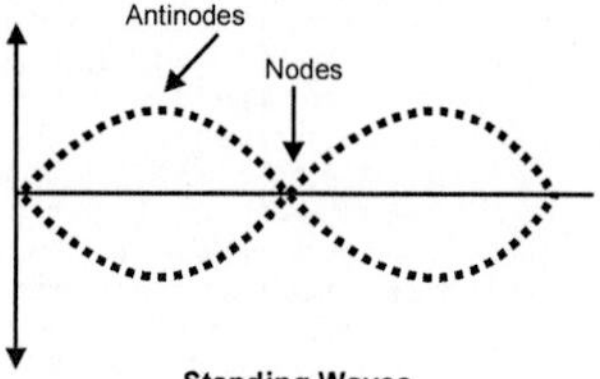

Standing Waves

Standstill
An interval in the cycle of a variable star during which the brightness temporarily stops changing.

Star
A celestial object that generates energy by means of nuclear fusion at its core. To do this it must have more than about 0.08 the sun's mass. If, for instance, the planet Jupiter were some fifty to one hundred times more massive than it is, fusion reactions would transpire in its core and it would be a star.

Star cluster
A gravitationally bound aggregation of stars, smaller and less massive than galaxies. "Globular" clusters are the largest category; they are old, and may harbor hundreds of thousands to millions of stars, and are found both within and well away from the galactic disk. "Open" clusters are smaller, have a wide range of ages, and reside within the disk.

Star counts
Determination of the number of stars in a region of the sky as a function of apparent magnitude and sometimes color.

Star stream
Discovered by Kapteyn in 1902, a star stream is a group of stars traveling in more or less the same direction. Kapteyn found what he thought were two oppositely directed star streams, but astronomers now recognize that these simply reflect the tendency of stars to have their largest velocities in the U direction.

Star streaming
A phenomenon that arises because the mean random speeds of the stars are different in different directions. The direction of star streaming is the direction along which the mean random speed has a maximum value. The phenomenon is caused by the rotation of the Galaxy.

Star system
A few stars that orbit each other. For example, a double star system consists of two stars; a triple star system consists of three stars; and so on.

Starburst galaxy
Any galaxy in which an anomalously large rate of star formation is taking place.

Stark effect
Broadening or splitting of a spectral line caused when a radiating atom or ion is influenced by an electric field, which slightly changes the energy level of the atom. Stark broadening is proportional to the ion and electron density in a plasma and is a good indicator of atmospheric pressure in a stellar atmosphere and hence of the star's luminosity.

Starlight
Energy (seen as light) produced by a star through nuclear fusion.

Starlink
A software environment and suite of programs for astronomical data analysis developed in the UK and supported by the Rutherford-Appleton Labs.

Stat-coulomb
The unit of charge in the cgs electrostatic system. 1 stat-coulomb = 3.3×10^{-10} coulombs.

State of motion
When a body changes it's position with respect to a fixed point in it's surroundings then it is said to be in a state of motion. The states of rest and motion are relative to the frame of reference.

State of rest
When a body does not change its position with respect to a fixed point in it's surrounding, then it is said to be in a state of rest. The states of rest and motion are relative to the frame of reference.

State space
The mathematical space whose points represent the states of a physical system.

Static electricity
Electricity at rest.

Static equilibrium
The state of an object when all forces acting on it sum to zero.

Static friction
If two surfaces are pressed together and a force is exerted to slide one surface over the other, there will be a resistance force called the force of friction. When the surfaces are not sliding, this force is called the force of static friction. The force of static friction will equal the force exerted to cause the sliding until the applied force reaches a magnitude that static friction can no longer resist. This is where the surfaces are on the verge of sliding, and this force is proportional to the normal force pressing the surfaces together. The constant of proportionality is called the coefficient of static friction, $ì_s$. After sliding commences, the resistance force will be that of kinetic friction.

Static limit
In the Kerr solution to Einstein's equations, a surface on which a particle would have to travel at the local light velocity in order to appear stationary to an observer at infinity, and just inside which no particle can remain stationary as viewed from infinity. The stationary limit lies outside the event horizon, touching it only at the poles.

Static universe
A Universe whose radius of curvature is constant and independent of time, as in the Einstein Universe.

Stationary limit
In the Kerr solution to Einstein's equations, a surface on which a particle would have to travel at the local light velocity in order to appear stationary to an observer at infinity, and just inside which no particle can remain stationary as viewed from infinity. The stationary limit lies outside the event horizon, touching it only at the poles. (In the Schwarzschild solution, the stationary limit coincides with the event horizon.).

Stationary nonequilibrium state
Time-independent state of a system subjected to fixed constraints.

Stationary point

(Of a planet): The position at which the rate of change of the apparent right ascension.

Stationary wave

A standing wave; the pattern formed when two waves of the same amplitude and frequency move simultaneously through a medium in opposite directions.

Statistical distribution

The range of variation of some quantity in a population, obtained by sampling many members of the population. For example, the statistical distribution of the height of American males could be obtained by sampling 10,000 randomly chosen males and counting the number of them within each range of heights. In cosmology, the distance between pairs of galaxies, averaged over a large number of galaxies, would constitute a statistical distribution.

Statistical equilibrium

A state in which the average density of atoms per cubic centimeter in any atomic state does not change with time and in which, statistically, energy is equally divided among all degrees of freedom if classical concepts prevail.

Statistical error

The uncertainty resulting from a measurement of purely random events. Such an uncertainty is defined as bracketing a range of values within which the correct value has a 66% chance of lying. For example, a value of (100 ± 10) obtained from a given measurement means that the true value has a 66% chance of lying between 90 and 110, and a 34% chance of being either above or below this range.

Statistical mechanics

The area of physics that analyzes the behavior of a system with very many members, such as a gas with many individual molecules. In such a situation, the behavior of the whole system is obtained by averaging over the behavior of individual members.

Statistical parallax

The mean parallax for a group of stars which are all at approximately the same distance, determined from their radial velocities and from the tau components of their proper motion.

Statistical weight

The probability that the state will appear under a given set of conditions. Usually, the number of ordinarily degenerate substates contained in the state; e.g., the $(2l + 1)m$ states of an atom in the absence of a magnetic field.

Status display unit

A set of LED's that is interfaced to several Unibus cards in the PEX box which indicates the activity of the processor or external interrupts. This unit may be found interfaced to all PDP-11's.

Steady state theory

(a) Theory that the expanding Universe was never in a state of appreciably higher density - i.e., that there was no "big bang" - and that matter is constantly being created out of empty space in order to maintain the cosmic matter density.

(b) A cosmological theory propounded by Bondi, Gold, and Hoyle in which the Universe has no beginning and no end and maintains the same mean density, in the face of its observed expansion, by the continuous creation of matter at the current rate of 2.8×10^{-46} g cm^{-3} s^{-1} (or roughly one nucleon per cubic kilometer per year). Discovery of the microwave background has persuaded most astronomers to reject the steady-state theory.

Steam point

It is the temperature of steam over pure boiling water under 1 atm pressure. The steam point is taken as the upper fixed point (100° C or 212° F) for temperature scales.

Stefan-Boltzmann law

The amount of energy radiated per second per unit

area of a perfectly black body is directly proportional to the fourth power of the absolute temperature of the surface of the body.

Stellar evolution

(a) How a star changes with time.
(b) The building of complex atomic nuclei from simpler nuclei in stars, with the result that succeeding generations of stars and planets contain a greater variety of chemical elements than did their predecessors.

Stellar population

A Galaxy-wide group of stars of all types that have similar ages, locations, kinematics, and metallicities. As astronomers presently know the Milky Way, they recognize four stellar populations: the thin disk; the thick disk; the stellar halo; and the bulge.

Stellar wind

A steady or unsteady outflow of material from the surface of a star. In many classes of star hot coronae are observed and these are believed to be due to heating by waves generated in the upper layers of the star. This results in the outflow of mass in the form of a stellar wind.

Stellarator

A type of plasma machine. It has a twisted-field configuration in the form of a figure 8 to fold the plasma back on itself; therefore, unlike a pinch machine. It has no ends where the plasma can leak out. Stellarators and tokomaks resemble each other in that both are toroidal devices that attain equilibrium and MHD stability through rotational transform and shear; they differ mainly in the way they attain these properties.

Stem-box cover

A cover over the tops of the Linac drift-tube stems that protrude from the top of a linac RF cavity. The Stem- box cover may be evacuated to prevent vacuum leaks around the stems.

Stephan's quintet

A highly disturbed cluster of five peculiar galaxies (NGC 7317, NGC 7318A, NGC 7318B, NGC 7319, NGC 7320) in Pegasus which seem to exhibit gaseous connecting bridges. Four have large redshifts (of the order of 5700-6700 km s^{-1}), but the fifth member (NGC 7320) has a much smaller redshift (800 km s^{-1}).

Stepping motor

A motor which rotates a small specific amount in response to an encoded bit of information. It allows beam-line elements to be moved precise distances.

Steradian

A unit of solid (three-dimensional) angular measure. One steradian is equal to the angle subtended at the centre of a sphere by an area of surface equal to the square of the radius. The name for the unit seems to have come into use about 1880 and was comparatively common by the turn of the century. The surface of a sphere subtends an angle of 4 steradians at its centre.

Sterotactic radiosurgery

This involves the use of multiple small pencil of radiation fired from many different directions and all aimed at the tumor. Machines used include the "gamma-knife," with several hundred small, high-activity Cobalt-60 sources and conventional medical linear accelerators equipped with specially designed sterotactic hardware.

Sticking coefficient

The fraction of all atoms (e.g., hydrogen) incident on an interstellar dust grain that become adsorbed.

Stimulated emission

(a) Radiation emitted by a body, such as an atom, when it is bombarded by radiation. The stimulated radiation has the same wavelength and direction as the bombarding radiation.
(b) Incident radiation can induce an atom to radiate by stimulated emission at a rate which depends on the intensity of the incident light. Stimulated emission has a definite phase relationship with the incident light and is the driving force behind the laser, it was discovered by Einstein.

Stochastic, stochastic cooling

A random process. Stochastic cooling works through a series of beam pickups, electronics, trunk lines and kicker electrodes. Consider the case of an individual p-. The particle passes through a pickup and some position is detected. Depending on the location of the pickup in the lattice, the position can be translated into a transverse or momentum error. The signal from the pickup is massaged electronically and transported across the ring to more electronics which serve to insure that the error signal derived at the pickup arrives at the kicker just as the p- arrives at the kicker (at the correct amplitude and phase to correct the error). Real time feedback. The actual process is slightly more complicated, both in practice and due to the fact that more than one particle comprises the beam.

Stokes parameters

(a) A way of characterizing the polarization state of light which is closely related to actual measurements.

(b) Four parameters (I, Q, U, V) which must be evaluated to describe fully a beam of polarized light. They involve the maximum and minimum intensity, the ellipticity, and the direction of polarization. The nonvanishing of *V* indicates the presence of elliptical polarization.

Stopband

Vertical and horizontal tune values at which field errors can cause beam blow up in an accelerator. These stop bands have a definite width, so that the beam reaches resonance as the offending tune value is approached. Tevatron extraction is produced by widening the half-integer stop band.

Storage cell

An electrochemical cell in which the reacting materials are regenerated by the use of a reverse current from an external source.

Storage ring

A circular (or near circular) structure in which either high energy and/or positrons, or protons and/or antiprotons can be circulated many times and thus "stored". Used to achieve high energy collisions. Because of the very different masses of protons and electrons a storage ring must be designed for one or the other type and cannot work for both.

Storage scope

Any oscilloscope or display which retains a trace for an indefinite length of time. There are several portable scopes available for diagnostics as well as at least one at most ACNET consoles in the MCR. Sometimes the term refers specifically to the Tektronix 613 storage scope at each ACNET console.

Store

To inject circulating beam into an accelerator and keep it there for long periods of time. In the Tevatron this means to inject protons and pbar bunches, cog the bunches to their proper collision points, ramp the Tev to 900 geV, turn on the low beta quadrupoles to bring the injected beam to low beta, and the collider detector experiments are taking data. In the antiproton source, it means that an antiproton stack is established.

Stp

Standard Temperature and Pressure. 0°c and 1 atmosphere.

Straggling

Because of the statistical nature of the collisions of charged particles with atomic electrons, the range of the charged particles is not unique, but is actually a mean value R. Fluctuations about R is called straggling.

Strain

Strain is the deformation of matter that results from stress. If a body experiences uniform compressive stress on all sides (hydrostatic pressure), it will maintain its shape (if it is uniform in makeup). In general, however, strain means a deformation of the size *and* shape of a body or collection of matter.

The easiest strain to understand is elastic strain, where the deformation is proportional to the stress applied. (Double the stress, double the deformation.) The elastic response of substances to stress is characterized by elastic moduli, which are analogous to the force constant of a spring.

Strange attractor

(a) A path in phase space that is not closed. Strange attractors are characteristic of chaotic behavior.

(b) An attractor in the phase space of some dynamical system having fractional dimensionality. Strange attractors are associated with chaotic dynamics.

Strange particles

The collective name for a group of strongly interacting particles possessing the property of strangeness. According to one theory, the strange particles are regarded as the higher quantum states of the nucleus.

Strange quark

The third flavor of quark (in order of increasing mass), with electric charge -1/3.

Strangeness

(a) A property of hadrons which may have a zero or non-zero value, depending on their rate of decay.

(b) A property ascribed to certain hyperons whose lifetimes before decay are abnormally long (about 10^{-8} to 10^{-10} seconds) relative to their rates of production (about one every 10^{-23} seconds). Like parity, strangeness is conserved in strong interactions but not in weak ones.

(c) A quantum number associated with the strange quark. Strangeness is conserved by the strong nuclear force.

(d) A property possessed by all matter containing a strange quark. This quark has charge -1/3 and partners the charmed quark in the second generation of particles.

Stratosphere

The region of Earth's atmosphere immediately above the troposphere. It starts at a height of about 15 km and goes to a height of about 50 km. The temperature increases from about 240 K to about 270 K.

Streamer chamber

A streamer chamber is a wide-gap chamber which records a three-dimensional image of a particle trajectory. An electron avalanche develops along the trail of ions, as in a narrow gap chamber, but because of a short pulse duration, this is arrested at an early stage, so the "track" appears as a row of short streamers extending typically a few millimeters. If the plate electrodes are transparent, the streamers may be viewed along the field and then appear as a series of dots similar to a track in a bubble chamber.

Streamer chamber

A streamer chamber is a wide-gap chamber which records a three-dimensional image of a particle trajectory. An electron avalanche develops along the trail of ions, as in a narrow gap chamber, but because of a short pulse duration, this is arrested at an early stage, so the "track" appears as a row of short streamers extending typically a few millimeters. If the plate electrodes are transparent, the streamers may be viewed along the field and then appear as a series of dots similar to a track in a bubble chamber.

Streamline

(a) A line following the direction of the fluid in laminar or *streamline flow*. Where the speed increases, as it does in a narrower section of a pipe, the streamlines are closer together.

(b) Path followed by a moving particle in a fluid when the flow is laminar - i.e., nonturbulent. It is a line in a fluid such that the tangent to it at every point is in the direction of the velocity flow.

Stress

If you feel bent out of shape, then you should blame

stress, not your physics professor, because that's what stress does. It deforms matter. Stress is the force per unit area acting on a surface. The surface may be an actual one between two different substances or an imaginary one like the distinction between the U.S. Constitution and the Supreme Court during Presidential elections.

String

(a) Fundamental one-dimensional object that is the essential ingredient in string theory.

(b) Nambu's original idea that the elementary particles could be described as extended, one dimensional objects was called string theory. Since the ends of Nambu's strings whipped around at the speed of light they were also called light strings. Later attempts to include the spin half fermions within a string theory led to the term spinning strings. Strings that possess supersymmetry are called superstrings. Heterotic strings combine spaces of two different dimensionalities. The term string is used in a generic way to describe all these different variations, including superstrings.

(c) The hypothesized, basic constituents of matter, according to new theories of physics. In earlier theories of physics, the basic constituents of matter were point-like particles, such as electrons, which interacted with other particles at a point. According to the string theory, the basic constituents are 1-dimensional structures called strings. There are completely different strings, called cosmic strings, which can form according to some theories and which may extend for great distances in space. Postulated to have formed as a result of processes in the early Universe, cosmic strings are 1-dimensional structures of enormous energy, extending for perhaps thousands or millions of light years in space. There is no good observational evidence that either kind of strings exist.

String coupling constant

A positive number that governs how likely it is for a given string to split apart into two strings or for two strings to join together into one-the basic processes in string theory. Each string theory has its own string coupling constant, the value of which should be determined by an equation; currently such equations are not understood well enough to yield any useful information.

String mode

A possible configuration (vibrational pattern, winding configuration) that a string can assume.

String theory

(a) A theory in which the fundamental constituents of matter are not particles but tiny one-dimensional objects, which we can think of as strings. These strings are so minute (only 10^{-33} cm long) that, even at current experimental energies, they seem to behave just like particles. So, according to string theory, what we call "elementary particles" are actually tiny strings. each of which is vibrating in a way characteristic of the particular "elementary particle".

(b) Unified theory of the Universe postulating that fundamental ingredients of nature are not zero-dimensional point particles but tiny one-dimensional filaments called strings. String theory harmoniously unites quantum mechanics and general relativity the previously known laws of the small and the large, that are otherwise incompatible. Often short for superstring theory.

(c) Theory that subatomic particles actually have extension along one axis, and that their properties are determined by the arrangement and vibration of the strings.

(d) The latest theory of fundamental physics in which the basic entity is a one-dimensional object rather than the 'zero-dimensional' point of conventional elementary particle physics.

(e) A theory of elementary particles incorporating relativity and quantum mechanics in which the particles are viewed not as points but as extended objects. String theory is a possible framework for constructing unified theories which include both the microscopic forces and gravity.

Strong focusing

A system for focusing charged particles in which the particles pass alternately through non-uniform electric or magnetic fields having gradients of opposite sign. Strong focusing is employed in the Fermilab Main Ring and Tevatron where quadrupole magnets of alternating signs provide the focusing for the circulating protons.

Strong force

The fundamental strong force is the force between quarks and Gluons that makes them combine to form the observed hadrons, such as protons and neutrons. It also causes forces between hadrons, such as the strong nuclear force that makes protons and neutrons bind together to form nuclei.

Strong force symmetry

Gauge symmetry underlying the strong force, associated with invariance of a physical system under shifts in the color charges of quarks.

Strong interaction

(a) The short-range nuclear force which is assumed to be responsible for binding the nucleus together. Strong interactions are so called because they occur in the extremely short time of about 10^{-23} seconds. Strong interactions can occur only when the particles involved are less than 3 fermis apart.

(b) The short-range nuclear interactions responsible for holding nuclei together. The characteristic range of the strong interaction is 10^{-13} cm, and the time scale over which it operates is 10^{-33} second.

(c) The interactions which bind quarks together to form rotons, neutrons, and other particles. The residual effects of these forces are responsible for the forces between protons and neutrons.

Strong nuclear force

(a) One of the four fundamental forces of nature. It governs the interaction between particles in atomic nuclei.

(b) Fundamental force of nature that binds quarks together, and holds nucleons (which are comprised of quarks) together as the nuclei of atoms. Portrayed in quantum chromodynamics as conveyed by quanta called gluons.

Strong nuclear interaction

The interaction that holds the particles of the nucleus together and is independent of charge.

Strongly coupled

Theory whose string coupling constant is larger than 1.

Strong-weak duality

Situation in which a strongly coupled theory is dual-physically identical-to a different, weakly coupled theory.

Strontium

A soft low-melting reactive metal. The electronic configuration is that of krypton with two additional outer 5s electrons.

Structure

Objects have structure if they have parts - that is, if they are made of other things. Whether objects have structure can be learned from experiments that probe them with projectiles. Over the past century, each stage of matter that was found as it became possible to search for ever-smaller things turned out to have structure. Quarks and leptons appear not to have structure, so perhaps the search for the basic constituents has finally ended. There are also theoretical arguments that quarks and leptons are the basic constituents.

Su(3)

Symmetrical Unitary of Order 3: A symmetry found in sub-nuclear spectra. It is a concept in group theory, by which Gell-Mann and others, using eight quantum numbers, have been able to combine particles into family groups or supermultiplets, as the lowest-lying eightfold group of the nucleon doublet, the singlet, the triplet, and the doublet. The SU(3) theory applies only to the strongly interacting particles.

Su(5)

The symmetrical Unitary of Order 5: The simplest type of grand unified theory, proposed in the 1970s.

Su(n)

The mathematical structure known as a 'group' that describes operations on N objects. Examples include SU(2) applied to the two quarks or two leptons in a generation and SU(3) applied to the three colors of quark. The three colors and two flavors have recently been combined to yield a set of live entities that can be described by a grand unified theory exploiting SU(5).

Sub-atomic

Of a scale smaller than that of an atom.

Subatomic particle

Any particle that is contained in an atom, or any particle that can be created in collisions of such particles, is loosely called subatomic, whether it is composite like a proton or elementary like a quark or electron.

Subcooled

The temperature difference between a liquid temperature and the (greater) equilibrium vapor pressure temperature.

Subcooler

A device to subcool liquid. Accomplished by providing heat exchange to a bath of significantly reduced pressure, equilibrium liquid. Often from the same source.

Subcritical

Describing an arrangement of fissile material that does not permit a sustained chain reaction because too many neutrons are absorbed without causing fission or otherwise lost.

Subdwarf (sd)

(a) A metal-poor main-sequence star. On the H-R diagram, subdwarfs lie slightly below the metal-rich Main Sequence, because they are fainter than metal-rich main-sequence stars of the same color.

(b) A star whose luminosity is 1.5 to 2 magnitudes lower than that of main-sequence stars of the same spectral type. Subdwarfs are primarily Population II and lie just below the Main Sequence on the H-R diagram.

(c) Late-type object whose observed color and absolute magnitude place it below the Main Sequence.

Subgiant

A star whose position on the H-R diagram is intermediate between that of main-sequence stars and normal giants of the same spectral type.

Sublattice magnetization

In an antiferromagnet the magnetic atoms can be divided into two equivalent classes, each magnetized in opposite directions. The total magnetization of one of these classes is the sublattice magnetization.

Sublimation

The change of a solid to a gaseous phase without passing through the liquid phase.

Sublimation (pump)

Sputter ion pumps as found in the Main Ring are not sufficient to achieve the ultra high vacuum needed in the Accumulator ring ($3X10^{-10}$ T), so titanium sublimation pumps are also employed. Sublimation pumps are a form of retainment pump. Retainment pumps operate by capturing gas molecules and retaining them on a surface. The p-source uses Titaniumsublimation pumps: a titanium filament is heated so as to cause the titanium to sublime and deposit on the nearby walls as a thin film. This fresh layer of titanium acts as a getter, passing gas molecules react with the Ti and are captured on the surface. Periodically a fresh film must be deposited. This is known as 'sublimating'.

Sub-luminous stars

Stars fainter than those on the main sequence. Subluminous stars are stars whose age divided by their life span is close to unity.

Sub-pulse

The weaker component of the pulse of a pulsar.

Subsonic

Describing a speed that is less than the speed of sound in the medium concerned.

Subspace

A subset of a vector space which is closed under the operations of vector addition and scalar multiplication.

Substorm

a process by which plasma in the magnetotail becomes energized at a fast rate, flowing Earthward and producing bright auroras and large Birkeland currents, for typical durations of half an hour.

Sum-over-histories

Probabilistic interpretation of a system's past, in which quantum indeterminacy is taken into account and the history is reconstructed in terms of each possible path and its relative likelihood.

Sum-over-paths

Formulation of quantum mechanics in which particles are envisioned to travel from one point to another along all possible paths between them.

Sun's corona

The luminous irregular envelope of highly ionized gas outside the chromosphere of the sun.

Sunspot

An intensely magnetic area on the Sun's visible face. For unclear reasons, it is slightly cooler than the surrounding photosphere (perhaps because the magnetic field somehow interferes with the outflow of solar heat in that region) and therefore appears a bit darker. Sunspots tend to be associated with violent solar outbursts of all kinds.

Sunspot cycle (or solar cycle)

An irregular cycle, averaging about 11 years in length, during which the number of sunspots (and of their associated outbursts) rises and then drops again. Like the sunspots, the cycle is probably magnetic in nature, and the polar magnetic field of the Sun also reverses each solar cycle.

Sunspot radiation

Intense, variable, circularly polarized radio waves in a noise storm.

Sun-synchronous orbit

a near-Earth orbit resembling that of a polar satellite, but inclined to it by a small angle. With the proper inclination angle, the equatorial bulge causes the orbit to rotate during the year once around the polar axis. Such a satellite then maintains a fixed position relative to the Sun and can, for instance, avoid entering the Earth's shadow.

Sunyaev-zel'dovich process

Compton scattering between the photons of the cosmic microwave background radiation and electrons in galaxy clusters.

Super critical

Pressures, Temperatures, or both above the critical point parameters.

Super heat

The difference between a gas temperature and the lower equilibrium vapor pressure temperature.

Super heater

A device specifically designed to provide some degree of super heat. see Vaporizer.

Super insulation

Multiple reflective layers of aluminized Mylar to reduce cryogenic radiation heat transfer.

Superbucket

A superbucket is an R.F. bunch in the extracted beam containing a substantially larger number of particles than the average R.F. bunch. A superbucket arises when the accelerated beam undergoes oscillations which do not effect all bunches equally; typically there is a periodicity of every 3rd or every 7th bunch over a train of thousands or millions of bunches. The term is to some extent a misnomer because "bucket" applies only within the accelerator whereas the effect is most talked about as observed in the experimental area.

Supercluster

A cluster of clusters of galaxies. Superclusters are typically about one hundred million (10^8) light-years in diameter and contain tens of thousands of galaxies.

Superconduct

To have no resistance. A perfect superconductor can carry an electrical current without losses.

Superconducting

Having no resistive component to electrical impedance.

Superconducting magnet

This is a magnet whose coils are made from superconducting material. Superconducting magnets reach much higher magnetic fields than conventional iron/copper magnets at a much lower electrical power cost. They must be cooled to 4 degrees K which is achieved by a continual flow of liquid helium through the magnets.

Superconducting super collider

A proposed accelerator of great size and high energy.

Superconducting transition temperature

This is the critical temperature below which a substance loses its electrical resistance and thus becomes a superconductor.

Superconducting wire

Wire made from materials which become superconducting at low temperatures and are thus able to carry very high currents without losses. Niobium-Titanium is a popular superconducting material that is used in the magnets for the Tevatron at Fermilab.

Superconductivity

This is a state of matter that many metals and alloys reach at sufficiently low temperatures (i.e. a few oK). This state is characterized by the total absence of electrical resistance thus making possible the conduction of electrical currents without any measurable loss. Superconductivity was discovered by Kammerlingh Onnes in the Netherlands in 1911. He was the first person to liquefy helium and was thus able to reach the extreme cold necessary to observe superconducting effects in mercury.

Superconductor

A substance which loses all electrical resistance when cooled to or below a critical temperature (typically 5-10 degrees Kelvin).

Supercooling

(a) The process by which a substance is cooled below the temperature at which a phase transition should occur, such as water that has been cooled to below zero degrees Centigrade but that has not yet formed ice.

(b) The phenomenon in which a system can be cooled below the normal temperature of a phase transition without the phase transition taking place. The original form of the inflationary Universe theory was based on the assumption that the Universe supercooled below the temperature of the grand unified theory phase transition.

Supercycle

The supercycle time is the amount of time required to complete all the different machine cycles that have been defined to operate periodically as a unit. This implies that the supercycle time is periodic and that its length is dependent on the number and duration of different machine cycles defined to occur within its period.

Supercycle reset

The starting point for all of the sequences in a supercycle. It is initiated by TCLK event 00 and takes place automatically when the previous supercycle is complete.

Superfluid

A liquid which undergoes the phenomenon of superfluidity, below the temperature at which this phenomenon sets in.

Super-high frequency

SFH A radio frequency in the range between 30 GHz and 3 GHz (wavelength 1 to 10 cm).

Supernova

A star that explodes and becomes extremely luminous in the process.

Superperiod

The large scale repetitive lattice of the Main Ring and Tevatron accelerators which is made up of 14 normal cells, 1 long straight section cell, 1 medium straight, and 1 short straight section cell.

Superposition

The principle of superposition states that the various wave trains which, in their totality, make up a wave may be considered as mutually independent. The properties of the combined waves can be computed as the sum (phase and amplitude) of the effects of elementary waves, treating the latter as if each were present alone.

Surface plot

A three-dimensional plot mapping the intensity of radiation from a region as a distorted surface. More intense radiation is represented by higher points on the surface. Therefore, regions of intense radiation resemble mountains on the earth.

Surface tension

The tendency of a liquid surface to contract; the measure of this tendency in newtons per meter.

Surface tension

The property of a liquid due to which its surface behaves like a stretched membrane.

S-wave

Secondary Wave: A seismic shear wave that moves transversely through Earth. The s-waves cannot penetrate the core of the Earth, being totally reflected by the 2900-km discontinuity.

Swic

Segmented Wire Ionization Chamber. It is a device used to determine beam profiles in the Switchyard and beam lines.

Switchyard

A system of devices through which the primary proton beam is removed from the Tevatron accelerator and transported to the external targeting stations.

Switchyard front end

The computer which interfaces with the electronics which control and monitor Switchyard devices. It is presently a DEC PDP-11.

Swix

Signal SWitching MatrIX. A software controlled switch for signals to be put on an oscilloscope.

Synchrocyclotron

The synchrocyclotron is a frequency modulated cyclotron which is capable of reaching higher energies by compensating for relativistic effects with a variable frequency accelerating voltage.

Synchronous orbit

a circular orbit around the equator, at a distance of 6.6 Earth radii. At this distance the orbital period is 24 hours, keeping the satellite "anchored" above the same spot on Earth. This makes the synchronous orbit useful for communication satellites: a satellite transmitting TV programs to the US, for instance, will always be in touch with the US if "anchored" above it, and receiving antennas will only need to point to a fixed spot in the sky.

Synchronous particle

The hypothetical particle circulating in phase with the rf voltage about which other particles in the phase-space bucket would oscillate.

Synchronous phase angle

The phase of the RF field needed to provide the proper accelerating voltage. The synchronous phase angle must be nonzero for acceleration to take place. The synchronous phase angle is zero at injection (provided there is not a phase error) and varied as the bend field in the magnets is increased to provide a positive accelerating voltage.

Synchrotron

A circular machine that accelerates subatomic particles to high energy by the repeated action of electric forces on the particles at each revolution. The particles are made to move in constant circular orbits by magnetic forces that continually increase in magnitude. Fermilab's Booster accelerator, Main Ring, and Tevatron are synchrotrons.

Synchrotron frequency

Frequency of longitudinal oscillations of the bunches.

Synchrotron oscillation

Synchrotron oscillation is the longitudinal oscillation of particles in an accelerator about an equilibrium of the phase of accelerating voltage at the time the particles are crossing the accelerating gap. The restoring force for the oscillation is provided by a property (phase focusing) of synchronous acceleration that out of time particles receive greater or less acceleration than the in time particles with the correct sense to reduce the time error on the next crossing of the accelerating gap. In synchrotrons like the Fermilab Booster and Main Ring, a particle makes many revolutions around the accelerator in a single synchrotron oscillation period.

Synchrotron radiation

Whenever a charged particle undergoes accelerated motion it radiates electromagnetic energy. A common example is the emission of radio waves when electrons move back and forth in a radio antenna. A charged particle traveling in the arc of a circle is also undergoing acceleration, due to its change in direction. The radiation emitted by such particles is called synchrotron radiation and it is particularly intense and very directional when electrons traveling at close to the speed of light are bent in magnetic fields.

System ready

Sum of the second-level interlocks in the NTF interlock module. Two such sums ("A" and "B") are required to be present in order to make up the next level of interlocks.

Systematic error

This is an error that throws off a measurement's value the same way each time the measurement is taken. These errors do not tend to cancel out when the average is taken. However, once a systematic error has been discovered, and if it was the same throughout the measurement process, it can be corrected. That is, unless it is a systematic error made by a bureaucracy in its dealings with you. In that case an error was not really made, but if it was, it was your fault.

T

T_2^*

Pronounced T-2-star. The spin-spin relaxation time composed of contributions from molecular interactions and inhomogeneities in the magnetic field.

Tachyon

A hypothetical particle of imaginary mass whose velocity always exceeds the speed of light. Tachyons have never been observed.

Tagged photon lab

An experimental area using the Proton-East beam. Photons from the primary target make electron-positron pairs in a converter. The electrons are transported several hundred feet and then impinge on a thin sheet of lead in the Tagged Photon Lab. In passing through the lead, some of the electrons will be deflected, emitting a high energy photon in approximately the forward direction. The energy of these photons is determined by measuring the energy of the deflected electrons, i.e., the photons are "tagged". The tagged photons are then used in experiments.

Tagging

Tagging is a process that establishes the states of particles before they interact with a target. Information about these initial states combined with data on the final state enable the experimenter to study the details of a reaction.

Tail lobes

the two bundles of nearly-parallel magnetic field lines which stretch into the *magnetotail,* on opposite sides of the *plasma sheet.* The northern lobe contains field lines entering the north polar region of Earth, while the southern lobe contains lines emerging from the southern polar region.

Tangential

Tangent to a curve. In circular motion, used to mean tangent to the circle, perpendicular to the radial direction Cf. Radial.

Tangential acceleration

Tangential acceleration is the same as linear acceleration in the following sense. Linear acceleration is rate of change of the velocity of an object in straight-line motion. It is the same as rate of change of the speed of the object but with a plus or minus sign. The plus sign corresponds to the velocity becoming more positive (or less negative), and the negative sign to the velocity becoming less positive (or more negative).

Tarcus

Tevatron Automated Ramp Checkout and Startup. A program on the MCR consoles which automates the necessary programs and steps of turning on the Tevatron ramp.

Target

Object intentionally struck by the proton beam in

order to produce secondary particles which are then studied by experimenters.

Target box

The targeting systems in Proton-East and Proton-Centre are placed inside a steel box. Each box contains five sets of parallel rails. Components, which may be as simple as a block of steel or as complicated as a set of magnets, are mounted on steel plates (drawers) which slide along the rails on bearings.

Target train

A series of magnets, targets, collimators, and diagnostic equipment placed on small railroad flatcars. Temporary setups for one experiment can be built on one set of flatcars (train load) while beam is being delivered on another. There are target trains in the Meson and Neutrino Areas.

Target tuning; pbar

The process of moving the the position where Main Ring beam strikes the pbar target to maximize pbar production. If beam is too close to the edge of the target horizontally, not enough pbars are produced. If beam is too close to the centre horizontally then too many pbars are reabsorbed in the target material. Vertical position is sensitize to capture by the lithium lens. Beam is steered by means of trim magnets in the AP1 line upstream from the target.

Tau

The third charged lepton (in order of increasing mass), with electric charge -1.

Tecar

Tevatron Excitation Control And Regulation. The microprocessor system which sends phasing information to the Tevatron main power supplies.

Tecar

Tevatron Excitation Control And Regulation. The microprocessor system which sends phasing information to the Tevatron main power supplies.

Technology

The application of science to human needs and goals.

Tele

A prefix meaning at a distance, as in telescope, telemetry, television.

Temperature

What a thermometer measures. Objects left in contact with each other tend to reach the same temperature. Roughly speaking, temperature measures the average kinetic energy per molecule. For the distinction between temperature and heat, see the glossary entry for heat.

Temporary magnet

A magnet produced by induction.

Tensile strength

The force required to break a rod or wire of unit cross-sectional area.

Term

One of several quantities which are added together.

Terminal

The point at which the operator interacts with the computer system. It usually consists of a keyboard and either a typewriter or TV screen.

Terrella

A small magnetized sphere, used as laboratory model of the Earth.

Tesla

The S.I. unit of magnetic flux density, defined as the magnetic flux density of a magnetic flux of 1 Wb through an area of $1m^2$.

Tetrode

A thermionic emission tube with four electrodes: cathode, anode, grid, and screen.

Tev

Tera electron volt or 1012 electron volts. "T" is also conveniently the initial letter of trillion which in American terminology is 1012.

Tevatron

The liquid Helium (4.2 K) cooled ring used to accelerate protons and antiprotons from 120 gev up to 1 tev beam energy. The two huge collider experiments sit at a place on this ring where the two counter-circulating beams are allowed to collide together. The magnets are superconducting magnets which require such cold temperatures. The cooling system has won awards for its ingenious construction as it is the largest volume helium-cooled system operating in the world.

Tevatron clock

Is a 10 mhz encoded pulse train which carries the clock events for triggering the operation of accelerator electronics.

Tevatron front end

The computer which interfaces with the electronics which control and monitor Tevatron devices. It is presently a DEC PDP-11.

Theoretical

Describing an idea which is part of a theory, or a consequence derived from theory.

Theories of relativity

Einstein's extensions to classical mechanics and electromagnetism.

Theory

A well-tested mathematical model of some part of science. In physics a theory usually takes the form of an equation or a group of equations, along with explanatory rules for their application. Theories are said to be successful if: (1) they synthesize and unify a significant range of phenomena; (2) they have predictive power, either predicting new phenomena, or suggesting a direction for further research and testing.

Thermal capacity

The quantity of heat required to raise the temperature of the whole body by one degree (1K or 1deg C) is called its thermal capacity.

Thermal conductivity

K, The heat flow per unit length per unit temperature difference of a given material and temperature. Varies with the temperature range under consideration. (wcm°k)

Thermal conductivity integral

The heat flow per unit length of a given material between two particular temperature end points.

Thermal contact

Contact between objects that allows them to influence each other's temperatures.

Thermal contraction

The shrinkage for reductions in temperature, usually expressed as a dimensionless number x 10^{-5} D Length/Length over a stated temperature range. The coefficient of thermal contraction (a,Δλ/λ°k) is a function of temperature.

Thermal energy

Careful writers make a distinction between heat and thermal energy, but the distinction is often ignored in casual speech, even among physicists. Properly, thermal energy is used to mean the total amount of energy possessed by an object, while heat indicates the amount of thermal energy transferred in or out. The term heat is used in this book to include both meanings.

Thermal equilibrium

When the two bodies in contact are at the same temperature and there is no flow of heat between them, these are said to be in thermal equilibrium. The common temperature of the bodies in thermal equilibrium is called the equilibrium temperature.

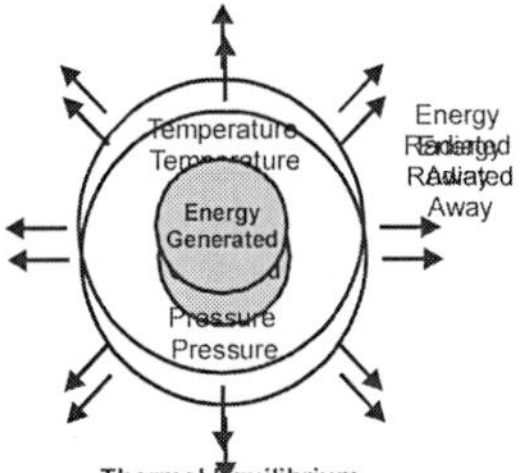

Thermal Equilibrium

Thermal expansion
The increase in the size of an object on heating is called thermal expansion.

Thermal gas
A collection of particles that collide with each other and exchange energy frequently, giving a distribution of particle energies that can be characterized by a single temperature.

Thermal particle
A particle that is part of a thermal gas.

Thermal radiation
Electromagnetic radiation emitted by electrons in a thermal gas.

Thermionic emission
The liberation of electrons from the surface of a hot body.

Thermocouple
An electric circuit composed of two dissimilar metals whose junctions are maintained at different temperatures .

Thermocouple gauge
Used to measure vacuum pressure. This type of gauge utilizes a thermocouple to measure the temperature of a heated element exposed to the vacuum. It is typically used down to about 1E-3 torr.

Thermodynamics
The branch of physics concerned with very general properties of matter and energy. It also describes the macroscopic properties of matter in terms of the microscopic properties of its components.

Thermoelectric effect
The production of an electron current in a closed circuit consisting of two dissimilar metals as a result of the emf developed when the two junctions are maintained at different temperatures.

Thermometer
It is a device used for numerical measurement of temperature. The commonly used thermometer is mercury thermometer.

Thermonuclear fusion
The combination of atomic nuclei at high temperatures to form more massive nuclei with the simultaneous release of energy. Thermonuclear fusion is the power source at the core of the Sun. Controlled thermonuclear fusion reactors, when successfully implemented, could become an attractive source of power on the Earth.

Third law of motion
Newton's first law of motion was really due to Galileo, his second law is a definition (and, actually, much more) and not exactly a law and therefore neither first nor second, so the third law of motion must really be his first and only law of motion. It might appear, therefore that Newton didn't do as much as claimed, but, in fact, he was the one who put physics on a modern footing. Theoretical physics can be thought of as beginning with the efforts of Sir Isaac, just as experimental physics began with Galileo. His "third law" expresses the idea that something cannot act on something else without being acted upon in turn. To whit: "If body A exerts a force on body B, then body B exerts an equal and opposite force on body A." These two equal and opposite forces are called an "action-reaction pair". Each member force of this pair is called an "action-reaction partner". Note that these forces *must* act on separate objects. A pair of forces acting on the same object is *not* an action-reaction pair. Also the action-reaction partners must be the same kind of force.

Third law of photoelectric emission
Within the region of effective frequencies, the maximum kinetic energy of photoelectrons varies directly with the difference between the frequency of the incident light and the cut-off frequency.

Thought experiment
An idealized experiment that cannot be performed under actual conditions.

Threshold frequency
The minimum frequency that light must have in

order to cause photoelectrons to be emitted by a given metal.

Threshold of hearing

The intensity of the faintest sound audible to the average human ear, 10^{-16} w/cm^2 at 10^3 hz.

Threshold of pain

For audible frequencies of sound, an intensity level above which pain results in the average human ear. Rock concert.

Thyratron

A gas-filled triode in which the voltage on the grid can trigger ionization of the gas in the tube. Once the gas is ionized, current flows from cathode to anode until the potential across the two falls below a certain level. In Linac the thyratrons are used as high-voltage relays in the chopper power supplies and in the RF modulators to trigger the ignitrons.

Thyratron

A gas-filled triode in which the voltage on the grid can trigger ionization of the gas in the tube. Once the gas is ionized, current flows from cathode to anode until the potential across the two falls below a certain level. In Linac the thyratrons are used as high-voltage relays in the chopper power supplies and in the RF modulators to trigger the ignitrons.

Tiger team

A U.S. Navy term for a highly specialized group with a special mission. Tiger Teams at Fermilab pamphlet.

Time dilation

Time dilation is an observed difference of elapsed time between two events as measured by observers either moving relative to each other or differently situated from gravitational masses. An accurate clock at rest with respect to one observer may be measured to tick at a different rate when compared to a second observer's own equally accurate clocks.

Time line generator

The module which encodes accelerator reset events on the Tevatron clock.

Time period (of a wave)

The time taken by a wave to travel through a distance equal to its wavelength is called its time period. It is denoted by T. Time period of a wave=1/ frequency of the wave.

Time period (of an oscillation)

The time taken to complete one oscillation is called the time period of an oscillation. The time period of a pendulum does not depend upon the mass of the bob and amplitude of oscillation. The time period of a pendulum is directly proportional to the square root of the length and inversely proportional to the square root of the acceleration due to gravity.

Timing diagram

A multiaxis plot of some aspects of a pulse sequence as a function of time.

TLG

Time Line Generator. It is a CAMAC 172 module controlled from page D69. The TLG defines the start time and the duration of cycle for each major system in the accelerator. Physically it resides in Rack 15 of the MAC room.

TLM

Total Loss Monitor. Any loss monitor which extends throughout an entire tunnel enclosure. TLM's give a good overall picture of losses in an area.

TM (010)

The transverse magnetic field configuration used in linear accelerators. This configuration has an axial electric field which is used to accelerate the particles.

TOF measurement

A time of flight (TOF) measurement takes advantage of the RF bunching in a beam to measure the time interval between a reference signal related to the production of particles in the target and the signal from detectors placed a known distance from the target. This method is frequently used to search for new particles.

Tolerance

The amount that the readback of a device can deviate from the nominal value before going into an alarm state.

Top quark

The sixth flavor of quark (in order of increasing mass) with electric charge +2/3.

Toroid

A device used to measure beam current in an accelerator; so named because it uses a toroidal winding on a core as a pickup.

Toroidal radius

In a solar loop structure, it is the distance from the axis of the loop to the centre of the "semi-circle" that the loop forms. Half of the distance from one loop footpoint to the other loop footpoint. For a doughnut, it is the distance from the centre of the doughnut hole to the centre (circular axis) of the pastry.

Torque

The rate of change of angular momentum; a numerical measure of a force's ability to twist on an object.

Torque arm

The perpendicular distance between the line of action of the torque producing force and the axis of rotation.

Torr

A practical unit of pressure equal to the amount of pressure required to support a column of mercury one millimeter high.

Total internal reflection

Condition where all light is reflected back from a boundary between materials; occurs when light travels from denser to rarer medium and angle of incidence is greater than the critical angle.

Total reflection

The reflection of light at the boundary of two transparent media when the angle of incidence exceeds the critical angle.

Touch panel

An accessory present at all ACNET consoles which allows the user to interact with an applications program by pressing a specified region on a touch-sensitive panel.

Tracer

A small amount of radioactive isotope introduced into a system in order to follow the behavior of some component of that system.

Track

The record of the path of a particle traversing a detector.

Trackball

An encoder at the ACNET consoles which allows the user to change the (x,y) position of the cursor on the TV and AEOLUS screens.

Tracking chamber

A section of a particle detector capable of detecting the passage of electrically charged particles.

Transfer hall

The section of the Main Ring where the Booster beam is transferred into the Main Ring. This is also the location of the extraction devices sending the beam into the switchyard.

Transfer line

A vacuum insulated, cryogenic radiation shielded, or concentric cryogenic pipe.

Transformation

The mathematical relationship between the variables such as x and t, as observed in different frames of reference.

Transformer

An electrical component consisting of two or more coils of wire placed in close proximity to each other such that the magnetic fields of each transformer overlap. Used to transfer electric energy from one alternating current circuit to one or more others. Often used to increase or decrease the voltage in the second circuit. Also used to physically isolate one circuit from another but still allow the transfer of AC power.

Transistor
A semiconductor device used as a substitute for vacuum tubes in electronic applications.

Transition
The point in a synchrotron machine's cycle at which all particles, regardless of their slight differences in momentum, take exactly the same amount of time to circle the machine. At this point the phase of the RF voltage with respect to the synchronous particle must be changed for the beam to remain stable. The energy at which this occurs is determined by the machine's lattice.

Transition energy (synchrotron)
The energy below which the particle rotation period decreases with increasing energy and above which the period increases with increasing energy. At this critical energy, a change in proton energy has no effect on the period. The RF electrical fields must be modified as the protons pass through the transition energy in order to assure stable acceleration to higher energies. The transition energy in the Fermilab Main Ring is 17 GeV.

Transition temperature
A specific temperature at which the resistivity of some materials drops suddenly to zero.

Translational equilibrium
The state of a body in which there are no unbalanced forces acting on it.

Transmission line
An electric line uniform in series resistance, series inductance, shunt inductance, and shunt capacitance. The transmission line from a PA to an RF cavity is coaxial in construction.

Transmission line
An electric line uniform in series resistance, series inductance, shunt inductance, and shunt capacitance. The transmission line from a PA to an RF cavity is coaxial in construction.

Transmutation
The transformation of one element into another by a nuclear reaction.

Transport line
A system of bending and focusing magnets used to transport beam from one area to another.

Transuranium elements
Elements with atomic number greater than 92.

Transverse magnetization
The XY component of the net magnetization.

Transverse wave
A wave in which the particles of the medium oscillate in a direction perpendicular of the direction of propagation of wave.

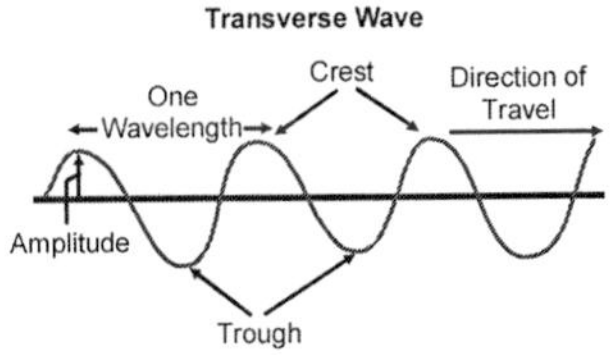

Trigger
An experimenter sets up 'a priori criteria' for accepting data. Once these criteria are met, an electronic signal allows events to be recorded. Not all triggers are legitimate events, however, but are the raw data recorded for computer analysis.

Trim
Small dipole magnet used for fine control of beam positions.

Triode
A thermionic emission tube with three electrodes: cathode, anode, and grid.

Triple point
The single condition of temperature and pressure at which the solid, liquid, and vapor phases of a substance can coexist in stable equilibrium.

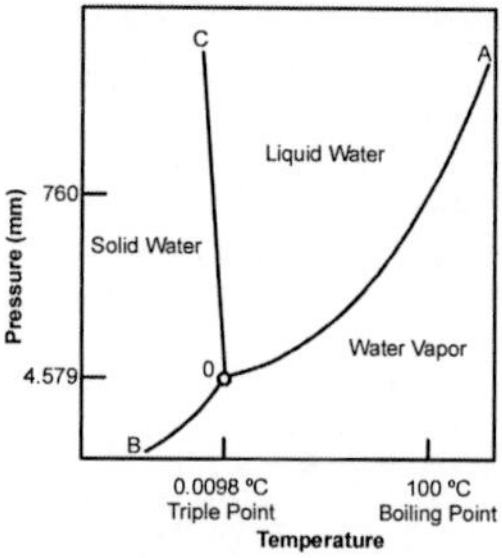

Triple point cells

Triple point cells are used in the calibration of thermometers. For exacting work, triple point cells are typically filled with a highly pure chemical substance such as hydrogen, argon, mercury, or water (depending on the desired temperature).

Triple point of water

The temperature of water at which ice, liquid water, and water vapor coexist at thermal equilibrium, defined as 0.01°C or 273.16 K. at 4.56 mm Hg (0.006 atm).

Triplet

A system of three quadrupoles of alternating polarity; it is used much like a doublet, but allows for coincidental focusing in the horizontal and vertical planes.

Triplet train

One of the target train systems in the Neutrino Area. It provides a broadband neutrino beam (a neutrino beam composed of a wide range of energies) using quadrupole focusing elements. The triplet train is compatible with operation of the muon beam N-1. "Triplet" refers to the three quadrupole magnet pairs used to focus the p and K particles produced at the target before they decay into the neutrinos and muons.

Trombone

Another name for a variable delay line. Trombones are used in the stochastic cooling systems to provide the proper delay between the pickups and the kickers. Trombones can also be found in the Linac gallery basement in series with every RF system PA to cavity transmission line.

Trough

A crest is the point on a wave with the maximum value or upward displace- ment within a cycle. A trough is the opposite of a crest, so the minimum or lowest point in a cycle.

Tscc link driver

Tevatron Serial Crate Controller. It handles the serial to parallel conversion, and vice-versa, when information is being passed between the parallel CAMAC dataway and a serial link.

Tss

Technical Support Section

TU77 tape drive

A high-performance, automatic-loading tape transport that uses recording densities of 800 bits/ inch or 1600 bits/inch, selectable under program control.

TU78 tape drive

A high-performance, automatic-loading tape that uses recording densities of 1600 bits/inch or 6250 bits/inch, selectable under program control.

Tune diagram

A plot of vertical tune values versus horizontal tune values with stop bands shown as solid or dashed lines.

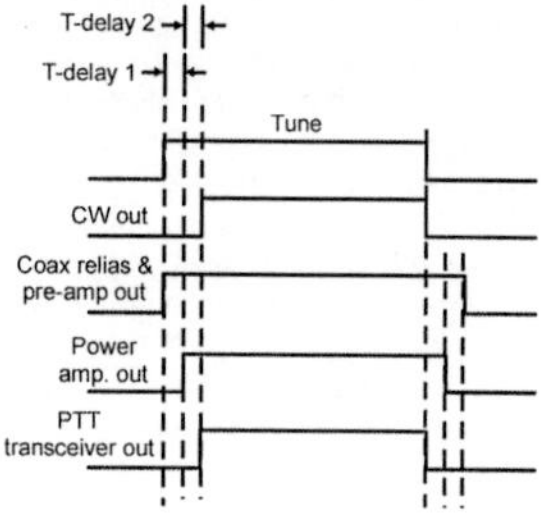

Tune of the accelerator

This is the number of betatron oscillations per Main Ring or Tevatron revolution. Presently the horizontal tune of the Main Ring is about 19.4

Tune

The number of betatron oscillations per revolution of the beam. There is a horizontal tune nx and a vertical tune ny. Its magnitude is primarily a function of quadrupole strengths. In operator parlance, tune is also used to mean the process of adjusting machine parameters to increase intensity or efficiency, or both.

Tuned circuit

A circuit that has its resistance, capacitance, and inductance adjusted so that it resonates at a certain frequency. See Resonance.

Tuner (R.F.)

An R.F. tuner is a variable reactance for changing the resonant frequency of an LC circuit or resonant cavity. As applied to the Fermilab Booster and Main Ring accelerating cavities the tuner consists of ferrite rings coupled to the accelerating cavity and biased by a programmed d.c. Current which flows in a toroidal winding around the rings to vary their magnetic permeability and hence their inductive loading of the cavity.

Tuning

The activity of adjusting magnets and other equipment which interact with a beam of particles in order to obtain a beam of desired characteristics, e.g., a beam focused onto a target with a small spot size.

Tuning fork

A metal two-prong fork that produces a sound of a definite pitch.

Tuning slug

Copper cylinders mounted in the wall of the Linac RF cavities that may be moved in and out to adjust cavity tune. Specifically, one motorized slug in each tank under the control of the low-level RF system.

Turbo molecular pump

A vacuum pump. It uses rapidly rotating vanes (turbines) to impart a momentum component to gas molecules, compressing them and making them easier to pump with a roughing pump. Used in the second stage of vacuum pump down, good down to about 10–9 torr. Ion pumps are used at operational pressures for the sake of economy and practicality.

Turnkey account

Also called captive account. An account which is open to any user. The password is publicly available information. Examples include the "Operator" account on the Operational VAX and the "DOSYL" account on the Development VAX.

Turn-on order

The order in which the Main Ring power supplies are phased on to ensure a minimal voltage to ground on the Main Ring bus.

Tvbs

Tevatron Beam Sync Clock. It is derived from a sub harmonic of the Tevatron RF frequency. See MRBS.

TWT

Travelling Wave Tube. TWT's are the final amplifiers for the stochastic cooling kickers. The Debuncher tubes can be found in the tunnel above the Debuncher kicker tanks. Accumulator TWT's are enclosed in racks in AP30 adjacent to the TWT power supplies. - Pbar Rookiebook

U

Ucd

Universal Clock Decoder. It is a card found in the PEX box of the PDP-11's. It generates a 15 Hz signal from the Tevatron clock for internal use. It can also be used to decode specific clock events and is used by the fast time plotting facility for that purpose.

Ultrasonic

Sound waves too high in frequency to be heard by the human ear; frequencies above 20,000Hz.

Ultrasonic range

Vibrations in matter above 20,000 vibrations/second.

Ultrasonic sound

Sound waves of frequencies above 20,000Hz.

Ultraviolet (UV)

electromagnetic radiation resembling visible light, but of shorter wavelength. The eye cannot see UV, and much of it is absorbed by ozone, a variant of oxygen, at altitudes of 30-40 km; satellite telescope, however, can and do view stars and the Sun in UV, and even in the extreme UV (EUV), the range between UV and X-rays.

Ultraviolet light

Electromagnetic radiations of shorter wavelength than visible light but longer than X rays.

Ultraviolet radiation

Electromagnetic radiation with a wavelength shorter than that of visible light, but longer than x-rays.

Umbra

The part of a shadow from which all light rays are excluded.

Unbalanced forces

When a number of forces act on a body and the resultant force is not zero, then the forces are said to be unbalanced.

Uncertainty

Synonym: error. A measure of the inherent variability of repeated measurements of a quantity. Aprediction of the probable variability of a result, based on the inherent uncertainties in the data, found from a mathematical calculation of how the data uncertainties would, in combination, lead to uncertainty in the result. This calculation or process by which one predicts the size of the uncertainty in results from the uncertainties in data and procedure is called error analysis. Uncertainties are always present; the experime- nter's job is to keep them as small as required for a useful result. We recognize two kinds of uncertainties: indeterminate and determinate. Indeterminate uncertainties are those whose size and sign are unknown, and are sometimes (misleadingly) called random. Determinate uncertainties are those of definite sign, often referring to uncertainties due to instrument miscalibration, bias in reading scales, or some unknown influence on the measurement.

Uncertainty principle

The statement that, due to the laws of quantum mechanics, it is impossible to simultaneously exactly measure a particle's position and momentum or to exactly measure a particle's energy for a finite amount of time.

Unibus box

The crate which houses the unibus cards. It communicates via a wire-wrapped backplane.

Unibus card

Any card designed specifically to reside in a Unibus box. They are found in the PEX boxes of each PDP-11 computer as well as in the VAX computers.

Unified field theory

A unified field theory is one that attempts to combine any two or more of the known interaction types (strong, electromagnetic, weak and gravitational) in a single theory so that the two distinct types of interaction are seen as two different aspects of a single mathematical structure. A 'grand unified' theory (or GUT) unifies three of the four types (strong, weak and electromagnetic interactions) in this way. The benefit is that the unification gives a simpler overall theory and predicts relationships between parameters that are otherwise independent.

Uniform acceleration

When the velocity of a body increases by equal amounts in equal intervals of time it is said to have uniform acceleration.

Uniform circular motion

If you've traveled much by air, you are familiar with this type of motion, encountered in holding patterns around airports. An object in uniform circular motion travels in a circle at constant speed. Although its speed is constant, it is nevertheless changing its direction of motion and hence its velocity. This change of the direction of motion results in centripetal acceleration, an acceleration that is directed toward the centre of the circle of motion. Therefore, as an air traveler you can take comfort that while in the holding pattern you are constantly accelerating toward the airport. Try not to think about the fact that, in spite of this, you are not getting any closer. The formula for the magnitude of this acceleration is: $a_c = v^2 / r$.

Uniform speed

When a body travels equal distances in equal intervals of time then it is said to have uniform speed.

Uniform velocity

When a body travels along a straight line in particular direction and covers equal distances in equal intervals of time it is said to have uniform velocity.

Unit magnetic pole

One that repels an exactly similar pole placed one centimeter away with a force of one dyne.

Units

Labels which distinguish one type of measurable quantity from other types. Length, mass and time are distinctly different physical quantities, and therefore have different unit names, meters, kilograms and seconds. We use several systems of units, including the metric (SI) units and a number of others of mainly historical interest.

Universal gas constant

Constant of proportionality, R, in the ideal gas equation.

Universal gravitational constant

Proportionality constant in Newton's law of universal gravitation, a fundamental constant of the universe, with the value 6.67×10-11 N-m2/kg.

Universal law of gravitation

Every object in the universe is attracted to every other object with a force directly proportional to the product of their masses and inversely proportional to the square of the distance between the centres of the two masses.

Universal time

The same as Greenwich Mean Time (GMT) in

England. Eastern Standard Time (EST) is five hours earlier than Universal Time.

Unpolarized light

Light consisting of transverse waves vibrating in all conceivable random directions.

Unstable

Matter that is capable of undergoing spontaneous change, as in a radioactive nuclide or an excited nuclear system. An unstable particle is any elementary particle that spontaneously decays into other particles.

Unstable equilibrium

One in which any deviation of the object from its equilibrium position results in a force pushing it even farther away.

UP quark

The first flavor of quark (in order of increasing mass), with electric charge +2/3.

Upstream

A relative term indicating the direction opposite to that in which the protons travel in that portion of the accelerator.

URA

University research association, inc.

User

High energy physics experimenter.

Utility crate

Obsolete. A modified CAMAC crate that was located in the "3 bay racks" of the Main Ring service buildings. These crates contained all the Main Ring link cards as well as the cards that controled and monitored such things as the LCW, correction elements, etc.

V

Vacuum

A space entirely devoid of matter (called also, by way of distinction, absolute vacuum). In a more general sense, a space, as the interior of a closed vessel, which has been exhausted to a high or the highest degree by an air pump or other artificial means.

Vacuum window

A thin piece of metal in the path of the beam which separates one portion of the beam tube vacuum from another.

Van allen belts

Two ring-shaped regions that girdle the Earth's equator in which electrically charged particles are trapped by the Earth's magnetic field.

Van de graaff generator

A particle accelerator that transfers a charge from an electron source to an insulated sphere by means of a moving belt composed of an insulating material.

Van der wall's force

General term for weak attractive intermolecular forces.

Vapor

The gaseous phase of a substance that exists as a liquid or solid under normal conditions.

Vapor pressure

The pressure as a function of temperature of a liquid in equilibrium with its own vapor.

Vaporization

The change in phase from a solid or a liquid to a gas. variation. See declination.

Vaporizer

A device to cause a heat input for the sole purpose of delivering the heat of vaporization and changing liquid to the gas phase.

Variable

A symbol representative of a set of numbers, points, values, etc. In science, variables represent values of measurements of quantities. Much confusion exists about the meanings of dependent and independent variables. In one sense this distinction hinges on how you write the relation between variables.

(1) If you write a function or relation in the form y = f(x), y is considered dependent on x and x is said to be the independent variable.

(2) If one variable (say x) in a relation is experimentally set, fixed, or held to particular values while measuring corresponding values of y, we call x the independent variable. We could just as well (in some cases) set values of y and then determine corresponding values of x. In that case y would be the independent variable.

(3) If the experimental uncertainties of one variable are smaller than the other, the one with the

smallest uncertainty is often called the independent variable.

(4) As a general rule independent variables are plotted on the horizontal axis of a graph, but this is not required if there's a good reason to do it otherwise.

VAX

VAX is an acronym for Virtual Address extension.

VAXAPM

The VAX applications Manager. A process on the Operational VAX which is somewhat analogous to the console APM. In particular, VAXAPM supports network services to start slave applications (such as ORBIT) in response to console requests.

VAXDPM

The VAX Data Pool Manager. A process internal to the OPER and DEVL VAX which accesses the datapool for applications programs on the VAX. It is identical in function to DPM on the consoles.

VCB

Vacuum Circuit Breaker. It connects 13.8 KV to a Main Ring or Tevatron power supply. A loss of the Power Supply Permit loop will open the VCB's thus disconnecting the power supplies.

VCO

Voltage Controlled Oscillator. It is used to produce the operating frequency for an RF system.

Vector

A vector is a quantity that has units and a numerical value plus a direction. Quantities like force and displacement have directions as well as magnitudes associated with them and are vectors. The magnitude of a vector is always a positive number and represents how big the vector is. A vector's direction can be described by angles (one angle in two dimensions and two angles in three dimensions). A vector can also be thought of as an ordered set of quantities. In two dimensions there are two of these, in three dimensions three - one quantity for each perpendicular direction (x, y, and z axes).

Vector component

A vector can be modeled as an arrow. Think of a vector as an arrow in a 3-D Cartesian coordinate system, with its tail at the origin. Conceptually, you can find its components like this. You proceed along the x axis (in either the positive or negative direction, as appropriate) until your line of sight to the tip of the arrowhead is perpendicular to this axis. Then you walk in the (+ or -) y direction until your line of sight to the tip is perpendicular to the y direction. (It will also be perpendicular to the x direction at this point.) Finally, you find you can walk in the (+/-) z direction directly to the tip of the arrow. The three straight lines that made up your stroll are just the x, y, and z coordinates of the vector.

Vector quantity

A quantity, which needs both magnitude and direction to describe it, is called a vector quantity. Such a physical quantity should also follow the vector law of addition.

Velocity

Velocity is speed plus direction. Speed is the rate at which distance is being covered, but has no reference to direction. Like the old airline joke: "This is your captain speaking. I have good news and bad news. The good news is that we are making excellent time. The bad news is I have no idea which way we are going." Velocity is a vector, meaning it must have a direction as well as a magnitude. A airplane flying north at 200 mph would have the same speed as one traveling east at 200 mph; however, they would have different velocities.

Vernier magnet

Small dipole magnets in the external beam lines used for small corrections in beam positioning.

Vertex

The centre of a curved mirror.

VFC

Voltage to Frequency Converter. Device used to return cell voltages, power lead voltages, and voltage to ground to the QPM.

Vibration
A back and forth motion that repeats itself.

Virtual image
The point(s) from which light rays converge as they emerge from a lens or mirror. The rays do not actually pass through each image point, but diverge from it.

Virtual object
The point(s) to which light rays converge as they enter a lens. The rays do not actually pass through each object point.

Viscosity
The measure of resistance to flow. Some cryogenic fluids have amazingly low viscosities. (g/cm sec)

Vms
Virtual Memory System. The operating system for the vaxs used at Fermilab. Virtual systems allow programs requiring more physical memory than is actually available to be run (with degraded efficiency) by writing the surplus onto a disk.

Volt
The unit of potential difference. The potential difference between two points in an electric field such that one joule of work moves a charge of one coulomb between these points.

Voltage
A sort of "electric pressure", gauging the electric force acting on ions or electrons (or more accurately, the amount of energy they might obtain from that force). In electric devices such as are used in the home, increasing the voltage increases the electric current just as increasing the pressure driving water through a pipe increases its flow rate. (The scientific term is "potential" or "potential difference".)

Voltage drop
The electric potential difference across a resistor or other part of a circuit that consumes power.

Voltage sensitivity
Voltage per unit scale division of an electric instrument.

Voltaic cell
A device that changes chemical into electric energy by the action of two dissimilar metals immersed in an electrolyte.

Voltmeter
An instrument used to measure the difference of potential between two points in an electric circuit.

Volume strain
The ratio of the decrease in volume to the volume before stress is applied.

VP curve
The plot of the gas liquid equilibrium in the PT plane. VP is an abbreviation for Vapor Pressure.

VPT
Vapor Pressure Thermometer. Measures temperature below the critical point by the VP curve relationship.

W

W boson
A carrier particle of the weak interaction.

W particle
The theoretical carrier for weak subatomic interactions.

Watchdog
A module which gives a permit for DC and RF gates in an RF high level system. Watchdogs monitor LCW temperatures, pressures, and conductivity, intermediate cylinder bias, etc. If faulted, the RF cavities are not allowed to be energized.

Water heater
Device which is used to tune the Tevatron RF cavities by varying the water temperature in them.

Water resistor
Plastic tubes running from the preaccelerator pit wall along the column and to the dome, used to control the potential drop among the column electrodes. The resistance of the tubes are controlled by LCW flowing through them. This resistance also has an effect on the current drawn by the Haefely power supply.

Watt
The SI unit of power, the rate of expenditure of energy, equalling the expenditure of one joule of energy each second. Named after James Watt, who didn't actually invent the steam engine, nor did he claim to have invented the steam engine. Instead, he improved steam engine technology and ran a series of TV ads that went something like this: "James Watt. I don't make the steam engines you buy; I make the steam engines you buy better."

Wave
A wave is a vibration of a medium that moves (propagates) from one point to another, carrying energy, but not the medium itself, with it. A wave pulse is a vibration that passes through a given point in the medium in a relatively short period of time. A periodic wave is a wave that repeats itself (both in space and time - think of a boat rising up and down on an "endless" sea of ocean swells).

Wave motion
The movement of a disturbance from one part of a medium to another involving the transfer of energy but not the transfer of matter.

Wave period
The time required for two successive crests or other successive parts of the wave to pass a given point.

Wave phase
Imagine two horizontal strings, tied securely at one end with the other end in the hands of a couple of physics students, who will be our shakers. By shaking their ends of the strings, they can cause harmonic waves to propagate down the strings to

the tied ends. "On your mark, get set, go!" They commence shaking and the waves begin to travel down the strings. They have the same wavelength and same speed. However, one student didn't start shaking as quickly as the other, and his wave is tardy, lagging behind the other by one-quarter of a wavelength. Now, one whole wavelength encompasses a complete oscillation of the string.

Wave velocity

The distance traveled by a wave in one second.

Waveform

A current or voltage (electrical signal) considered as a function of time.

Waveform generator/sequencer

A Linac module in the modulator pulse forming circuitry that generates RF system times in response to the RFON timing pulse. This module also forms the basic modulator waveform which is then passed to the amplitude control module.

Wavefront

Technically speaking, to mark off a wavefront you connect all adjacent points on a wave that have the same phase. For example, ocean swells are two-dimensional waves (more accurately, waves propagating along a two-dimensional surface), roughly sinusoidal in cross-section. All points along the crest of a particular swell would have the same phase and would therefore constitute a wavefront.

Waveguide

An evacuated rectangular copper tube that provides a path for microwaves to travel along. They are very carefully designed for a particular wavelength microwave, so as to transmit as much energy as possible.

Wavelength

the wavelength of a sinusoidal wave is the spatial period of the wave—the distance over which the wave's shape repeats. It is usually determined by considering the distance between consecutive corresponding points of the same phase, such as crests, troughs, or zero crossings, and is a characteristic of both traveling waves and standing waves, as well as other spatial wave patterns. Wavelength is commonly designated by the Greek letter lambda (l). The concept can also be applied to periodic waves of non-sinusoidal shape. The term wavelength is also sometimes applied to modulated waves, and to the sinusoidal envelopes of modulated waves or waves formed by interference of several sinusoids. The SI unit of wavelength is the meter.

Weak focusing

A system of focussing of particles in a circular accelerator in which all of the focussing fields are the same sign. The system is weakly focussing because only very weak focussing fields can be used without making the beam oscillations (betatron oscillations) become unstable.

Weak interaction

The interactions responsible for all processes in which flavor changes; hence for the instability of heavy leptons and quarks, and particles that contain them. Weak interactions that do not change flavor have also been observed.

Weak nuclear force

The force responsible for beta decay.

Weak nuclear interaction

The interaction that produces pairs of particles that have unusually long half-lives.

Weber

The unit of magnetic flux.

Weight

The force with which a body is attracted towards the centre of the earth is called its weight. The SI unit of weight is N. The gravitational units of weight are kg-wt and g-wt. The weight of a body of mass m is given by mg. Its value will depend upon the value of g at that place. The weight of a body is measured with a spring balance.

Weightlessness

When your apparent weight is zero, you are experiencing "weightlessness". This does *not* mean that you are actually weightless (hence the quotation marks), because that would mean the force of gravity acting on you would be zero. Consider the dude in the apparent weight discussion whose bathroom is in an elevator.

Weightlessness

The state when the apparent weight of a body becomes zero.

Wet engine

Cryogenic device which cools the helium by allowing it to do work against a piston. It is used to cool the primary helium flow to the magnets.

Wheatstone bridge

Instrument used for the measurement of electric resistance.

White light

Visible light that includes all colours and, therefore, all visible wavelengths.

Wien's displacement law

For a black body, the product of the wavelength corresponding to maximum radiance and its absolute temperature is constant.

Wire scanner

A single wire (in contrast to a multi-wire) which is stepped through a circulating beam; the signal it develops is read once per step by a computer and the readings are plotted to produce a beam profile.

Word

A unit for storing integer data in the computer. In many computers, such as the PDP's and VAX's, it has a length of two bytes (sixteen bits) and is stored in two's complement representation. It may have a value in the range -32768 to +32767.

Work

Something professors extol and students shun. Mental work, that is. When it comes to defining *mechanical* work we need physics, although, to be honest, it was probably the engineers of the nineteenth century that did the most to define work due to their efforts to understand machinery.

Work function

The difference in energy of the Fermi level of a solid and the energy of free space outside the solid. In this application, the amount of energy required to liberate an electron from a metal surface.

Work-energy theorem

This is really more than a theorem. It is also a way of looking at the relationship between force and energy. A net force acting on an object will cause the object to accelerate. If this force is not perpendicular to the motion, it will change the object's speed. (A force acting perpendicular to the motion causes centripetal, or radial, acceleration and will not change the object's speed, only its direction of motion, nor will it do any work on the object.) A net force that changes an object's speed also changes the value of $(1/2)mv^2$ for the object, the object's kinetic energy.

Working equation

The equation derived from a basic equation as an expression of the unknown quantity in a problem directly in terms of the unknown quantities stated in the problem. The working equation is the mathematical expression of the solution to the problem.

Working point

The point or region on a tune diagram (vertical vs. Horizontal tune) where an accelerator normally operates.

WZ sagittae

A recurrent DAe old nova (1913 and 1946) with the shortest known orbital period (about 80 minutes). It is almost certainly a close binary system in which mass is being transferred onto a white-dwarf primary.